CYCLOPS

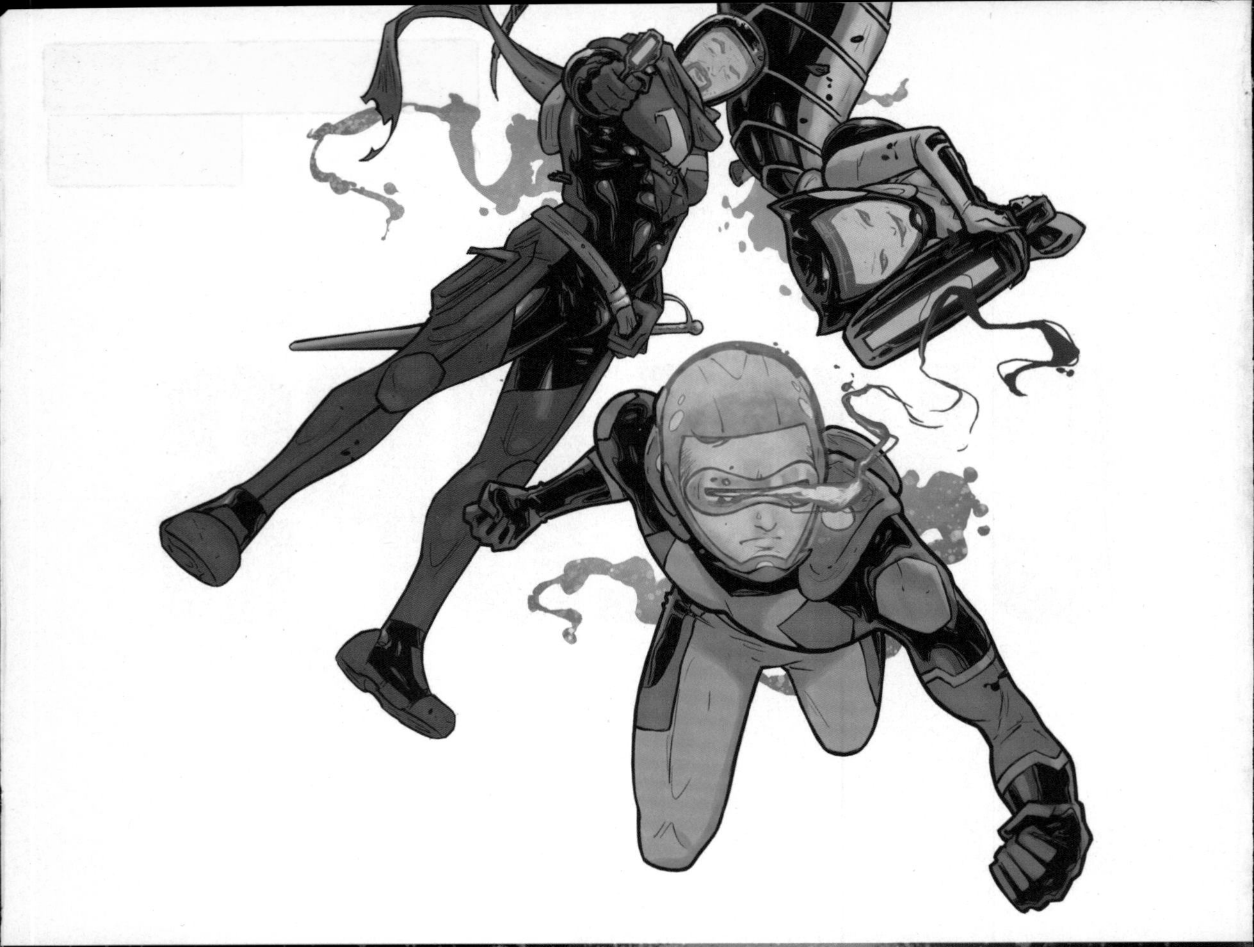

COLLECTION EDITOR: JENNIFER GRÜNWALD
ASSISTANT EDITOR: SARAH BRUNSTAD
ASSOCIATE MANAGING EDITOR: ALEX STARBUCK
EDITOR, SPECIAL PROJECTS: MARK D. BEAZLEY
SENIOR EDITOR, SPECIAL PROJECTS: JEFF YOUNGQUIST
SVP PRINT, SALES & MARKETING: DAVID GABRIEL
BOOK DESIGNER: JEFF POWELL

EDITOR IN CHIEF: AXEL ALONSO
CHIEF CREATIVE OFFICER: JOE QUESADA
PUBLISHER: DAN BUCKLEY
EXECUTIVE PRODUCER: ALAN FINE

CYCLOPS VOL. 1: STARSTRUCK. Contains material originally published in magazine form as CYCLOPS #1-5. First printing 2014. ISBN# 978-0-7851-9075-2. Published by MARVEL WORLDWIDE, INC., a subsidiary of MARVEL ENTERTAINMENT, LLC. OFFICE OF PUBLICATION: 135 West 50th Street, New York, NY 10020. **Printed in Canada.** ALAN FINE, EVP - Office of the President, Marvel Worldwide, Inc. and EVP & CMO Marvel Characters B.V.; DAN BUCKLEY, Publisher & President - Print, Animation & Digital Divisions; JOE QUESADA, Chief Creative Officer; TOM BREVOORT, SVP of Publishing; DAVID BOGART, SVP of Operations & Procurement, Publishing; C.B. CEBULSKI, SVP of Creator & Content Development; DAVID GABRIEL, SVP Print, Sales & Marketing; JIM O'KEEFE, VP of Operations & Logistics; DAN CARR, Executive Director of Publishing Technology; SUSAN CRESPI, Editorial Operations Manager; ALEX MORALES, Publishing Operations Manager; STAN LEE, Chairman Emeritus. For information regarding advertising in Marvel Comics or on Marvel.com, please contact Niza Disla, Director of Marvel Partnerships, at ndisla@marvel.com. For Marvel subscription inquiries, please call 800-217-9158. **Manufactured between 10/24/2014 and 12/1/2014 by SOLISCO PRINTERS, SCOTT, QC, CANADA.**

10 9 8 7 6 5 4 3 2 1

CYCLOPS

STARSTRUCK

WRITER
GREG RUCKA

ARTIST, #1-3
RUSSELL DAUTERMAN

PENCILER, #4-5
CARMEN CARNERO

INKER, #4-5
TERRY PALLOT

COLORIST
CHRIS SOTOMAYOR

LETTERER
VC'S JOE CARAMAGNA

COVER ART
ALEXANDER LOZANO

ASSISTANT EDITOR
FRANKIE JOHNSON

EDITORS
**NICK LOWE, JEANINE SCHAEFER,
TOM BRENNAN & KATIE KUBERT**

X-MEN GROUP EDITOR
MIKE MARTS

CYCLOPS CREATED BY STAN LEE & JACK KIRBY

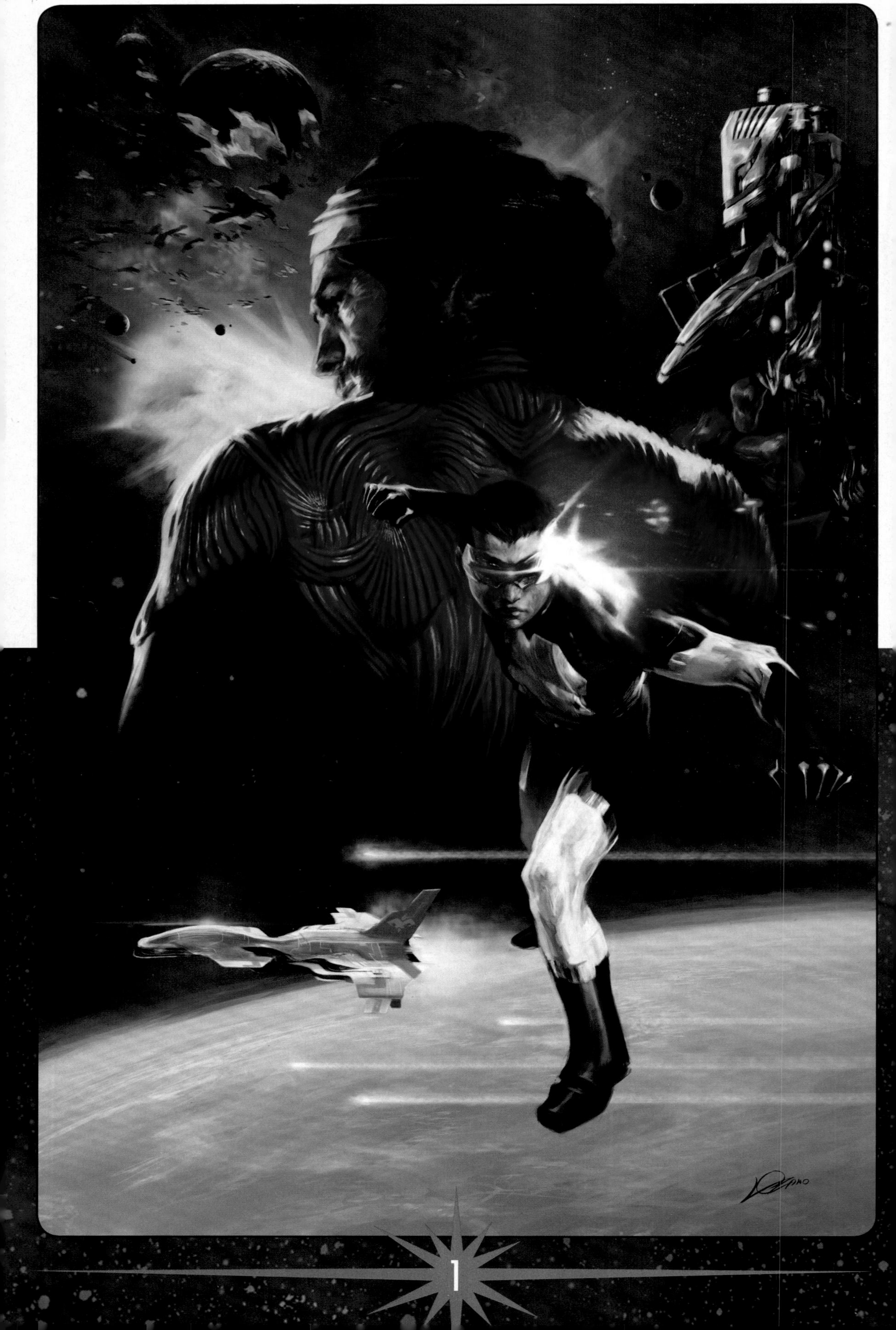

1

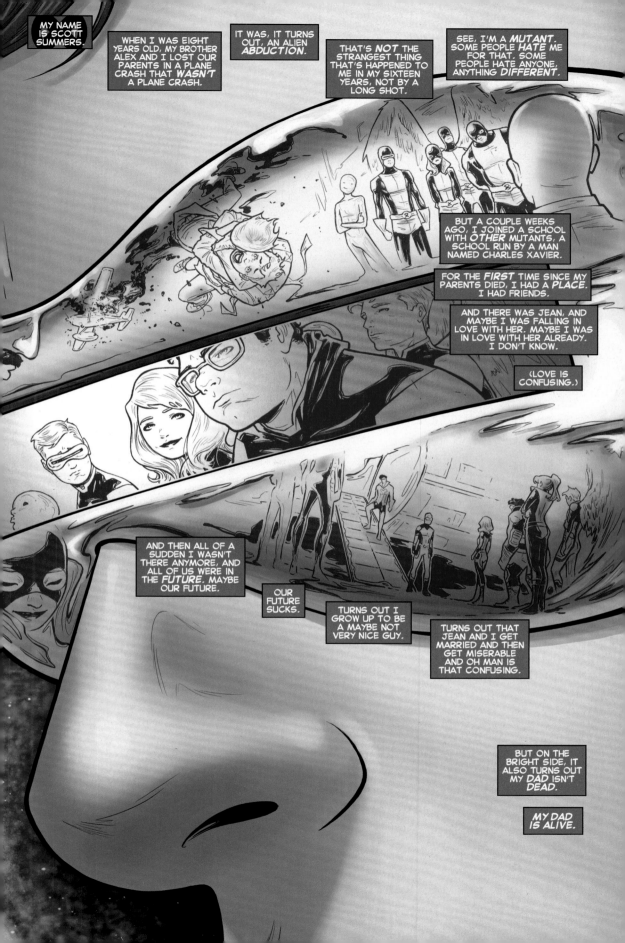

MY NAME IS SCOTT SUMMERS.

WHEN I WAS EIGHT YEARS OLD, MY BROTHER ALEX AND I LOST OUR PARENTS IN A PLANE CRASH THAT *WASN'T* A PLANE CRASH.

IT WAS, IT TURNS OUT, AN ALIEN *ABDUCTION.*

THAT'S *NOT* THE STRANGEST THING THAT'S HAPPENED TO ME IN MY SIXTEEN YEARS, NOT BY A LONG SHOT.

SEE, I'M A *MUTANT.* SOME PEOPLE *HATE* ME FOR THAT. SOME PEOPLE HATE ANYONE, ANYTHING *DIFFERENT.*

BUT A COUPLE WEEKS AGO, I JOINED A SCHOOL WITH *OTHER* MUTANTS, A SCHOOL RUN BY A MAN NAMED CHARLES XAVIER.

FOR THE *FIRST* TIME SINCE MY PARENTS DIED, I HAD A *PLACE.* I HAD FRIENDS.

AND THERE WAS JEAN, AND MAYBE I WAS FALLING IN LOVE WITH HER. MAYBE I WAS IN LOVE WITH HER ALREADY. I DON'T KNOW.

(LOVE IS CONFUSING.)

AND THEN ALL OF A SUDDEN I WASN'T THERE ANYMORE, AND ALL OF US WERE IN THE *FUTURE.* MAYBE OUR FUTURE.

OUR FUTURE SUCKS.

TURNS OUT I GROW UP TO BE A MAYBE NOT VERY NICE GUY.

TURNS OUT THAT JEAN AND I GET MARRIED AND THEN GET MISERABLE AND OH MAN IS THAT CONFUSING.

BUT ON THE BRIGHT SIDE, IT ALSO TURNS OUT MY *DAD* ISN'T *DEAD.*

MY DAD IS ALIVE.

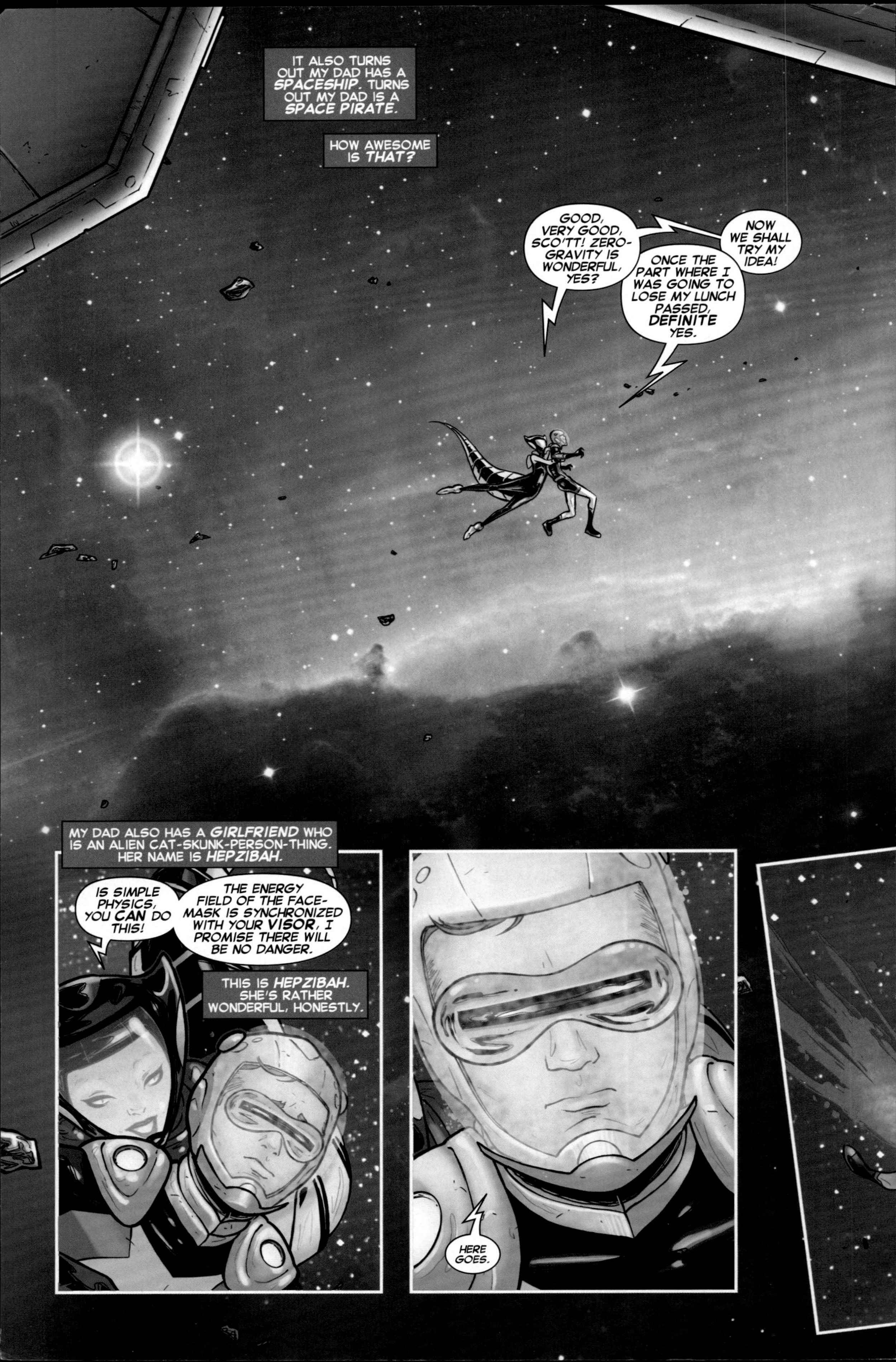
IT ALSO TURNS OUT MY DAD HAS A SPACESHIP. TURNS OUT MY DAD IS A SPACE PIRATE.
HOW AWESOME IS THAT?
GOOD, VERY GOOD, SCO'TT! ZERO-GRAVITY IS WONDERFUL, YES?
NOW WE SHALL TRY MY IDEA!
ONCE THE PART WHERE I WAS GOING TO LOSE MY LUNCH PASSED, DEFINITE YES.
MY DAD ALSO HAS A GIRLFRIEND WHO IS AN ALIEN CAT-SKUNK-PERSON-THING. HER NAME IS HEPZIBAH.
IS SIMPLE PHYSICS, YOU CAN DO THIS!
THE ENERGY FIELD OF THE FACE-MASK IS SYNCHRONIZED WITH YOUR VISOR, I PROMISE THERE WILL BE NO DANGER.
THIS IS HEPZIBAH. SHE'S RATHER WONDERFUL, HONESTLY.
HERE GOES.

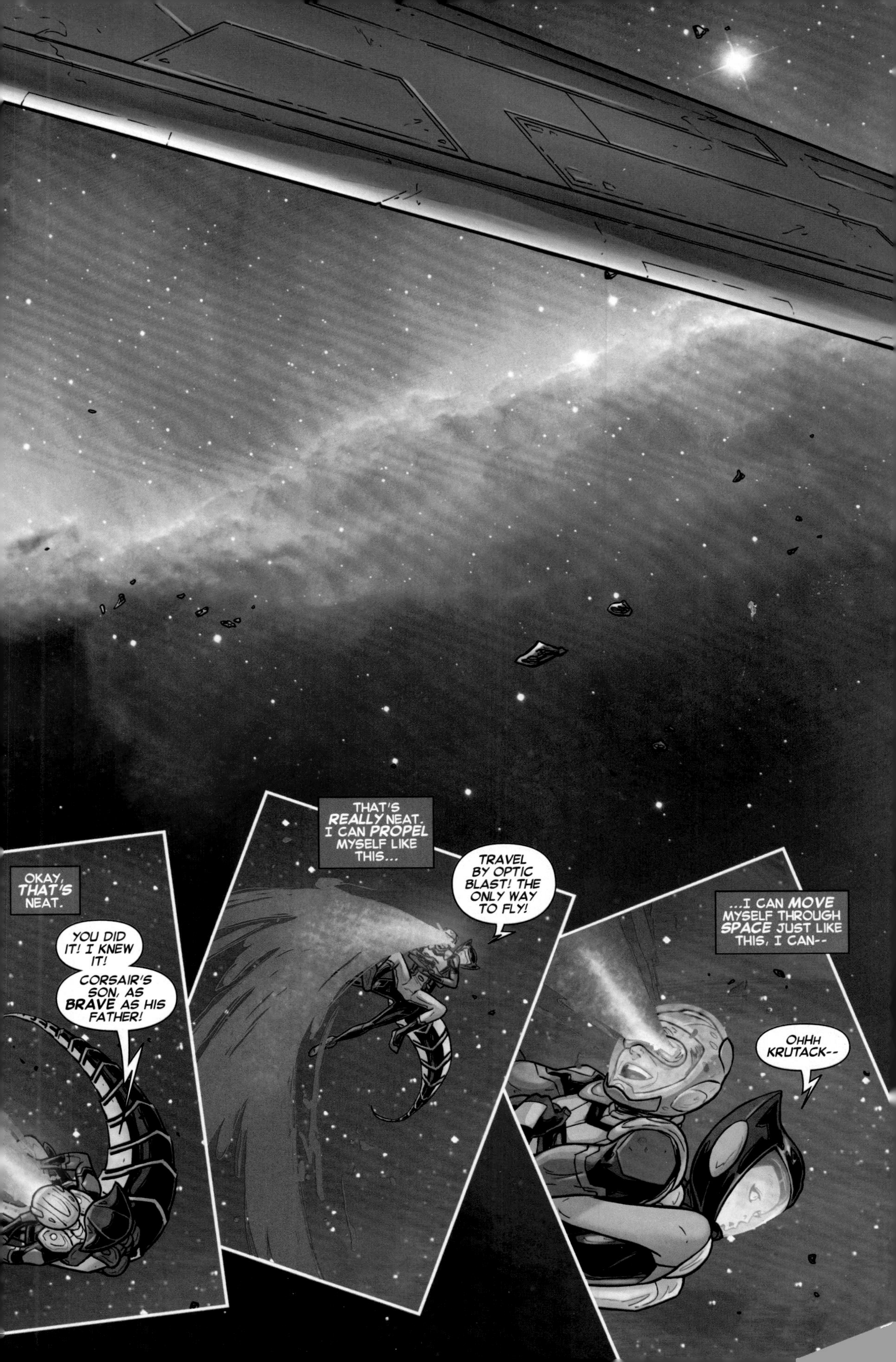
OKAY, THAT'S NEAT.
YOU DID IT! I KNEW IT!
CORSAIR'S SON, AS BRAVE AS HIS FATHER!
THAT'S REALLY NEAT. I CAN PROPEL MYSELF LIKE THIS...
TRAVEL BY OPTIC BLAST! THE ONLY WAY TO FLY!
...I CAN MOVE MYSELF THROUGH SPACE JUST LIKE THIS, I CAN--
OHHH KRUTACK--

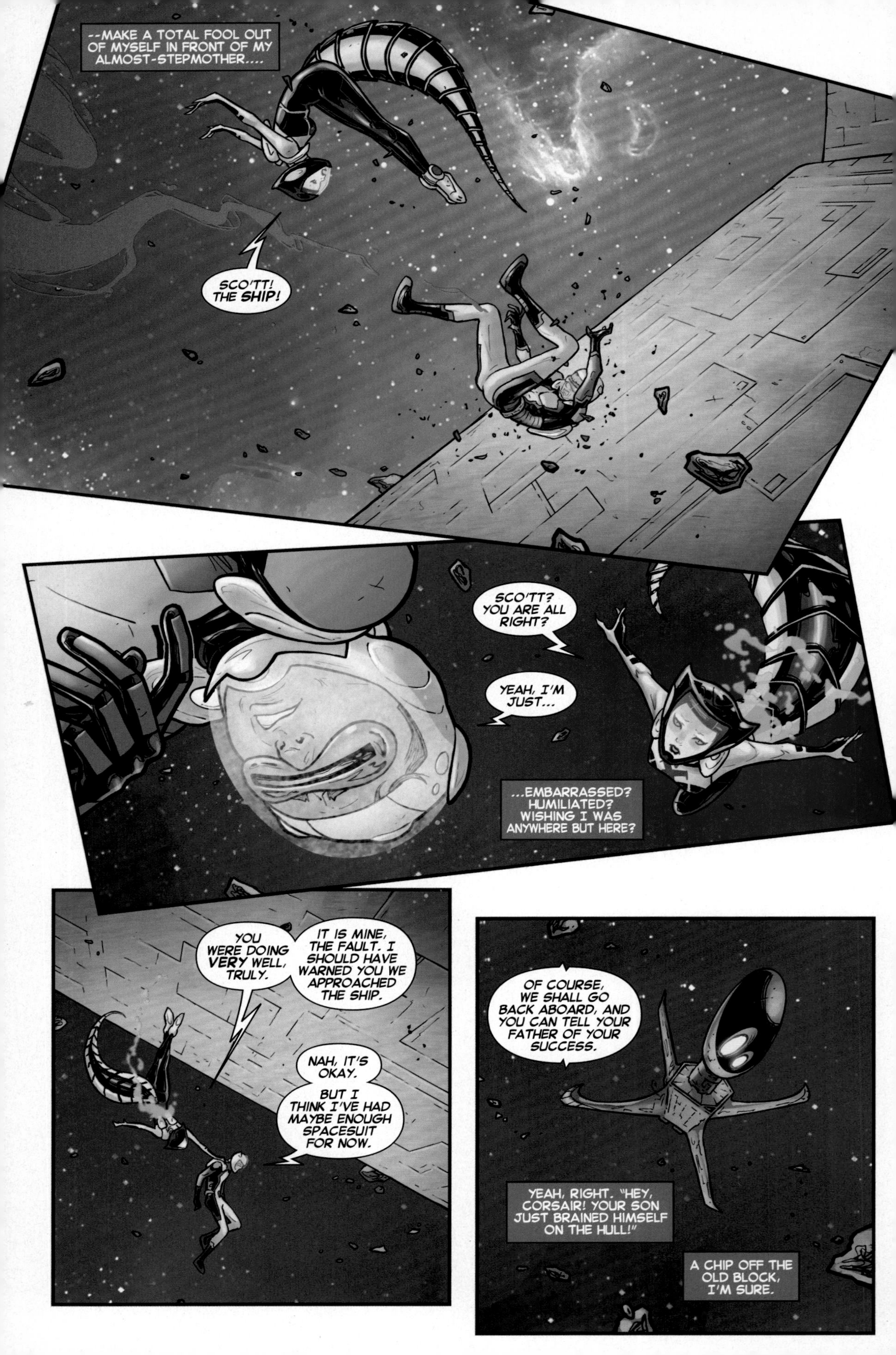
--MAKE A TOTAL FOOL OUT OF MYSELF IN FRONT OF MY ALMOST-STEPMOTHER....
SCO'TT! THE SHIP!
SCO'TT? YOU ARE ALL RIGHT?
YEAH, I'M JUST...
...EMBARRASSED? HUMILIATED? WISHING I WAS ANYWHERE BUT HERE?
YOU WERE DOING VERY WELL, TRULY.
IT IS MINE, THE FAULT. I SHOULD HAVE WARNED YOU WE APPROACHED THE SHIP.
NAH, IT'S OKAY.
BUT I THINK I'VE HAD MAYBE ENOUGH SPACESUIT FOR NOW.
OF COURSE, WE SHALL GO BACK ABOARD, AND YOU CAN TELL YOUR FATHER OF YOUR SUCCESS.
YEAH, RIGHT. "HEY, CORSAIR! YOUR SON JUST BRAINED HIMSELF ON THE HULL!"
A CHIP OFF THE OLD BLOCK, I'M SURE.

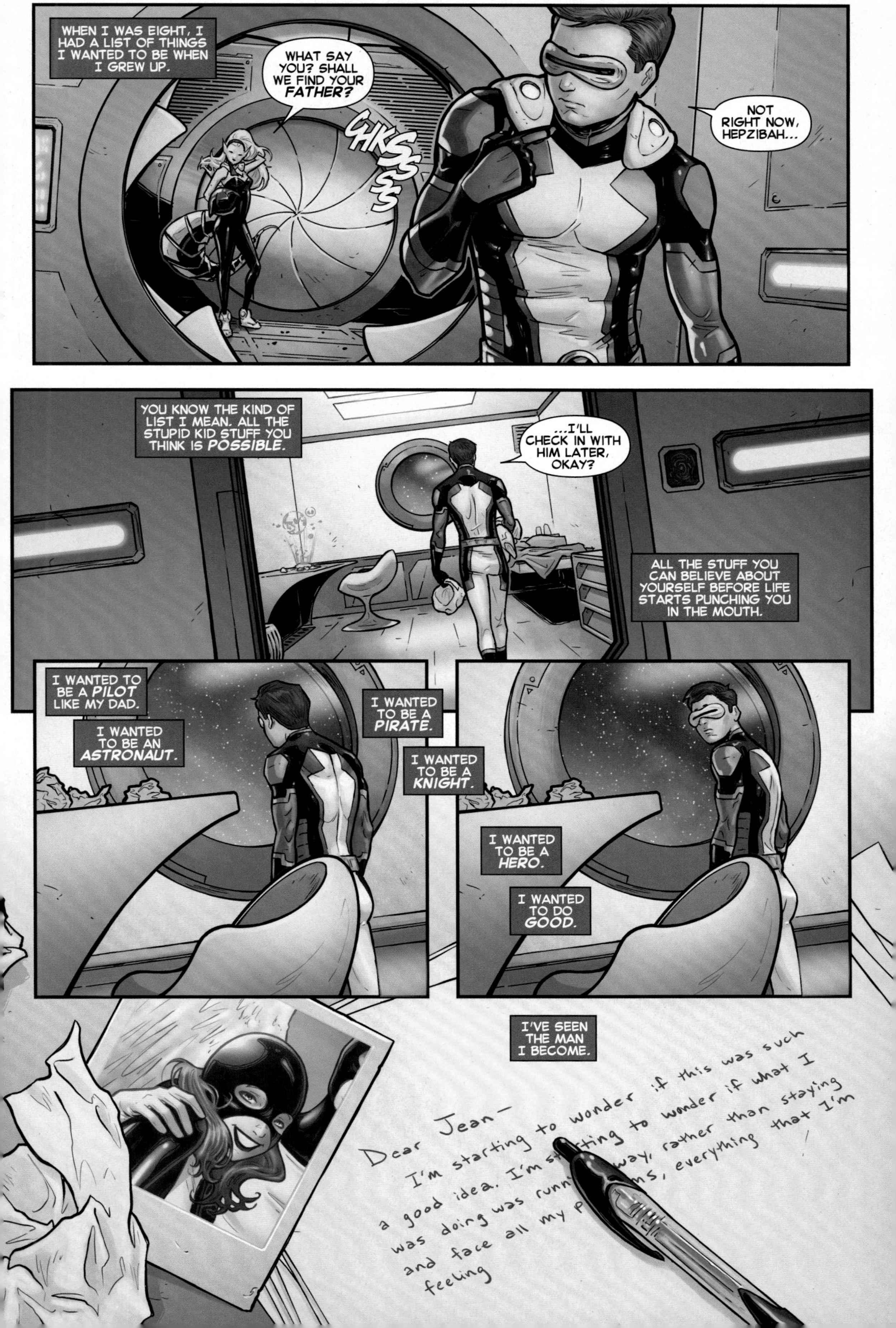
WHEN I WAS EIGHT, I HAD A LIST OF THINGS I WANTED TO BE WHEN I GREW UP.
WHAT SAY YOU? SHALL WE FIND YOUR FATHER?
CHKSSSSS
NOT RIGHT NOW, HEPZIBAH...
YOU KNOW THE KIND OF LIST I MEAN. ALL THE STUPID KID STUFF YOU THINK IS POSSIBLE.
...I'LL CHECK IN WITH HIM LATER, OKAY?
ALL THE STUFF YOU CAN BELIEVE ABOUT YOURSELF BEFORE LIFE STARTS PUNCHING YOU IN THE MOUTH.
I WANTED TO BE A PILOT LIKE MY DAD.
I WANTED TO BE AN ASTRONAUT.
I WANTED TO BE A PIRATE.
I WANTED TO BE A KNIGHT.
I WANTED TO BE A HERO.
I WANTED TO DO GOOD.
I'VE SEEN THE MAN I BECOME.
Dear Jean—
I'm starting to wonder if this was such
a good idea. I'm st ting to wonder if what I
was doing was runn way, rather than staying
and face all my p ms, everything that I'm
feeling

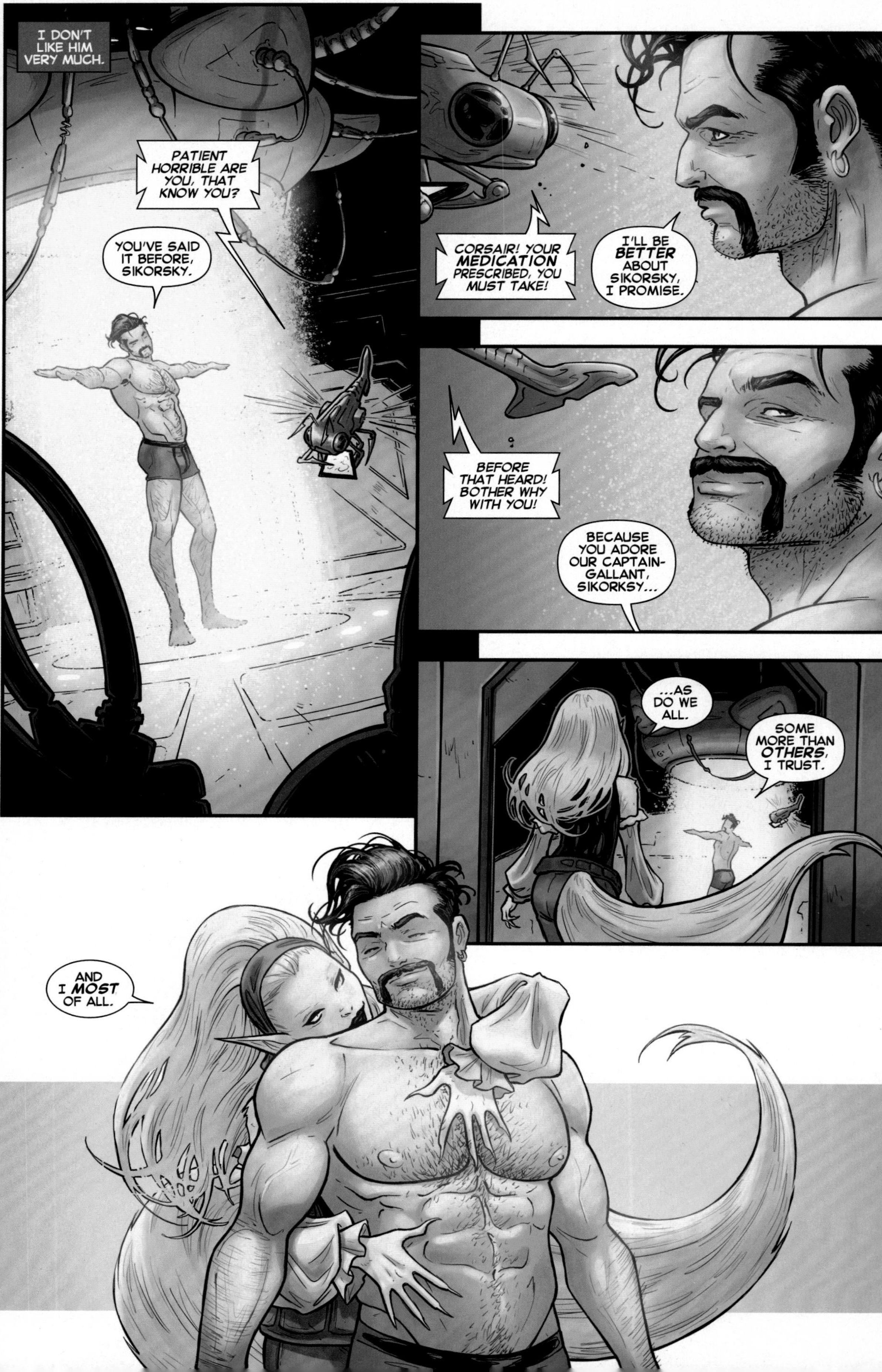
I DON'T LIKE HIM VERY MUCH.
PATIENT HORRIBLE ARE YOU, THAT KNOW YOU?
YOU'VE SAID IT BEFORE, SIKORSKY.
CORSAIR! YOUR MEDICATION PRESCRIBED, YOU MUST TAKE!
I'LL BE BETTER ABOUT SIKORSKY, I PROMISE.
BEFORE THAT HEARD! BOTHER WHY WITH YOU!
BECAUSE YOU ADORE OUR CAPTAIN-GALLANT, SIKORKSY...
...AS DO WE ALL.
SOME MORE THAN OTHERS, I TRUST.
AND I MOST OF ALL.

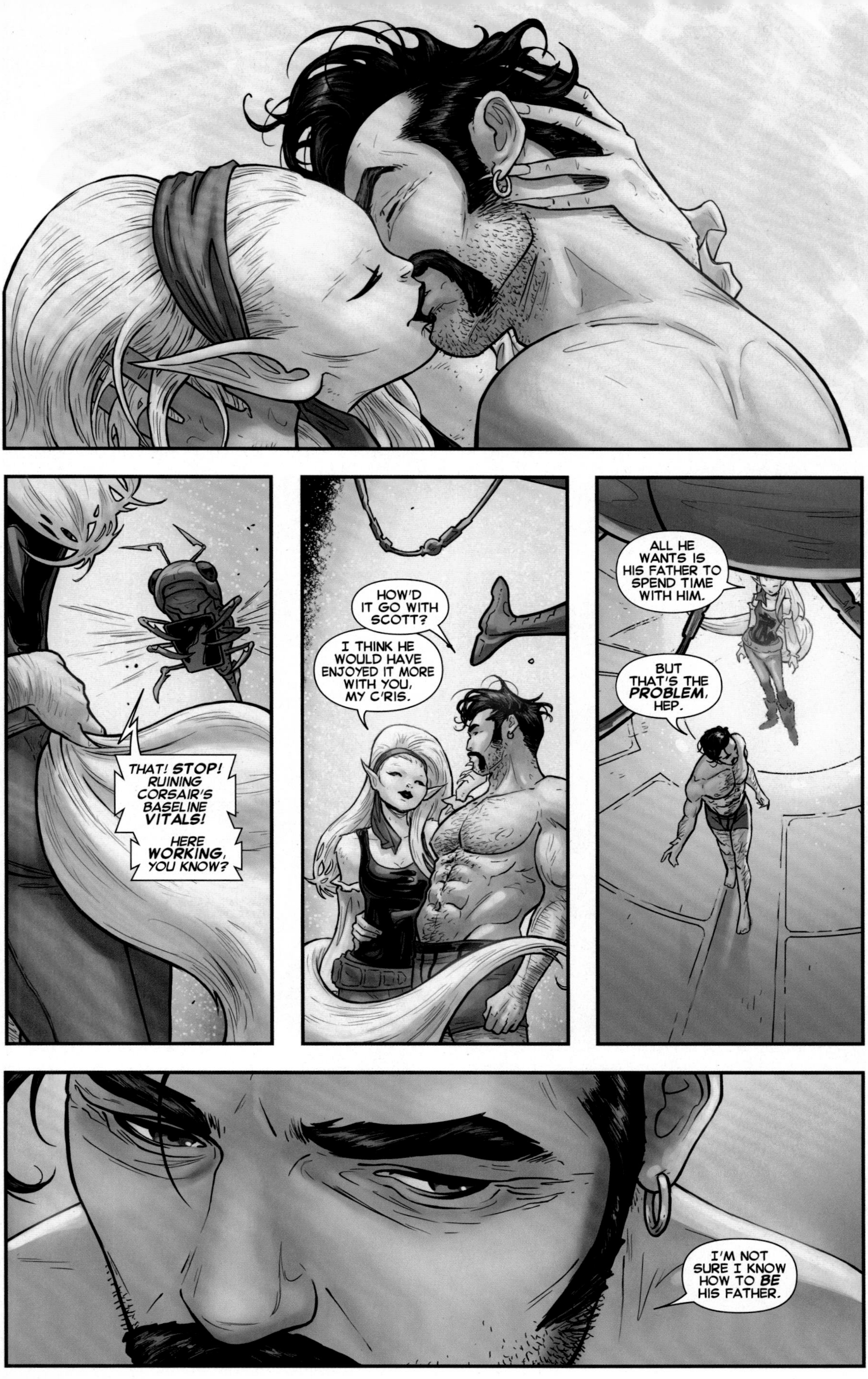
THAT! STOP! RUINING CORSAIR'S BASELINE VITALS!
HERE WORKING, YOU KNOW?
HOW'D IT GO WITH SCOTT?
I THINK HE WOULD HAVE ENJOYED IT MORE WITH YOU, MY C'RIS.
ALL HE WANTS IS HIS FATHER TO SPEND TIME WITH HIM.
BUT THAT'S THE PROBLEM, HEP.
I'M NOT SURE I KNOW HOW TO BE HIS FATHER.

DEAR JEAN,

I'VE STARTED THIS LETTER SIX TIMES, AND EACH TIME I STALL OUT.

WHEN WE PARTED, I MEANT WHAT I SAID, THAT I WANTED EACH OF US TO HAVE A CHANCE AT HAPPINESS...

...I REALLY DID MEAN IT, BUT I'M BEGINNING TO WONDER IF THAT'S EVEN POSSIBLE, IF...IF...

...

GAH!

ᛉᛉᛉᛉ ᚺᚲᛉᛉᛏ ᛉᚲᛉᛉ ᚲᛉᛉᚺᚺᛉ

OH, HEY, SORRY.

DIDN'T SEE YOU DOWN THERE.

AR

WOULDN'T HAPPEN TO HAVE ANY ADVICE ABOUT ROMANCE, WOULD YOU, CR'REEE?

ᚲᛉᛉᚷ ᚺᛉᛏᚲᚷ ᛉᚲᛉᛉ ᚷᚲᛏᛏᛉᛏᚺ ᛏᛉᛉ ᛉᚺᚺᚺ ᛉᛉᚺᚺ ᚺᛉᛉ ᛉᛉᛉᚷᚺᛉᛉᚲᛏᚺ ᛉ ᛉᛏᛉᚺ.

I WOULD NOT TAKE OUGHT HE SAYS TO HEART, LAD...

...HE WOULD SAY *ANYTHING* TO KEEP YOU PETTING HIM.

I WAS MOSTLY JOKING, CH'OD.

I CAN'T UNDERSTAND A THING CR'REEE SAYS, TO BE HONEST.

TO BE HONEST, NEITHER CAN I, SCOTT.

GKWLECY IE CYEN X MILX IX OCSEIWA.

SO I AM GIVEN TO UNDERSTAND THE ENERGY FIELD FOR YOUR VACCSUIT HELMET WORKED AS INTENDED.

POTENTIALLY VERY USEFUL, I SHOULD THINK.

OH, YEAH, IT'LL BE *BRILLIANT* TACTICALLY.

SEE, BECAUSE IT'LL LOOK LIKE I'M RUNNING *AWAY*...

...BUT YOU'LL ACTUALLY HEADING *TOWARDS* THEM.

YOU HAVE YOUR *FATHER'S* SENSE OF H--

DREEEET DREEEET DREEEET

--UMOR BATTLE STATIONS!

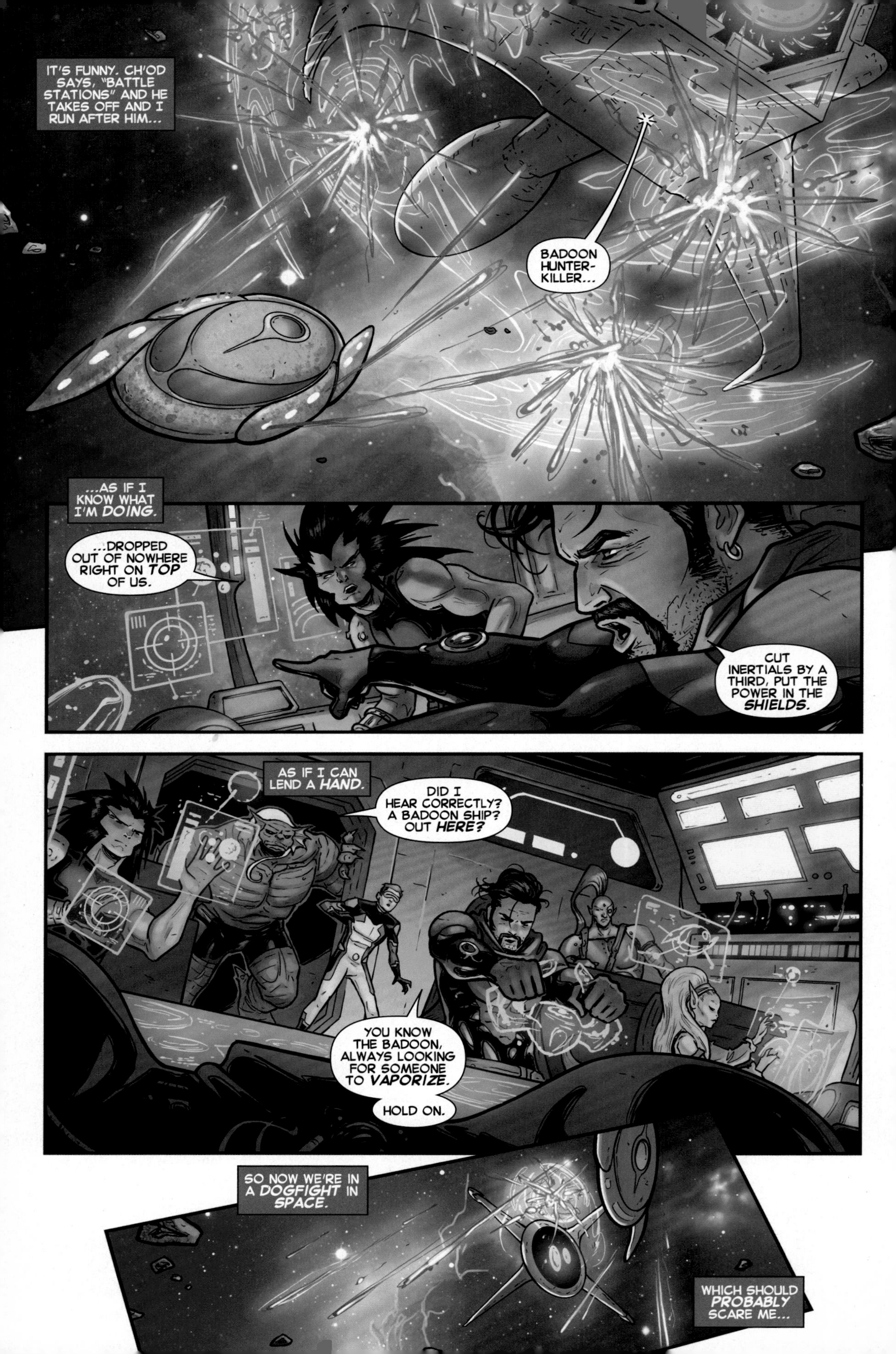
IT'S FUNNY. CH'OD SAYS, "BATTLE STATIONS" AND HE TAKES OFF AND I RUN AFTER HIM...
BADOON HUNTER-KILLER...
...AS IF I KNOW WHAT I'M DOING.
...DROPPED OUT OF NOWHERE RIGHT ON TOP OF US.
CUT INERTIALS BY A THIRD, PUT THE POWER IN THE SHIELDS.
AS IF I CAN LEND A HAND.
DID I HEAR CORRECTLY? A BADOON SHIP? OUT HERE?
YOU KNOW THE BADOON, ALWAYS LOOKING FOR SOMEONE TO VAPORIZE.
HOLD ON.
SO NOW WE'RE IN A DOGFIGHT IN SPACE.
WHICH SHOULD PROBABLY SCARE ME...

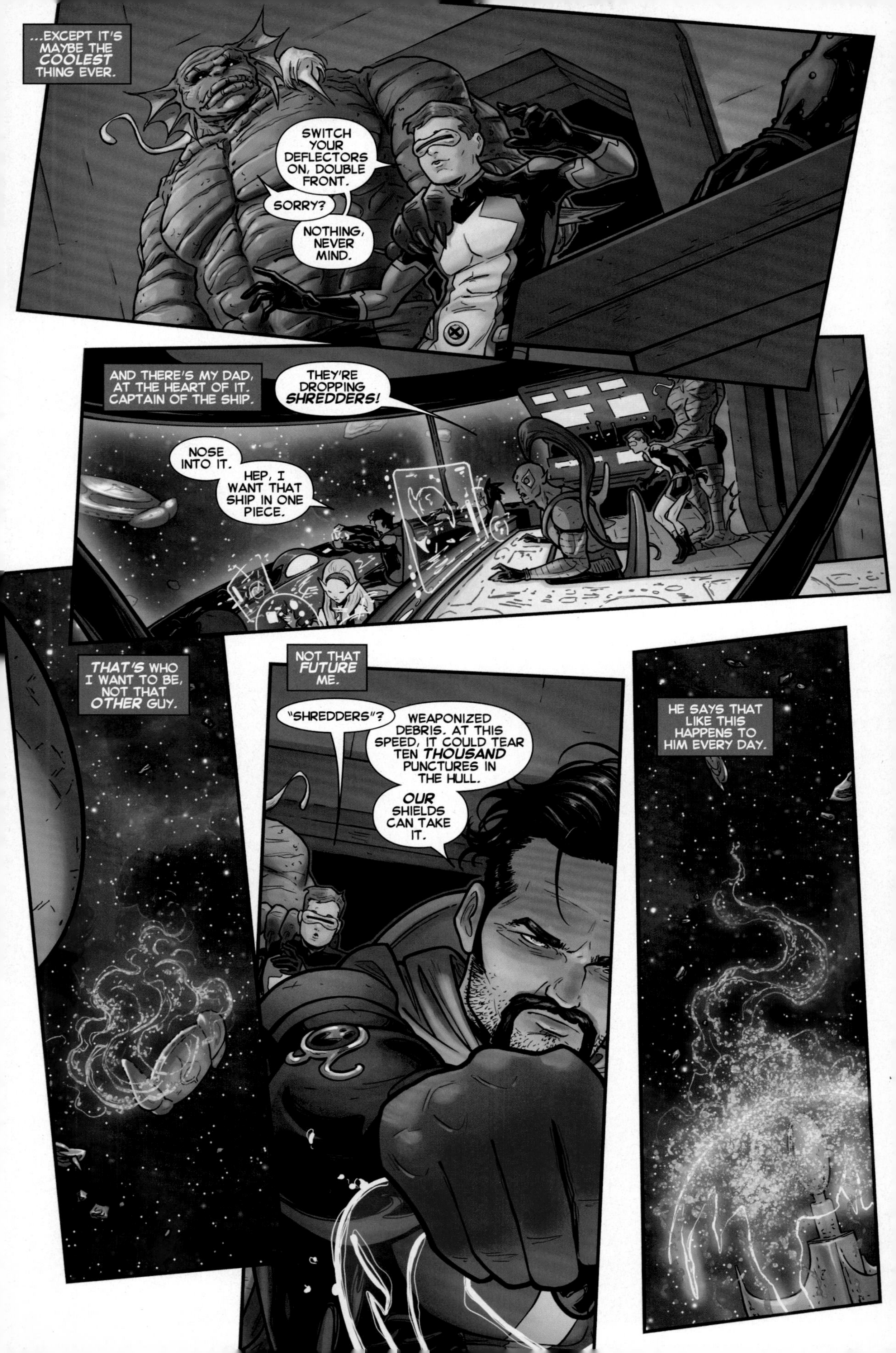
...EXCEPT IT'S MAYBE THE COOLEST THING EVER.
SWITCH YOUR DEFLECTORS ON, DOUBLE FRONT.
SORRY?
NOTHING, NEVER MIND.
AND THERE'S MY DAD, AT THE HEART OF IT. CAPTAIN OF THE SHIP.
THEY'RE DROPPING SHREDDERS!
NOSE INTO IT.
HEP, I WANT THAT SHIP IN ONE PIECE.
THAT'S WHO I WANT TO BE, NOT THAT OTHER GUY.
NOT THAT FUTURE ME.
"SHREDDERS"?
WEAPONIZED DEBRIS. AT THIS SPEED, IT COULD TEAR TEN THOUSAND PUNCTURES IN THE HULL.
OUR SHIELDS CAN TAKE IT.
HE SAYS THAT LIKE THIS HAPPENS TO HIM EVERY DAY.

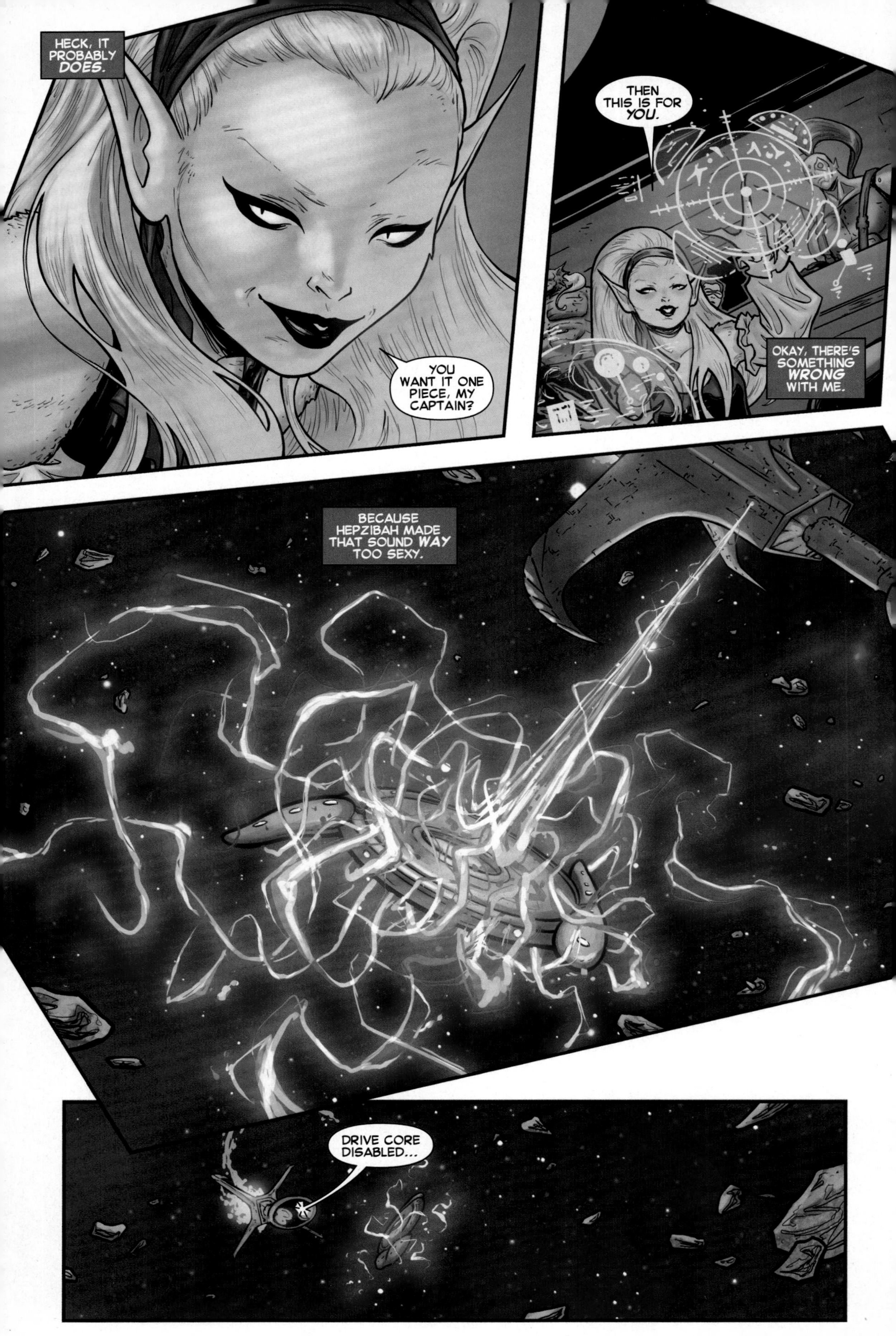
HECK, IT PROBABLY DOES.
YOU WANT IT ONE PIECE, MY CAPTAIN?
THEN THIS IS FOR YOU.
OKAY, THERE'S SOMETHING WRONG WITH ME.
BECAUSE HEPZIBAH MADE THAT SOUND WAY TOO SEXY.
DRIVE CORE DISABLED...

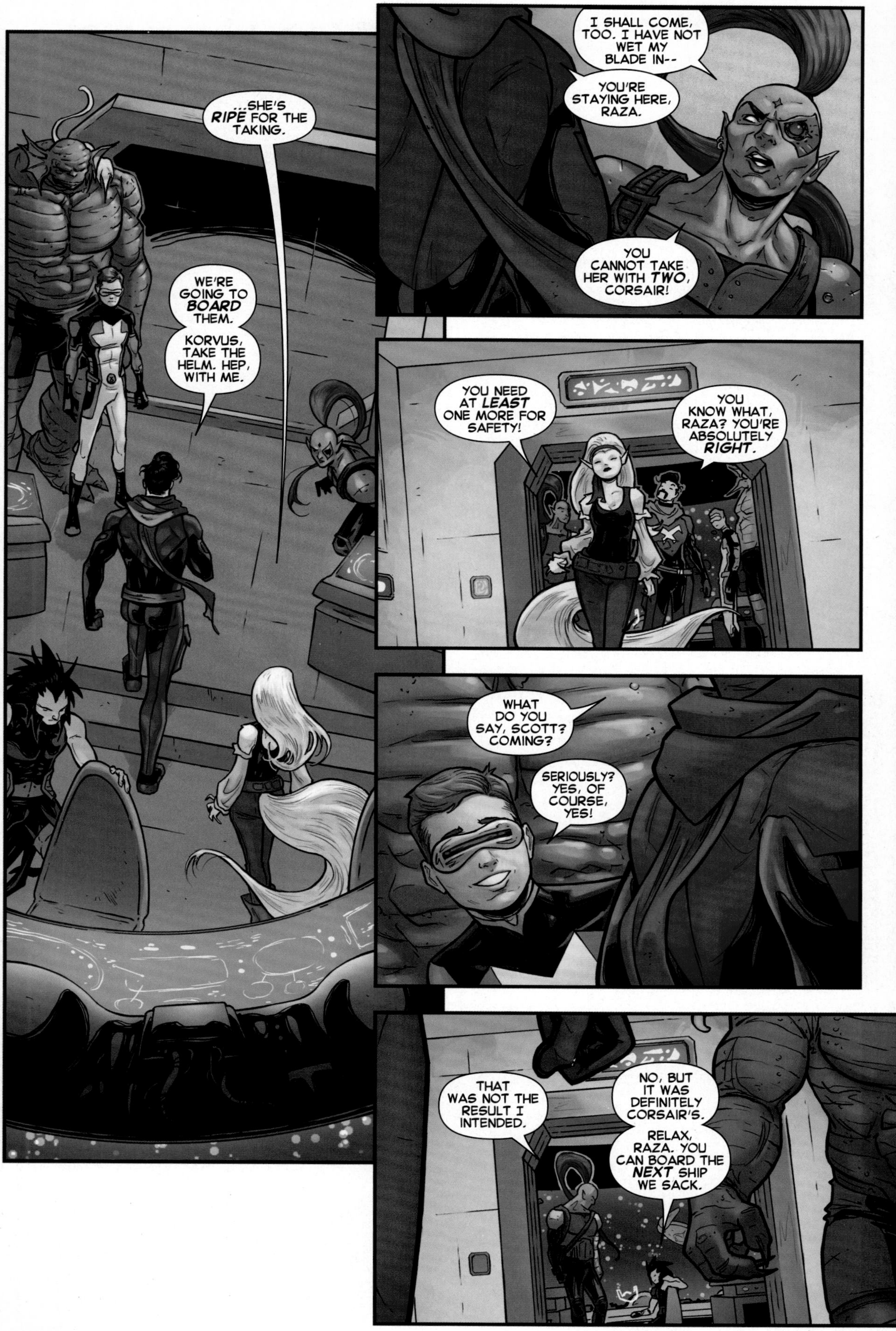
...SHE'S RIPE FOR THE TAKING.
WE'RE GOING TO BOARD THEM.
KORVUS, TAKE THE HELM. HEP, WITH ME.
I SHALL COME, TOO. I HAVE NOT WET MY BLADE IN--
YOU'RE STAYING HERE, RAZA.
YOU CANNOT TAKE HER WITH TWO, CORSAIR!
YOU NEED AT LEAST ONE MORE FOR SAFETY!
YOU KNOW WHAT, RAZA? YOU'RE ABSOLUTELY RIGHT.
WHAT DO YOU SAY, SCOTT? COMING?
SERIOUSLY? YES, OF COURSE, YES!
THAT WAS NOT THE RESULT I INTENDED.
NO, BUT IT WAS DEFINITELY CORSAIR'S.
RELAX, RAZA. YOU CAN BOARD THE NEXT SHIP WE SACK.

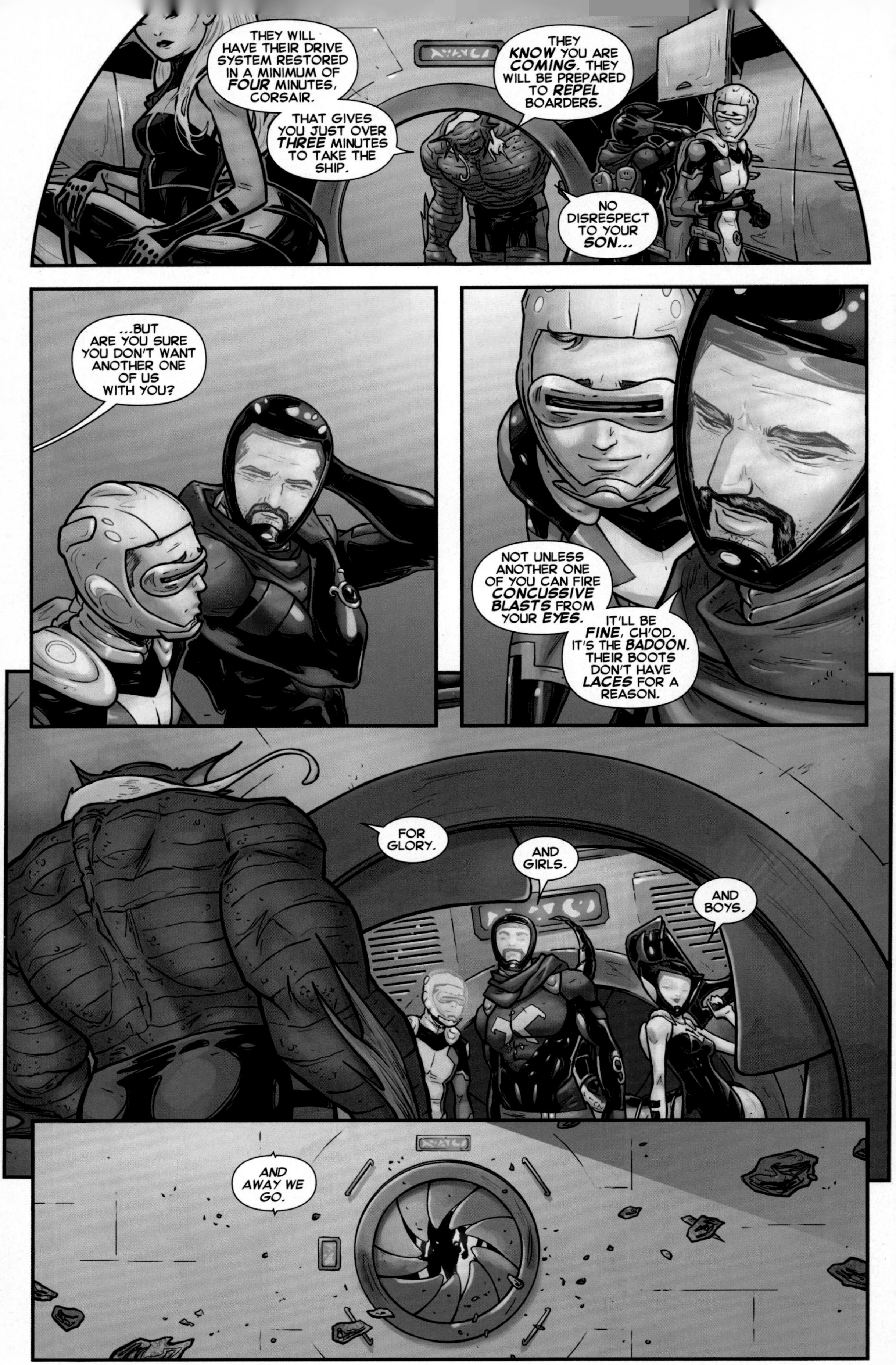
THEY WILL HAVE THEIR DRIVE SYSTEM RESTORED IN A MINIMUM OF FOUR MINUTES, CORSAIR.
THAT GIVES YOU JUST OVER THREE MINUTES TO TAKE THE SHIP.
THEY KNOW YOU ARE COMING. THEY WILL BE PREPARED TO REPEL BOARDERS.
NO DISRESPECT TO YOUR SON...
...BUT ARE YOU SURE YOU DON'T WANT ANOTHER ONE OF US WITH YOU?
NOT UNLESS ANOTHER ONE OF YOU CAN FIRE CONCUSSIVE BLASTS FROM YOUR EYES.
IT'LL BE FINE, CH'OD. IT'S THE BADOON. THEIR BOOTS DON'T HAVE LACES FOR A REASON.
FOR GLORY.
AND GIRLS.
AND BOYS.
AND AWAY WE GO.

MAKE FOR THE AIRLOCK, THERE, YOU SEE IT, SC'OTT?

I SEE IT.

SO... WHAT DO WE DO? I MEAN, CAN YOU OPEN THE DOOR OR--

NO, NO DOORS. THAT'S WHAT THEY'RE WAITING ON.

RULE OF LIFE, RULE OF WAR, REMEMBER THIS, SON:

NEVER DO WHAT THEY EXPECT YOU TO DO.

OR IN OTHER WORDS...

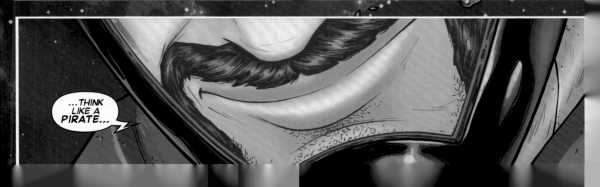

...THINK LIKE A PIRATE...

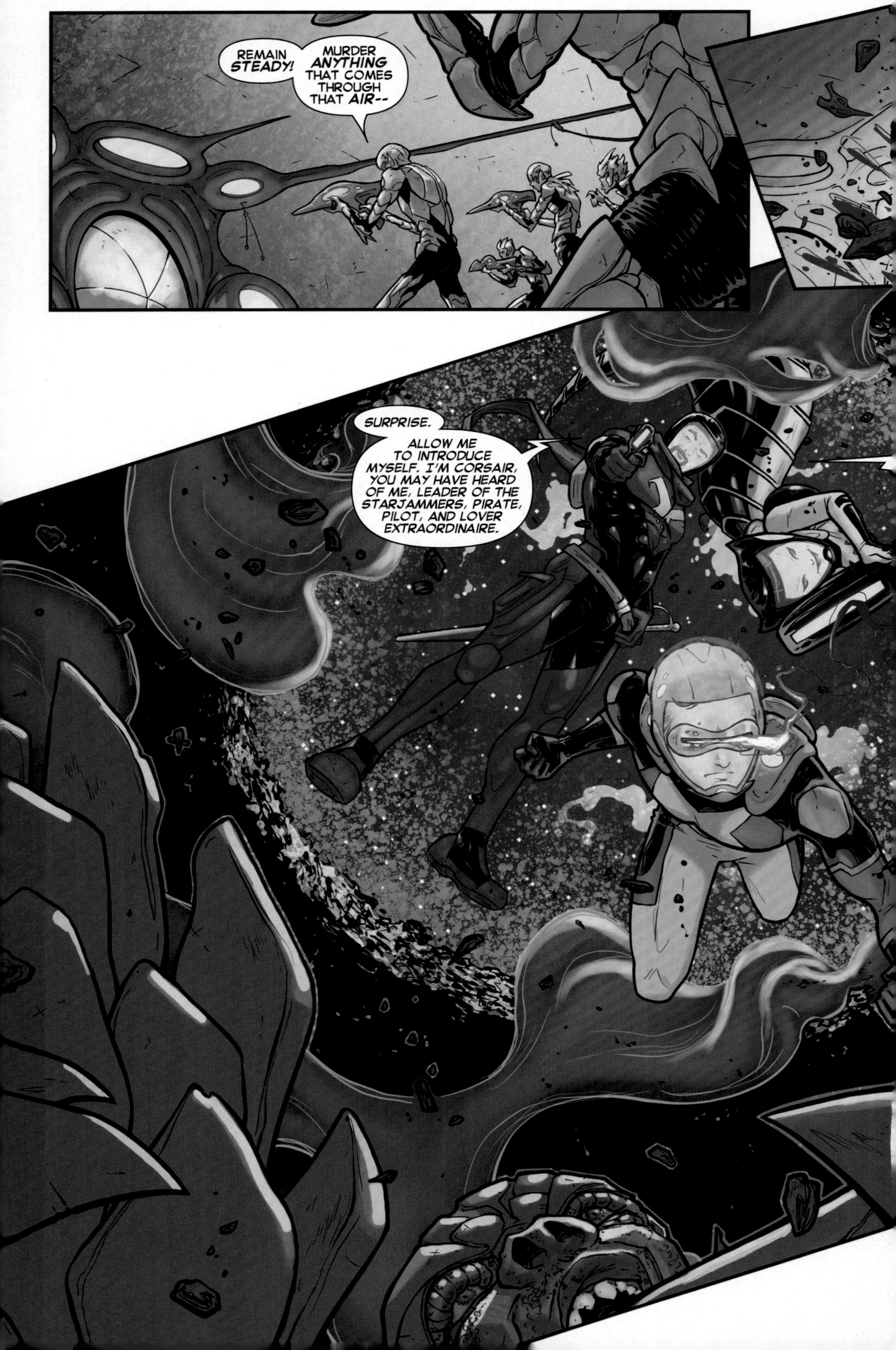

REMAIN STEADY!
MURDER ANYTHING THAT COMES THROUGH THAT AIR--
SURPRISE.
ALLOW ME TO INTRODUCE MYSELF. I'M CORSAIR, YOU MAY HAVE HEARD OF ME, LEADER OF THE STARJAMMERS, PIRATE, PILOT, AND LOVER EXTRAORDINAIRE.

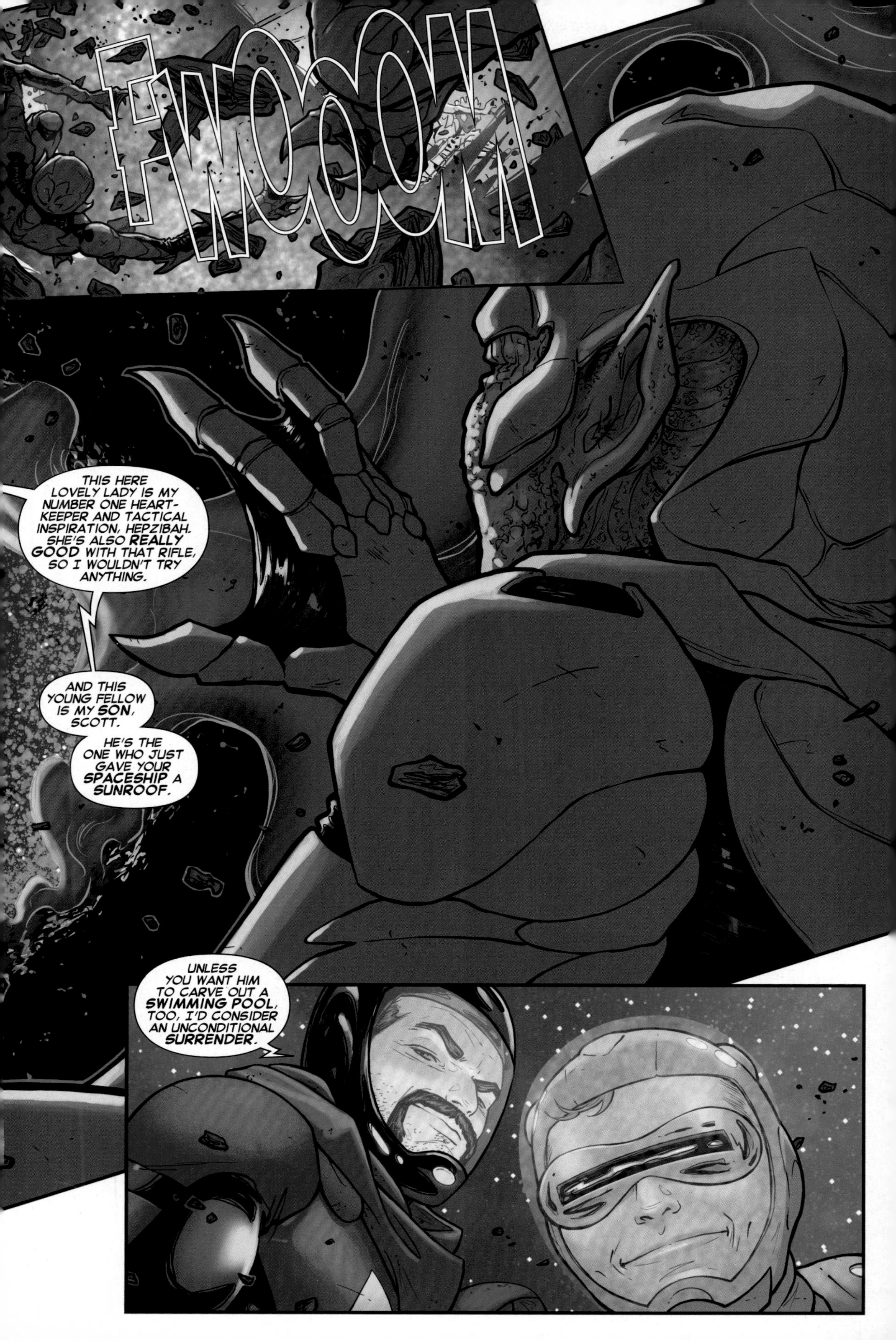
FWOOOOM
THIS HERE LOVELY LADY IS MY NUMBER ONE HEART-KEEPER AND TACTICAL INSPIRATION, HEPZIBAH. SHE'S ALSO REALLY GOOD WITH THAT RIFLE, SO I WOULDN'T TRY ANYTHING.
AND THIS YOUNG FELLOW IS MY SON, SCOTT.
HE'S THE ONE WHO JUST GAVE YOUR SPACESHIP A SUNROOF.
UNLESS YOU WANT HIM TO CARVE OUT A SWIMMING POOL, TOO, I'D CONSIDER AN UNCONDITIONAL SURRENDER.

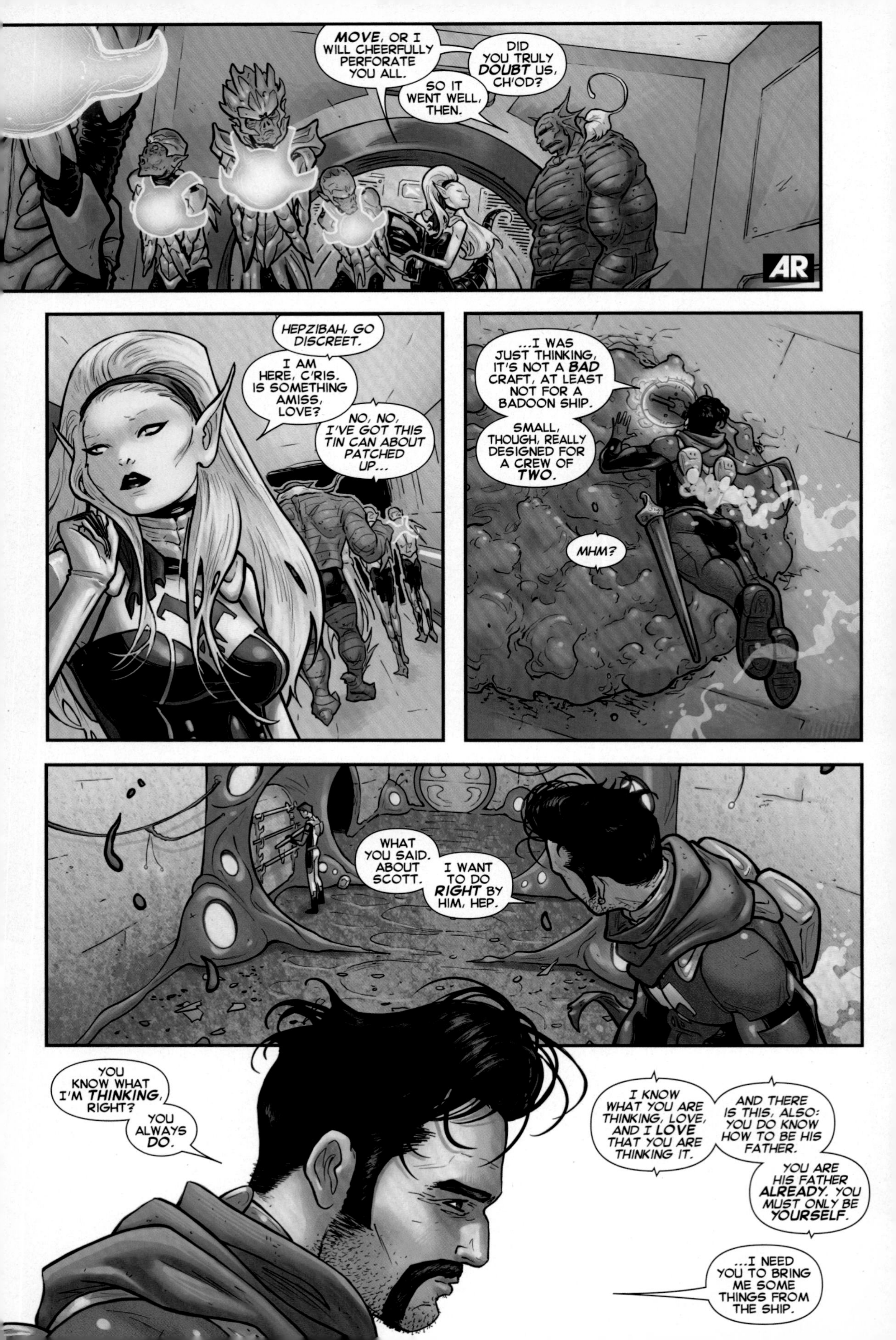

MOVE, OR I WILL CHEERFULLY PERFORATE YOU ALL.
SO IT WENT WELL, THEN.
DID YOU TRULY DOUBT US, CH'OD?
AR
HEPZIBAH, GO DISCREET.
I AM HERE, C'RIS. IS SOMETHING AMISS, LOVE?
NO, NO, I'VE GOT THIS TIN CAN ABOUT PATCHED UP...
...I WAS JUST THINKING, IT'S NOT A BAD CRAFT, AT LEAST NOT FOR A BADOON SHIP.
SMALL, THOUGH, REALLY DESIGNED FOR A CREW OF TWO.
MHM?
WHAT YOU SAID. ABOUT SCOTT.
I WANT TO DO RIGHT BY HIM, HEP.
YOU KNOW WHAT I'M THINKING, RIGHT?
YOU ALWAYS DO.
I KNOW WHAT YOU ARE THINKING, LOVE, AND I LOVE THAT YOU ARE THINKING IT.
AND THERE IS THIS, ALSO: YOU DO KNOW HOW TO BE HIS FATHER.
YOU ARE HIS FATHER ALREADY. YOU MUST ONLY BE YOURSELF.
...I NEED YOU TO BRING ME SOME THINGS FROM THE SHIP.

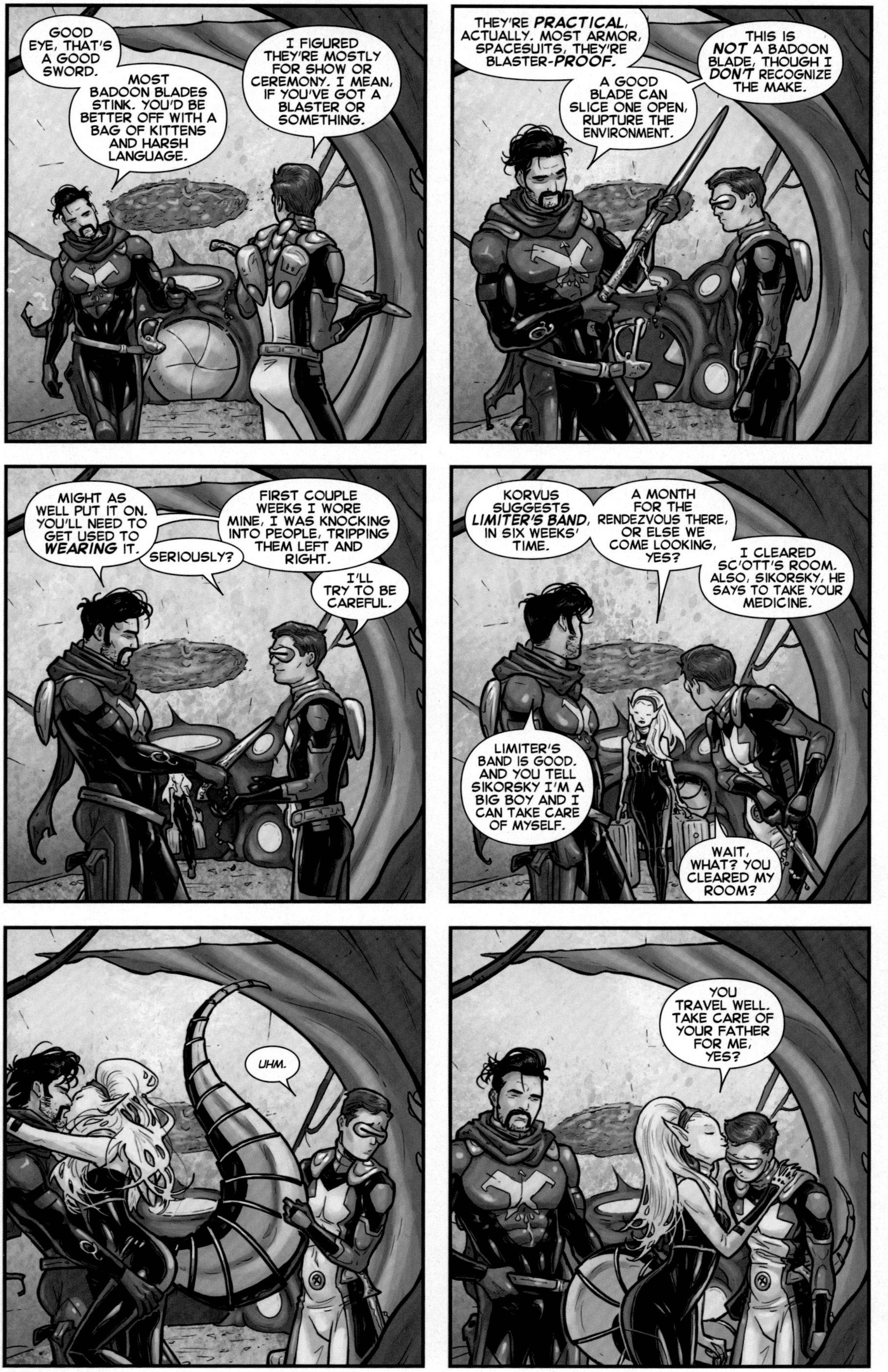
GOOD EYE, THAT'S A GOOD SWORD.
MOST BADOON BLADES STINK. YOU'D BE BETTER OFF WITH A BAG OF KITTENS AND HARSH LANGUAGE.
I FIGURED THEY'RE MOSTLY FOR SHOW OR CEREMONY. I MEAN, IF YOU'VE GOT A BLASTER OR SOMETHING.
THEY'RE PRACTICAL, ACTUALLY. MOST ARMOR, SPACESUITS, THEY'RE BLASTER-PROOF.
A GOOD BLADE CAN SLICE ONE OPEN, RUPTURE THE ENVIRONMENT.
THIS IS NOT A BADOON BLADE, THOUGH I DON'T RECOGNIZE THE MAKE.
MIGHT AS WELL PUT IT ON. YOU'LL NEED TO GET USED TO WEARING IT.
SERIOUSLY?
FIRST COUPLE WEEKS I WORE MINE, I WAS KNOCKING INTO PEOPLE, TRIPPING THEM LEFT AND RIGHT.
I'LL TRY TO BE CAREFUL.
KORVUS SUGGESTS LIMITER'S BAND, IN SIX WEEKS' TIME.
A MONTH FOR THE RENDEZVOUS THERE, OR ELSE WE COME LOOKING, YES?
I CLEARED SC'OTT'S ROOM. ALSO, SIKORSKY, HE SAYS TO TAKE YOUR MEDICINE.
LIMITER'S BAND IS GOOD. AND YOU TELL SIKORSKY I'M A BIG BOY AND I CAN TAKE CARE OF MYSELF.
WAIT, WHAT? YOU CLEARED MY ROOM?
UHM.
YOU TRAVEL WELL. TAKE CARE OF YOUR FATHER FOR ME, YES?

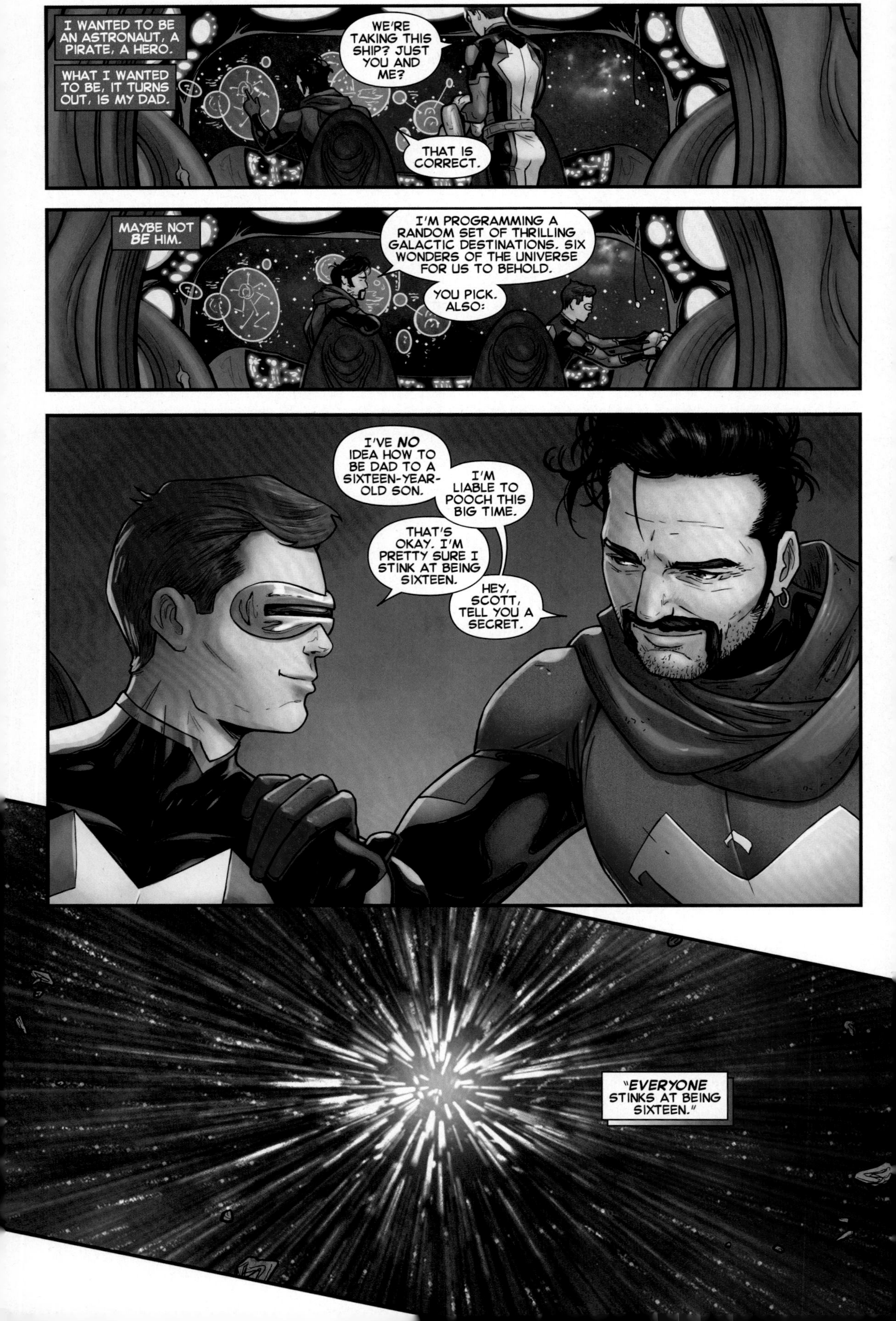

I WANTED TO BE AN ASTRONAUT, A PIRATE, A HERO.
WHAT I WANTED TO BE, IT TURNS OUT, IS MY DAD.
WE'RE TAKING THIS SHIP? JUST YOU AND ME?
THAT IS CORRECT.
MAYBE NOT *BE* HIM.
I'M PROGRAMMING A RANDOM SET OF THRILLING GALACTIC DESTINATIONS. SIX WONDERS OF THE UNIVERSE FOR US TO BEHOLD.
YOU PICK. ALSO:
I'VE **NO** IDEA HOW TO BE DAD TO A SIXTEEN-YEAR-OLD SON.
I'M LIABLE TO POOCH THIS BIG TIME.
THAT'S OKAY. I'M PRETTY SURE I STINK AT BEING SIXTEEN.
HEY, SCOTT, TELL YOU A SECRET.
"*EVERYONE* STINKS AT BEING SIXTEEN."

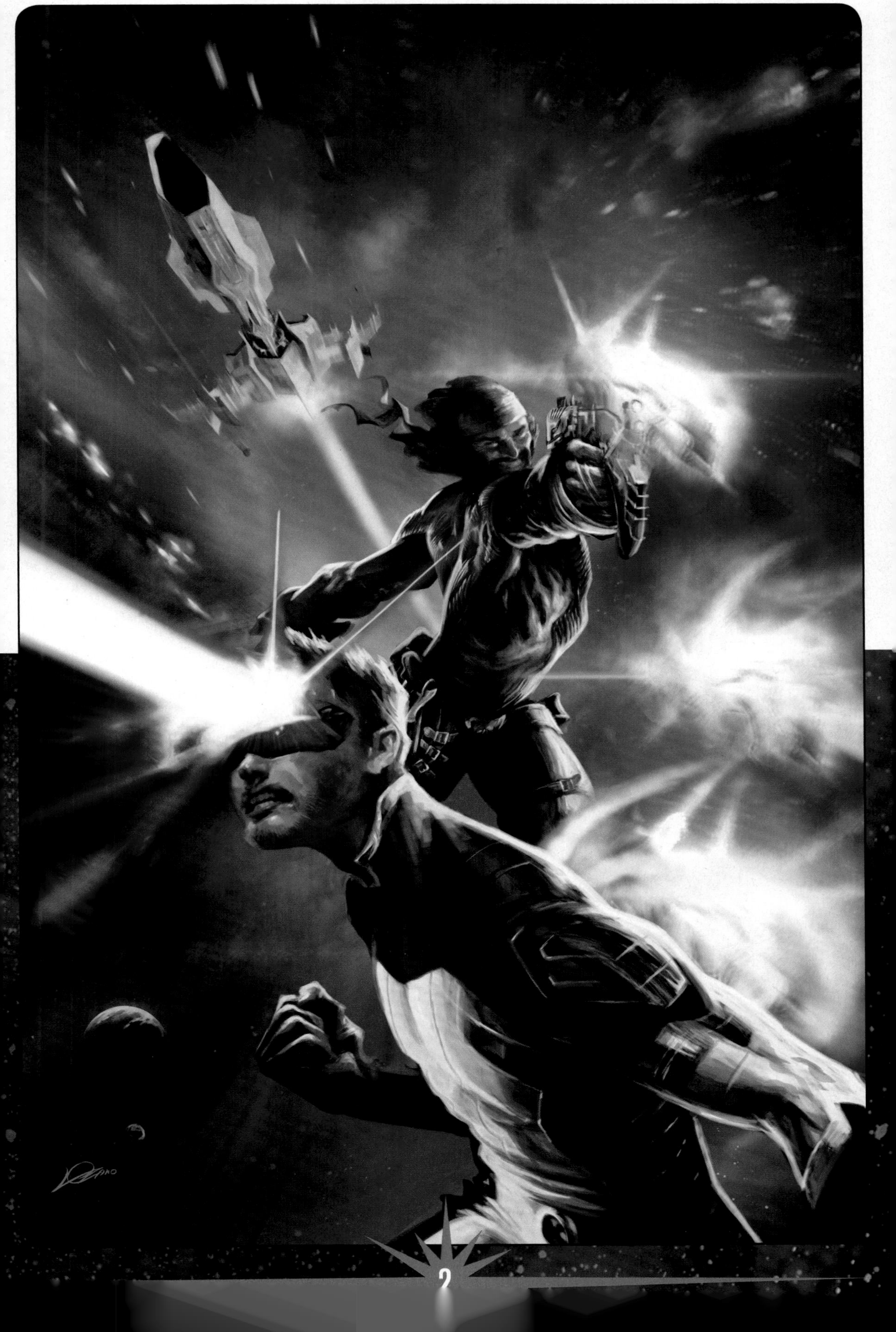

2

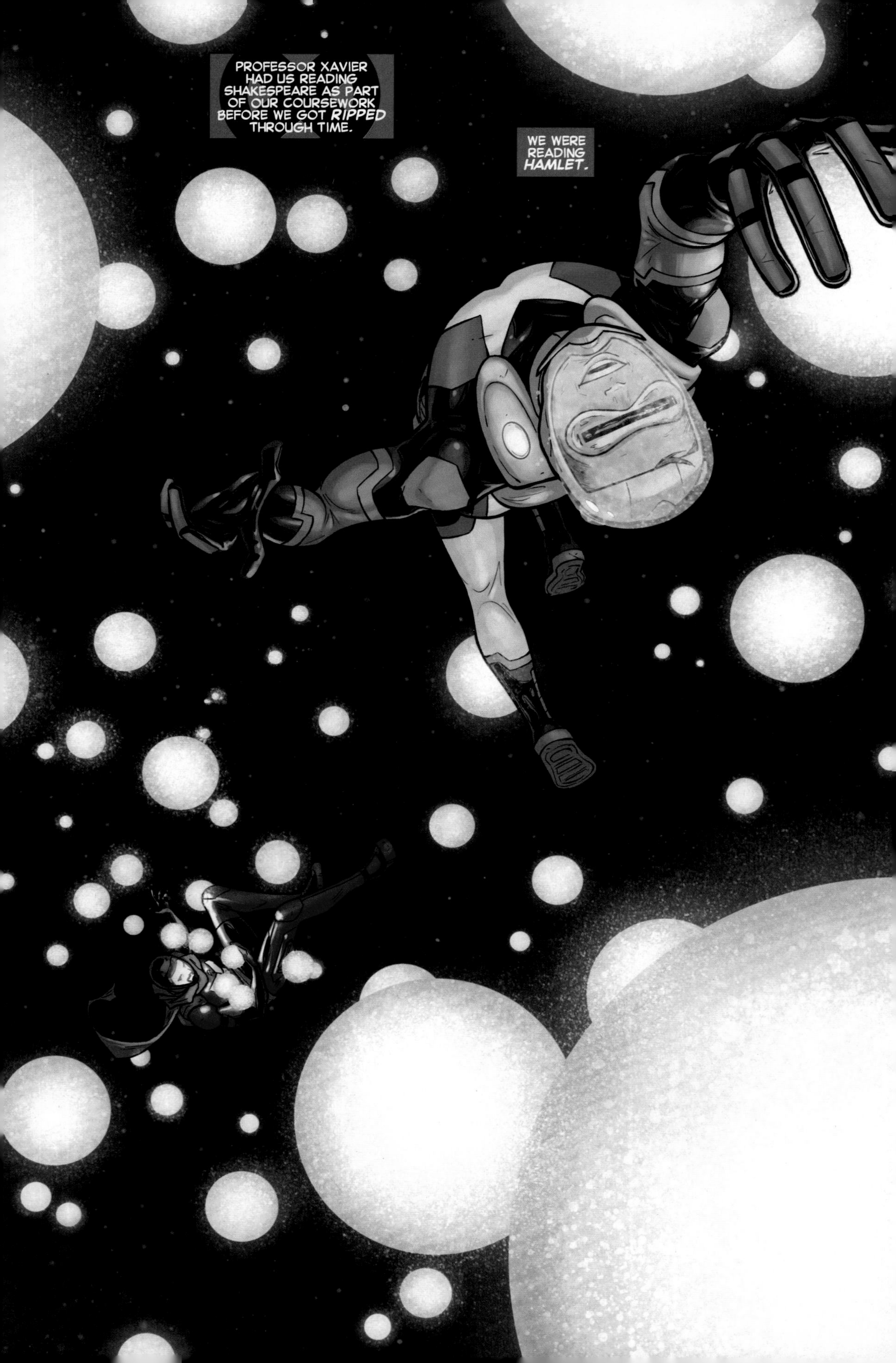
PROFESSOR XAVIER HAD US READING SHAKESPEARE AS PART OF OUR COURSEWORK BEFORE WE GOT *RIPPED* THROUGH TIME.
WE WERE READING *HAMLET*.

THE LAST COUPLE OF MONTHS, EVER SINCE ALL THIS HAPPENED, SINCE LEARNING ABOUT THE MAN I GROW UP TO *BECOME*...

...SINCE LEARNING ABOUT A FUTURE THAT IS ANYTHING BUT *GOOD* FOR ME AND MY FRIENDS AND *ESPECIALLY* JEAN...

...SINCE LEARNING THAT MY FATHER IS NOT ONLY STILL *ALIVE*, BUT HE'S BECOME A CROSS BETWEEN *JACK SPARROW* AND *HAN SOLO*...

...SINCE HEADING OUT ON A *TOUR* OF THE *GALAXY* WITH HIM, FOR PETE'S SAKE...

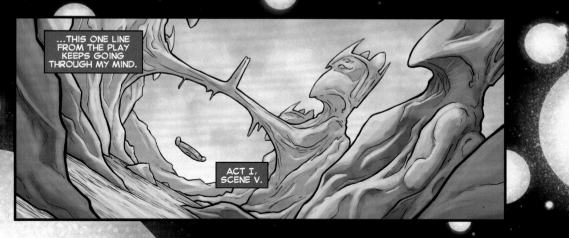

...THIS ONE LINE FROM THE PLAY KEEPS GOING THROUGH MY MIND.

ACT I, SCENE V.

"THERE ARE MORE THINGS IN HEAVEN AND EARTH, HORATIO, THAN ARE DREAMT OF IN YOUR PHILOSOPHY."

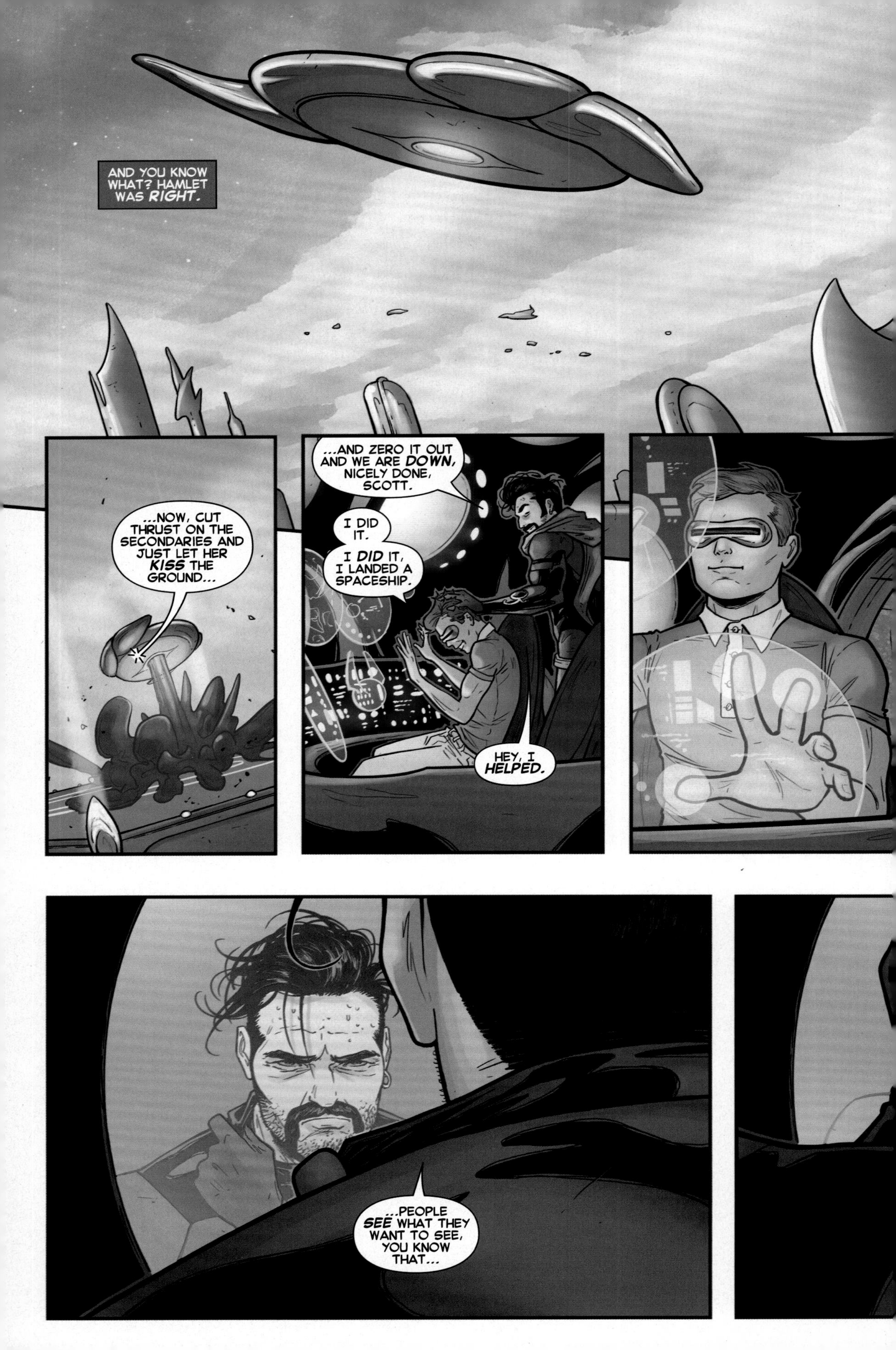
AND YOU KNOW WHAT? HAMLET WAS RIGHT.
...NOW, CUT THRUST ON THE SECONDARIES AND JUST LET HER KISS THE GROUND...
...AND ZERO IT OUT AND WE ARE DOWN, NICELY DONE, SCOTT.
I DID IT.
I DID IT, I LANDED A SPACESHIP.
HEY, I HELPED.
...PEOPLE SEE WHAT THEY WANT TO SEE, YOU KNOW THAT...

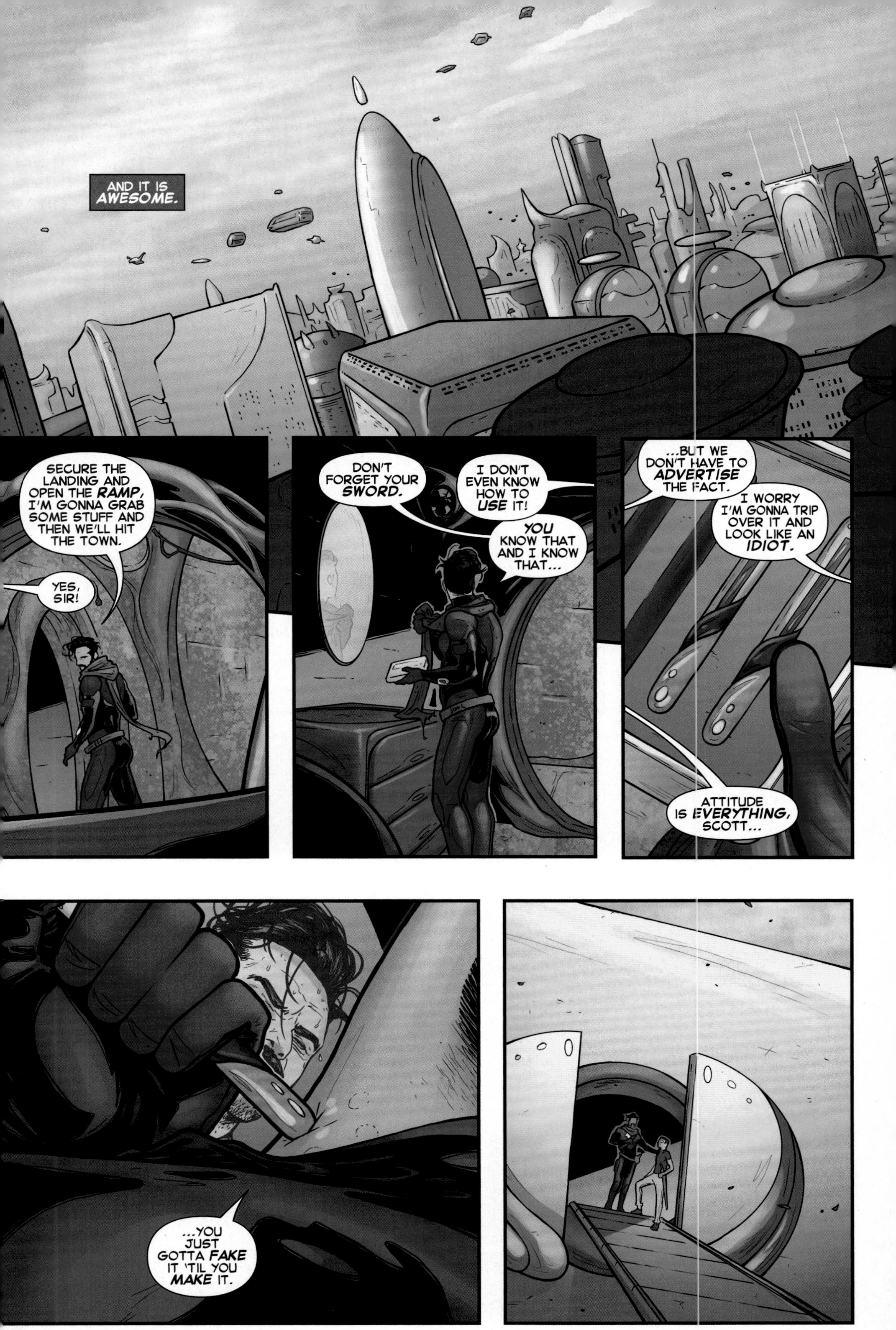
AND IT IS AWESOME.
SECURE THE LANDING AND OPEN THE RAMP, I'M GONNA GRAB SOME STUFF AND THEN WE'LL HIT THE TOWN.
YES, SIR!
DON'T FORGET YOUR SWORD.
I DON'T EVEN KNOW HOW TO USE IT!
YOU KNOW THAT AND I KNOW THAT...
...BUT WE DON'T HAVE TO ADVERTISE THE FACT.
I WORRY I'M GONNA TRIP OVER IT AND LOOK LIKE AN IDIOT.
ATTITUDE IS EVERYTHING, SCOTT...
...YOU JUST GOTTA FAKE IT 'TIL YOU MAKE IT.

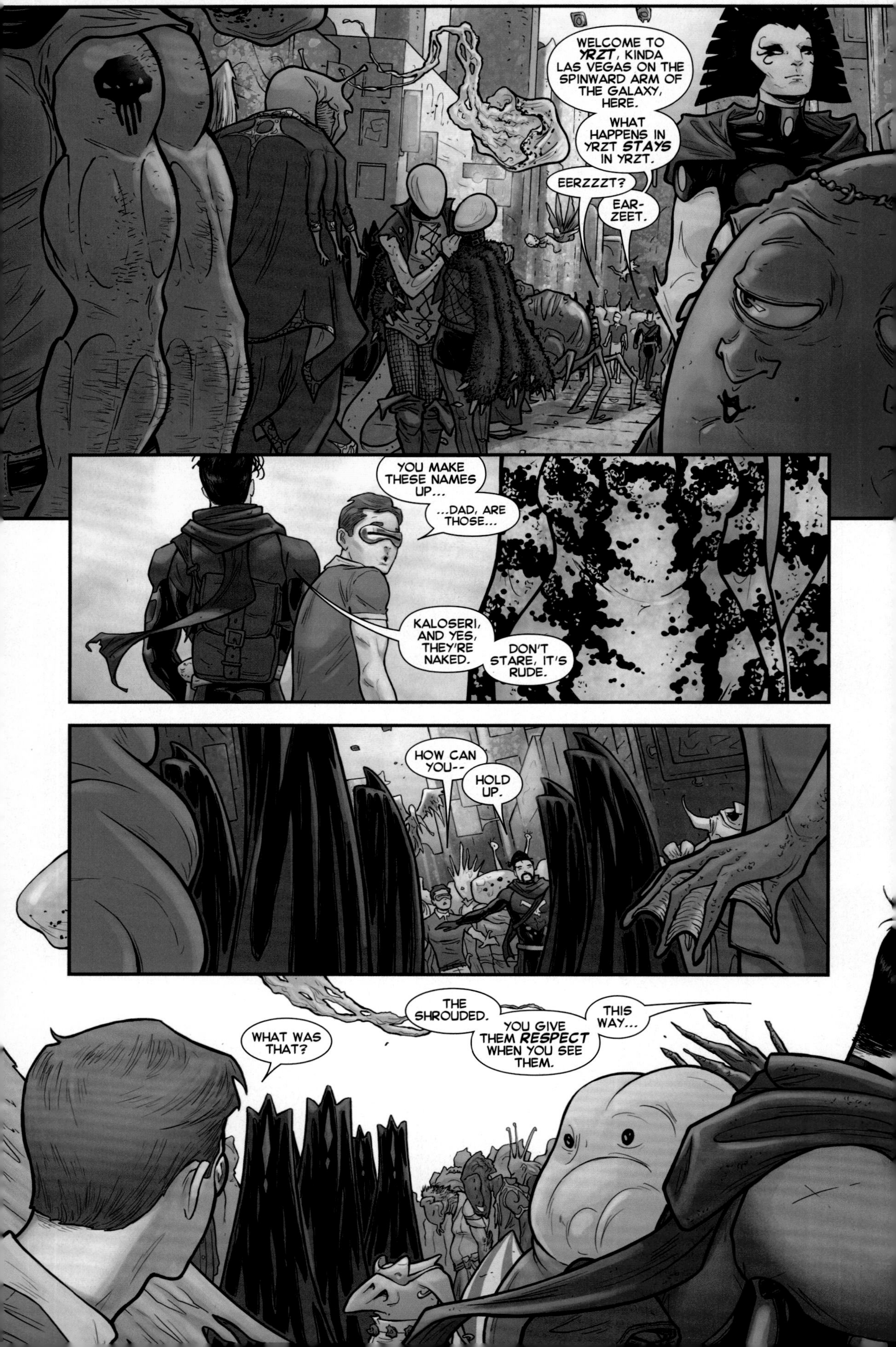
WELCOME TO YRZT, KINDA LAS VEGAS ON THE SPINWARD ARM OF THE GALAXY, HERE.
WHAT HAPPENS IN YRZT STAYS IN YRZT.
EERZZZT?
EAR-ZEET.
YOU MAKE THESE NAMES UP...
...DAD, ARE THOSE...
KALOSERI, AND YES, THEY'RE NAKED.
DON'T STARE, IT'S RUDE.
HOW CAN YOU--
HOLD UP.
WHAT WAS THAT?
THE SHROUDED.
YOU GIVE THEM RESPECT WHEN YOU SEE THEM.
THIS WAY...

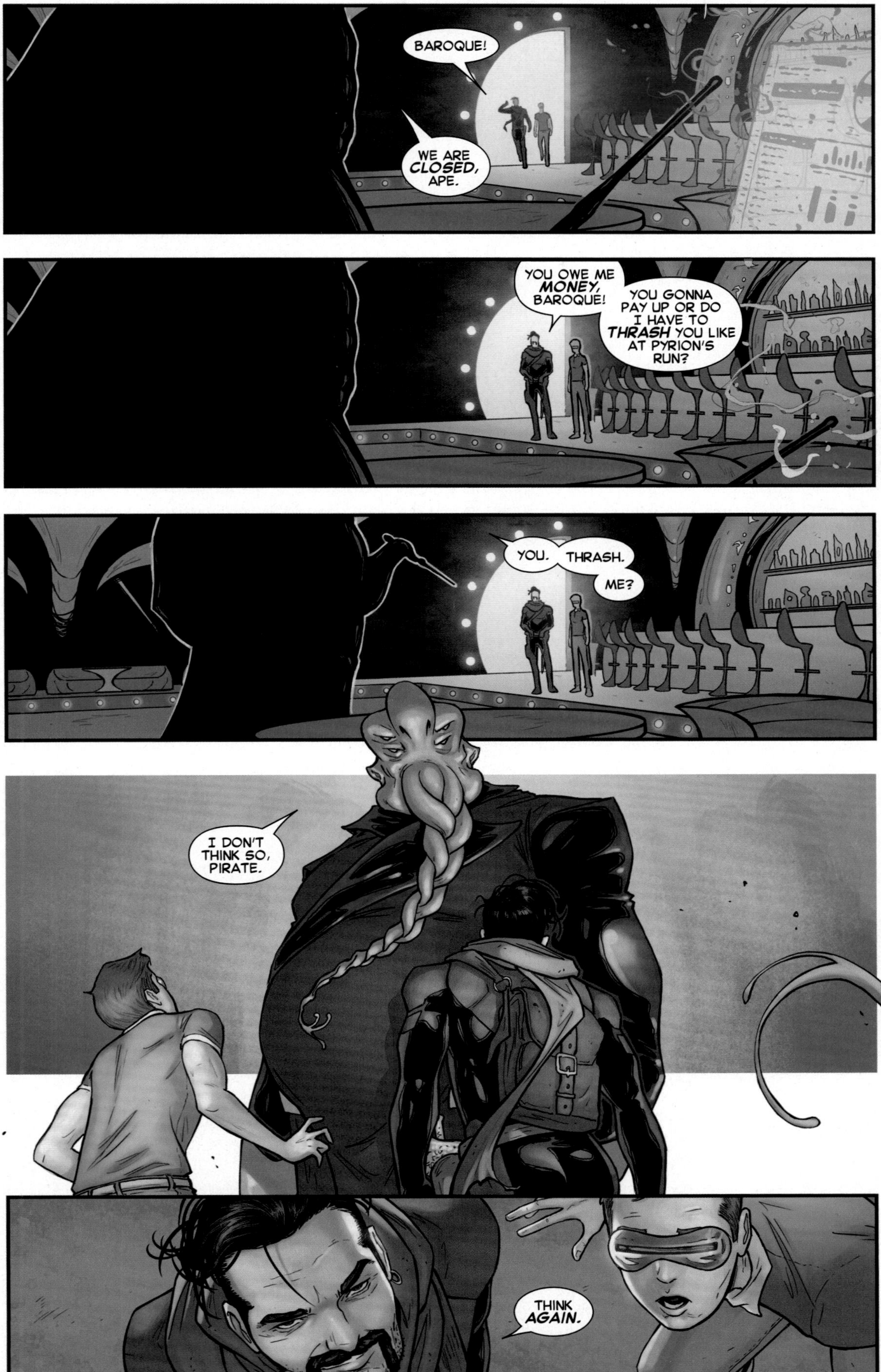

BAROQUE!
WE ARE CLOSED, APE.
YOU OWE ME MONEY, BAROQUE!
YOU GONNA PAY UP OR DO I HAVE TO THRASH YOU LIKE AT PYRION'S RUN?
YOU.
THRASH.
ME?
I DON'T THINK SO, PIRATE.
THINK AGAIN.

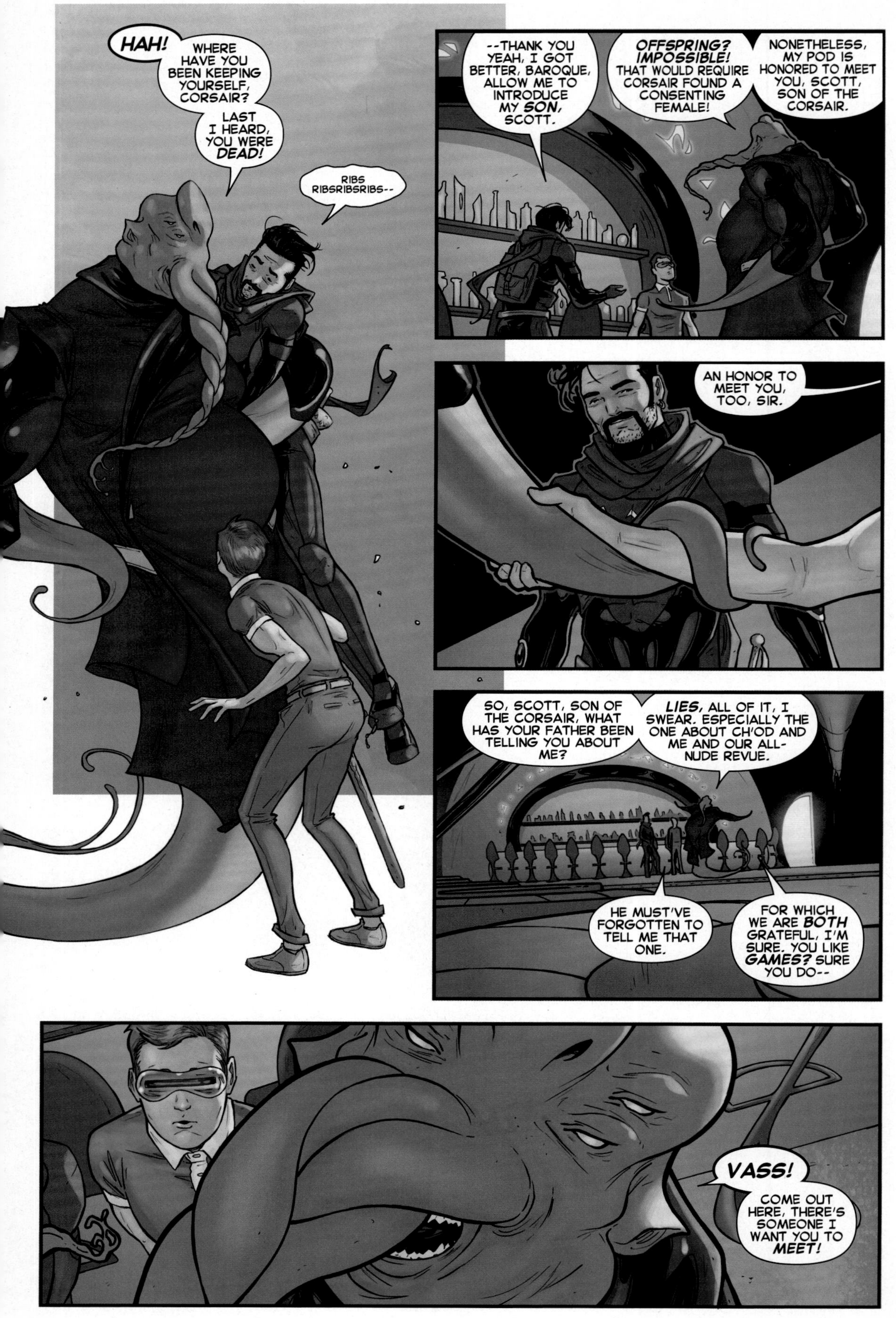
HAH!
WHERE HAVE YOU BEEN KEEPING YOURSELF, CORSAIR?
LAST I HEARD, YOU WERE DEAD!
RIBS RIBSRIBSRIBS--
--THANK YOU YEAH, I GOT BETTER, BAROQUE, ALLOW ME TO INTRODUCE MY SON, SCOTT.
OFFSPRING? IMPOSSIBLE! THAT WOULD REQUIRE CORSAIR FOUND A CONSENTING FEMALE!
NONETHELESS, MY POD IS HONORED TO MEET YOU, SCOTT, SON OF THE CORSAIR.
AN HONOR TO MEET YOU, TOO, SIR.
SO, SCOTT, SON OF THE CORSAIR, WHAT HAS YOUR FATHER BEEN TELLING YOU ABOUT ME?
LIES, ALL OF IT, I SWEAR. ESPECIALLY THE ONE ABOUT CH'OD AND ME AND OUR ALL-NUDE REVUE.
HE MUST'VE FORGOTTEN TO TELL ME THAT ONE.
FOR WHICH WE ARE BOTH GRATEFUL, I'M SURE. YOU LIKE GAMES? SURE YOU DO--
VASS!
COME OUT HERE, THERE'S SOMEONE I WANT YOU TO MEET!

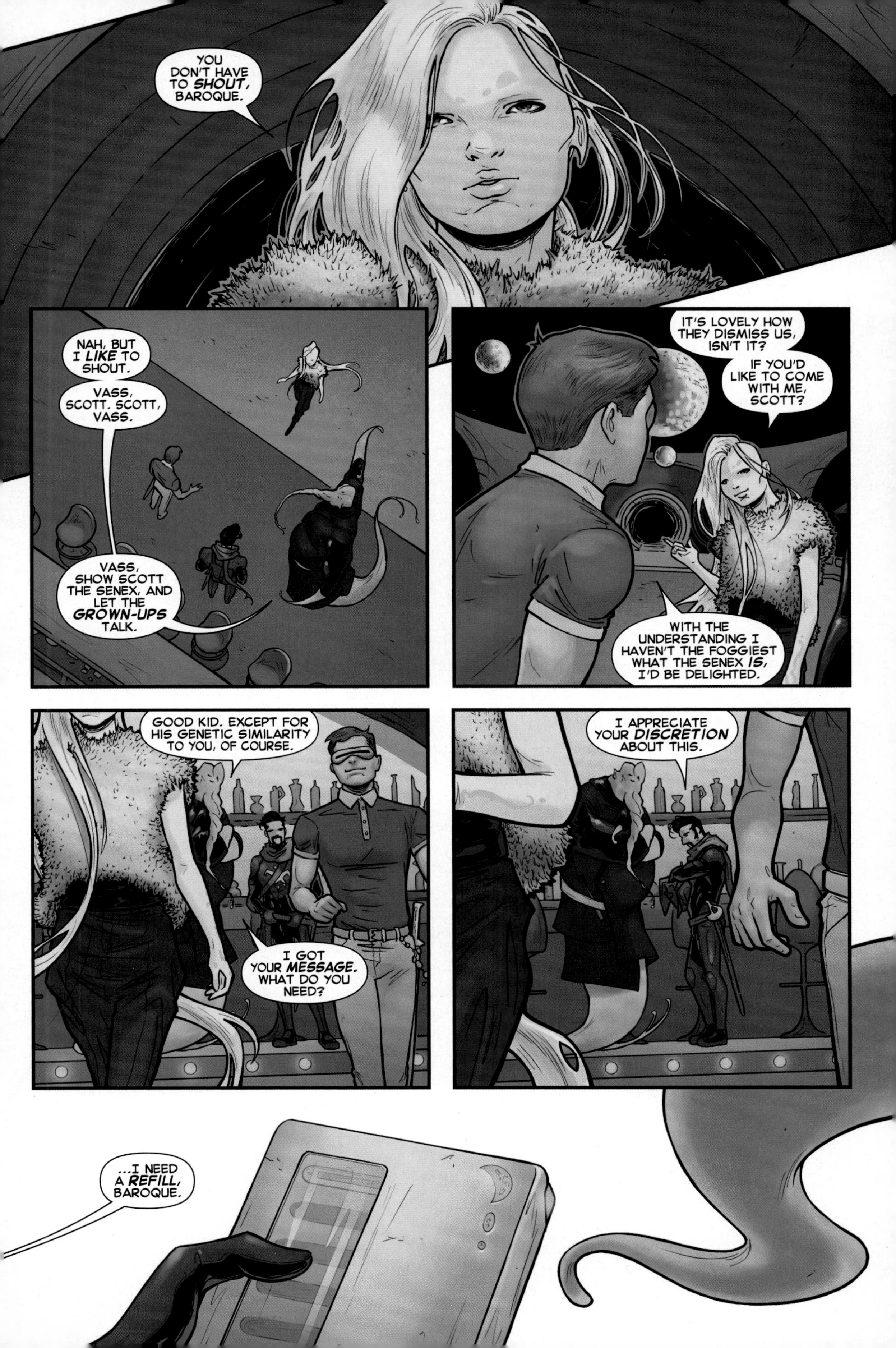
YOU DON'T HAVE TO SHOUT, BAROQUE.
NAH, BUT I LIKE TO SHOUT.
VASS, SCOTT. SCOTT, VASS.
VASS, SHOW SCOTT THE SENEX, AND LET THE GROWN-UPS TALK.
IT'S LOVELY HOW THEY DISMISS US, ISN'T IT?
IF YOU'D LIKE TO COME WITH ME, SCOTT?
WITH THE UNDERSTANDING I HAVEN'T THE FOGGIEST WHAT THE SENEX IS, I'D BE DELIGHTED.
GOOD KID. EXCEPT FOR HIS GENETIC SIMILARITY TO YOU, OF COURSE.
I GOT YOUR MESSAGE. WHAT DO YOU NEED?
I APPRECIATE YOUR DISCRETION ABOUT THIS.
...I NEED A REFILL, BAROQUE.

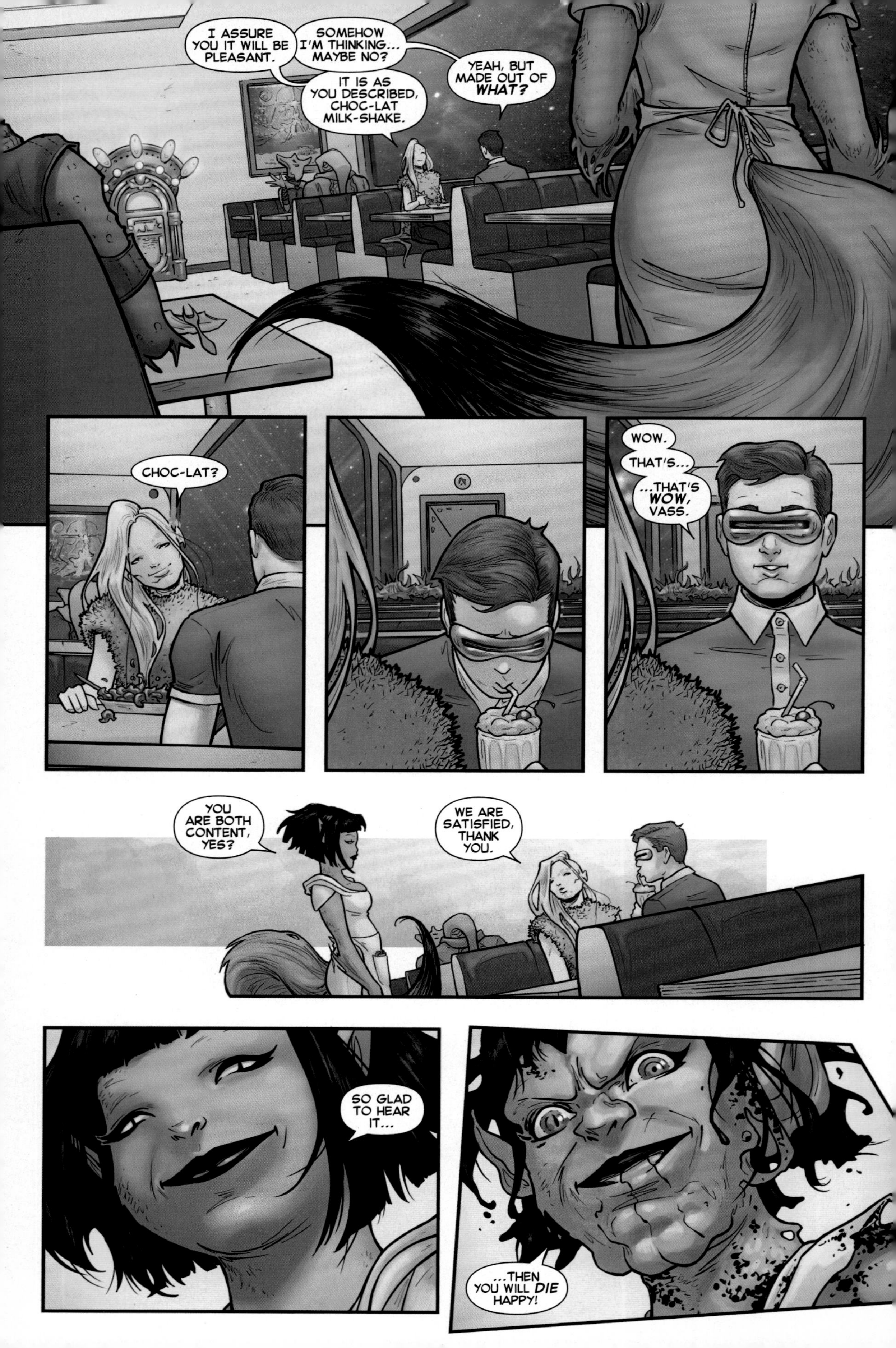
I ASSURE YOU IT WILL BE PLEASANT.
SOMEHOW I'M THINKING... MAYBE NO?
IT IS AS YOU DESCRIBED, CHOC-LAT MILK-SHAKE.
YEAH, BUT MADE OUT OF WHAT?
CHOC-LAT?
WOW.
THAT'S...
...THAT'S WOW, VASS.
YOU ARE BOTH CONTENT, YES?
WE ARE SATISFIED, THANK YOU.
SO GLAD TO HEAR IT...
...THEN YOU WILL DIE HAPPY!

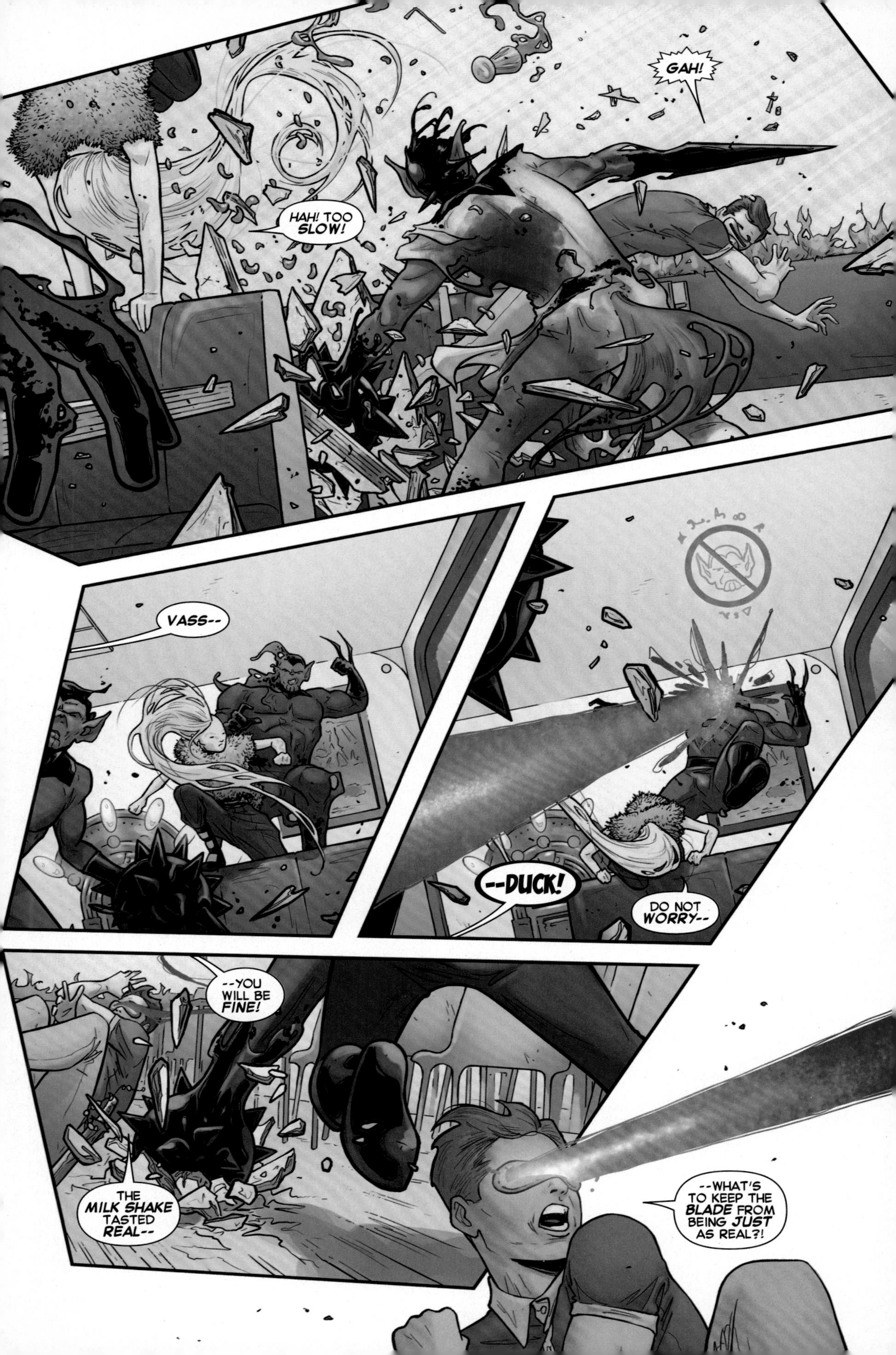
GAH!
HAH! TOO SLOW!
VASS--
--DUCK!
DO NOT WORRY--
--YOU WILL BE FINE!
THE MILK SHAKE TASTED REAL--
--WHAT'S TO KEEP THE BLADE FROM BEING JUST AS REAL?!

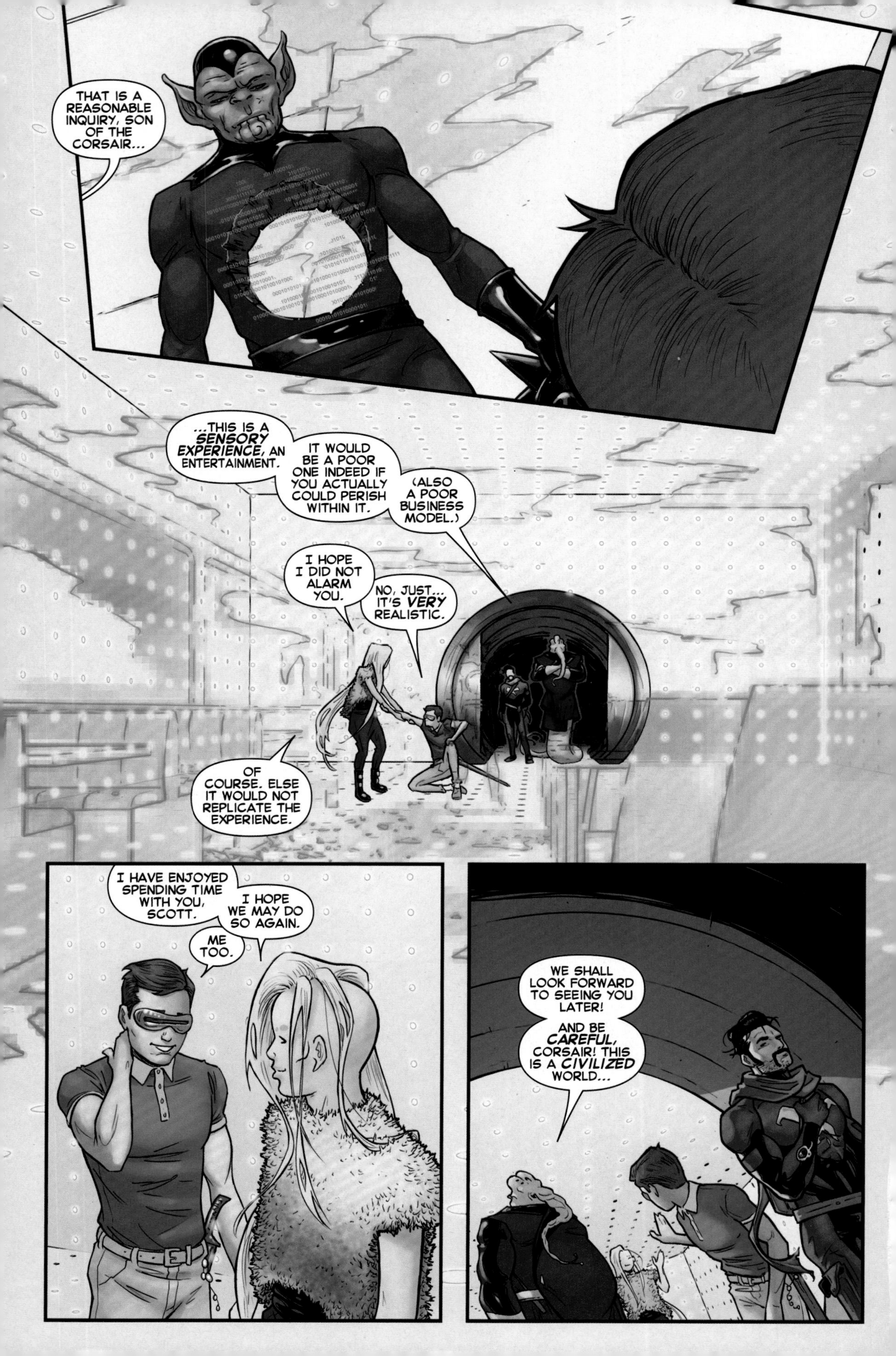
THAT IS A REASONABLE INQUIRY, SON OF THE CORSAIR...
...THIS IS A SENSORY EXPERIENCE, AN ENTERTAINMENT.
IT WOULD BE A POOR ONE INDEED IF YOU ACTUALLY COULD PERISH WITHIN IT.
(ALSO A POOR BUSINESS MODEL.)
I HOPE I DID NOT ALARM YOU.
NO, JUST... IT'S VERY REALISTIC.
OF COURSE. ELSE IT WOULD NOT REPLICATE THE EXPERIENCE.
I HAVE ENJOYED SPENDING TIME WITH YOU, SCOTT.
I HOPE WE MAY DO SO AGAIN.
ME TOO.
WE SHALL LOOK FORWARD TO SEEING YOU LATER!
AND BE CAREFUL, CORSAIR! THIS IS A CIVILIZED WORLD...

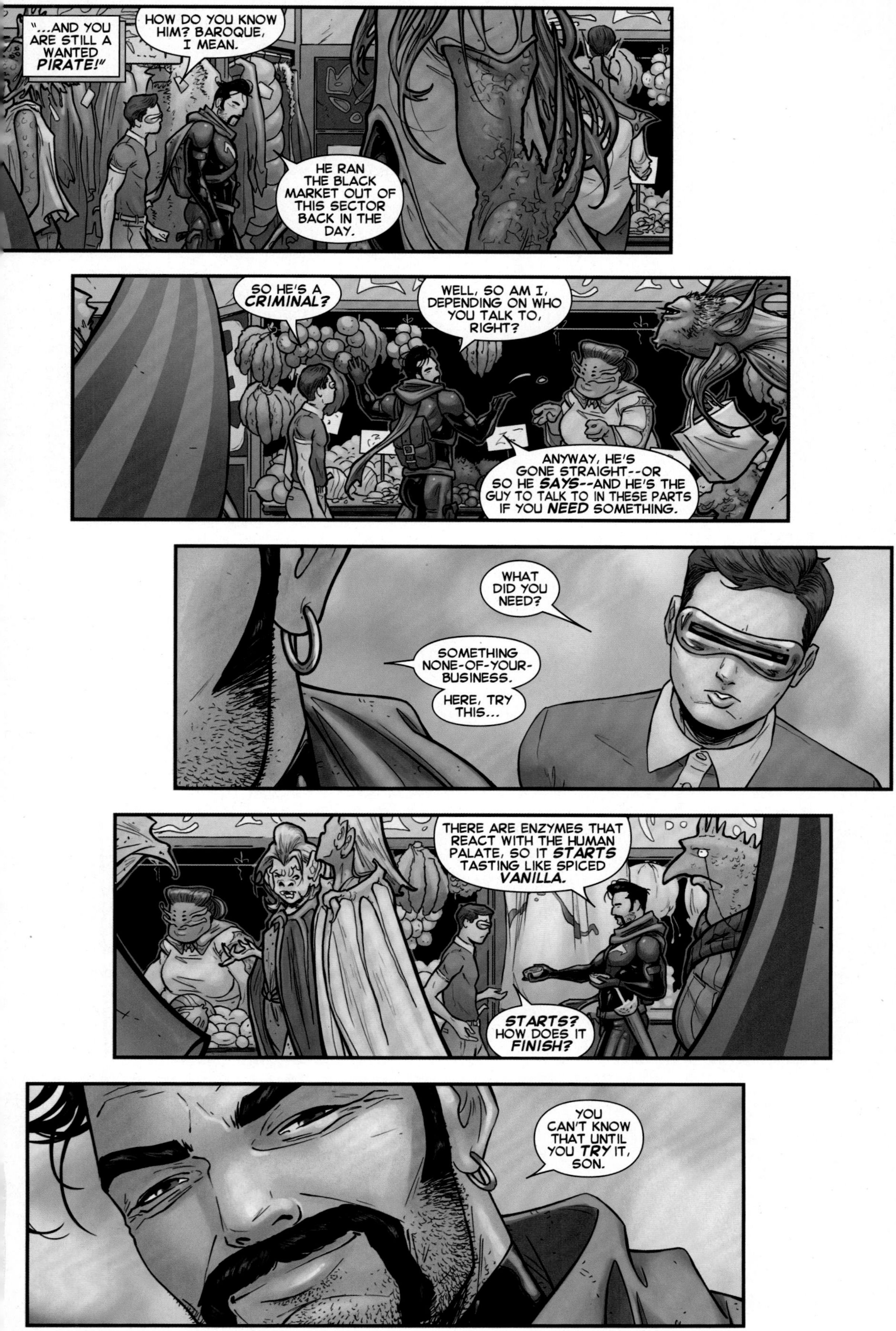
"...AND YOU ARE STILL A WANTED PIRATE!"
HOW DO YOU KNOW HIM? BAROQUE, I MEAN.
HE RAN THE BLACK MARKET OUT OF THIS SECTOR BACK IN THE DAY.
SO HE'S A CRIMINAL?
WELL, SO AM I, DEPENDING ON WHO YOU TALK TO, RIGHT?
ANYWAY, HE'S GONE STRAIGHT--OR SO HE SAYS--AND HE'S THE GUY TO TALK TO IN THESE PARTS IF YOU NEED SOMETHING.
WHAT DID YOU NEED?
SOMETHING NONE-OF-YOUR-BUSINESS.
HERE, TRY THIS...
THERE ARE ENZYMES THAT REACT WITH THE HUMAN PALATE, SO IT STARTS TASTING LIKE SPICED VANILLA.
STARTS? HOW DOES IT FINISH?
YOU CAN'T KNOW THAT UNTIL YOU TRY IT, SON.

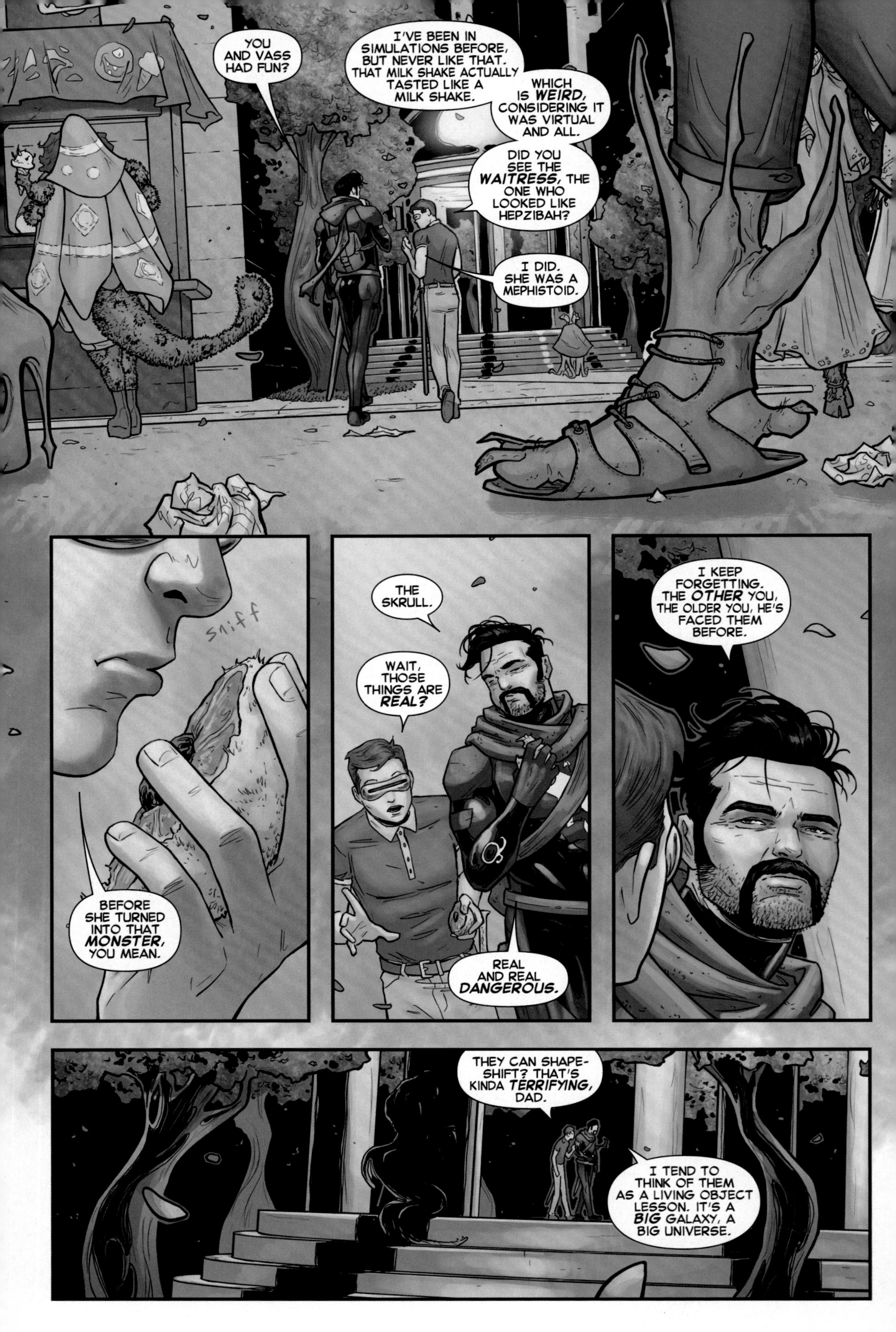
YOU AND VASS HAD FUN?
I'VE BEEN IN SIMULATIONS BEFORE, BUT NEVER LIKE THAT. THAT MILK SHAKE ACTUALLY TASTED LIKE A MILK SHAKE.
WHICH IS WEIRD, CONSIDERING IT WAS VIRTUAL AND ALL.
DID YOU SEE THE WAITRESS, THE ONE WHO LOOKED LIKE HEPZIBAH?
I DID. SHE WAS A MEPHISTOID.
sniff
BEFORE SHE TURNED INTO THAT MONSTER, YOU MEAN.
THE SKRULL.
WAIT, THOSE THINGS ARE REAL?
REAL AND REAL DANGEROUS.
I KEEP FORGETTING. THE OTHER YOU, THE OLDER YOU, HE'S FACED THEM BEFORE.
THEY CAN SHAPE-SHIFT? THAT'S KINDA TERRIFYING, DAD.
I TEND TO THINK OF THEM AS A LIVING OBJECT LESSON. IT'S A BIG GALAXY, A BIG UNIVERSE.

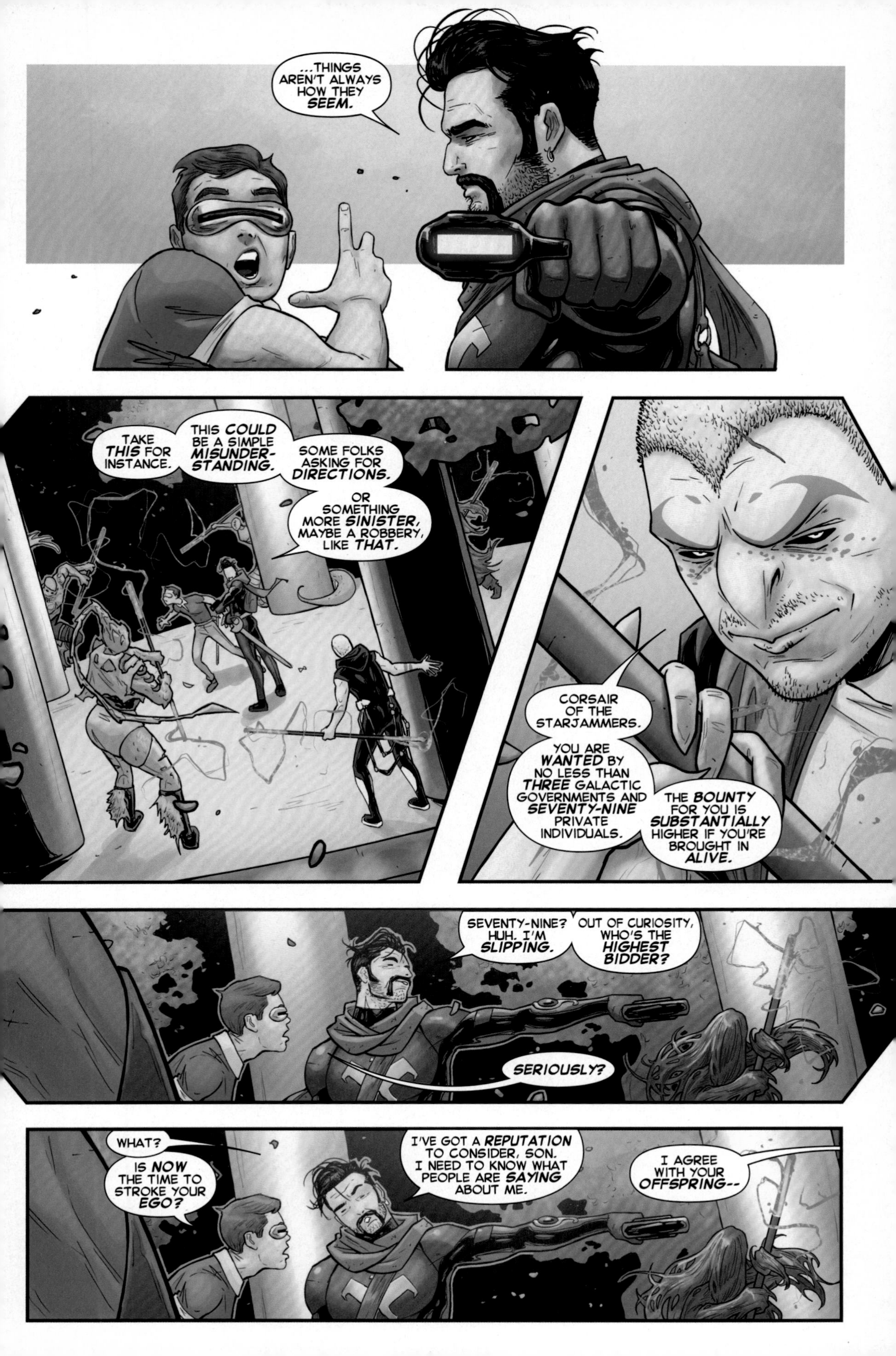
...THINGS AREN'T ALWAYS HOW THEY SEEM.
TAKE THIS FOR INSTANCE.
THIS COULD BE A SIMPLE MISUNDERSTANDING.
SOME FOLKS ASKING FOR DIRECTIONS.
OR SOMETHING MORE SINISTER, MAYBE A ROBBERY, LIKE THAT.
CORSAIR OF THE STARJAMMERS.
YOU ARE WANTED BY NO LESS THAN THREE GALACTIC GOVERNMENTS AND SEVENTY-NINE PRIVATE INDIVIDUALS.
THE BOUNTY FOR YOU IS SUBSTANTIALLY HIGHER IF YOU'RE BROUGHT IN ALIVE.
SEVENTY-NINE? HUH. I'M SLIPPING.
OUT OF CURIOSITY, WHO'S THE HIGHEST BIDDER?
SERIOUSLY?
WHAT?
IS NOW THE TIME TO STROKE YOUR EGO?
I'VE GOT A REPUTATION TO CONSIDER, SON. I NEED TO KNOW WHAT PEOPLE ARE SAYING ABOUT ME.
I AGREE WITH YOUR OFFSPRING--

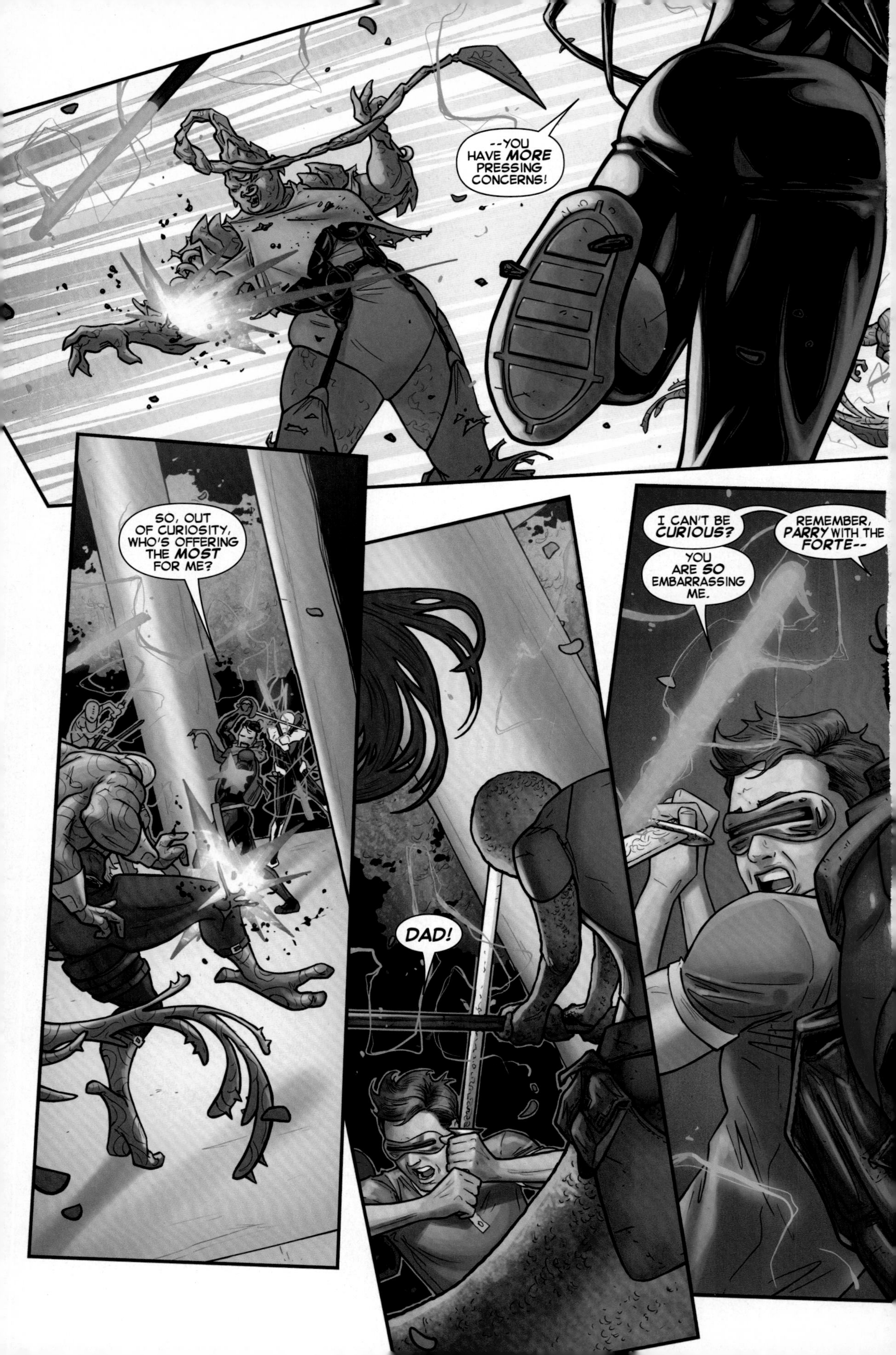
--YOU HAVE MORE PRESSING CONCERNS!
SO, OUT OF CURIOSITY, WHO'S OFFERING THE MOST FOR ME?
DAD!
I CAN'T BE CURIOUS?
YOU ARE SO EMBARRASSING ME.
REMEMBER, PARRY WITH THE FORTE--

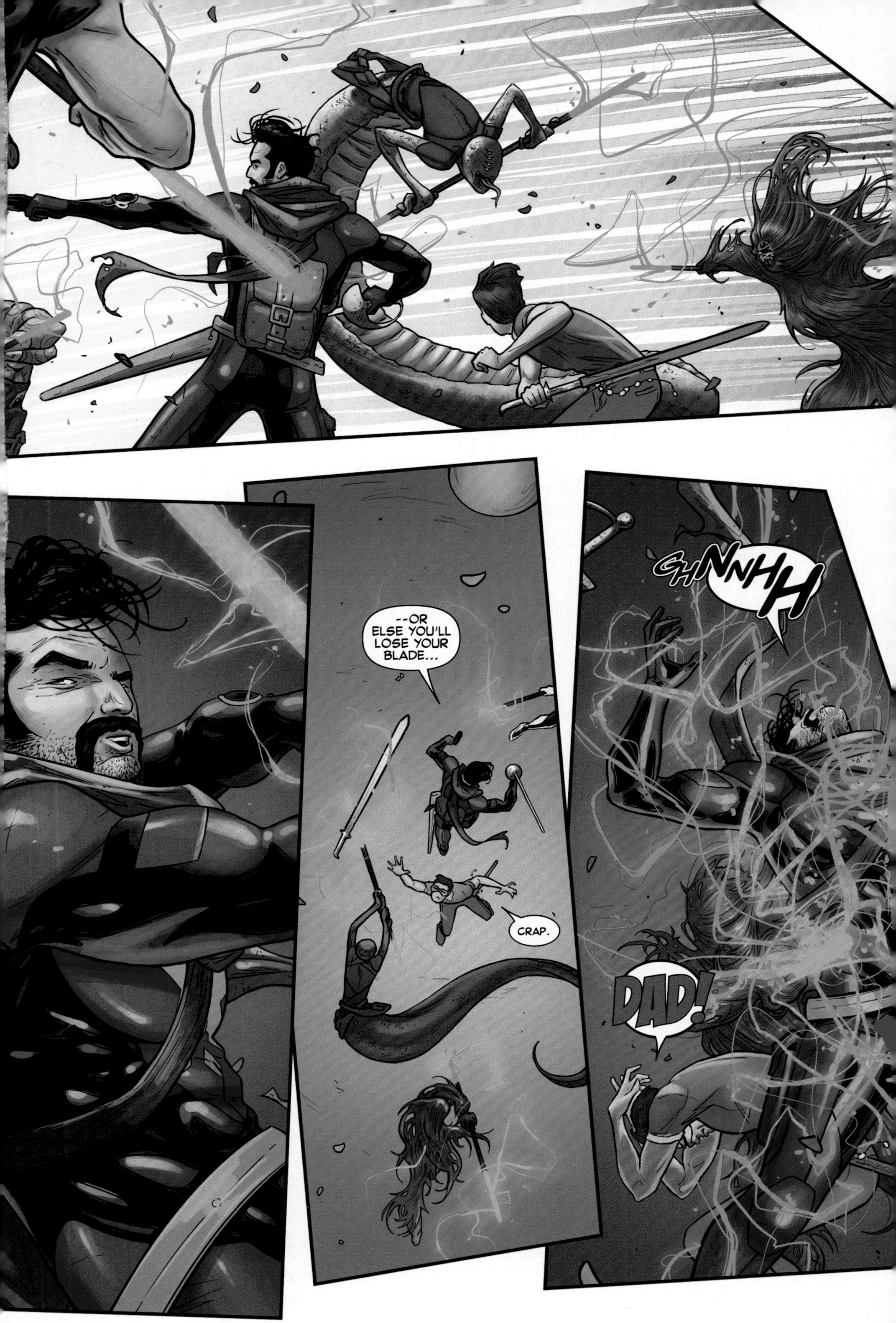
--OR ELSE YOU'LL LOSE YOUR BLADE...
CRAP.
GHNNHH
DAD!

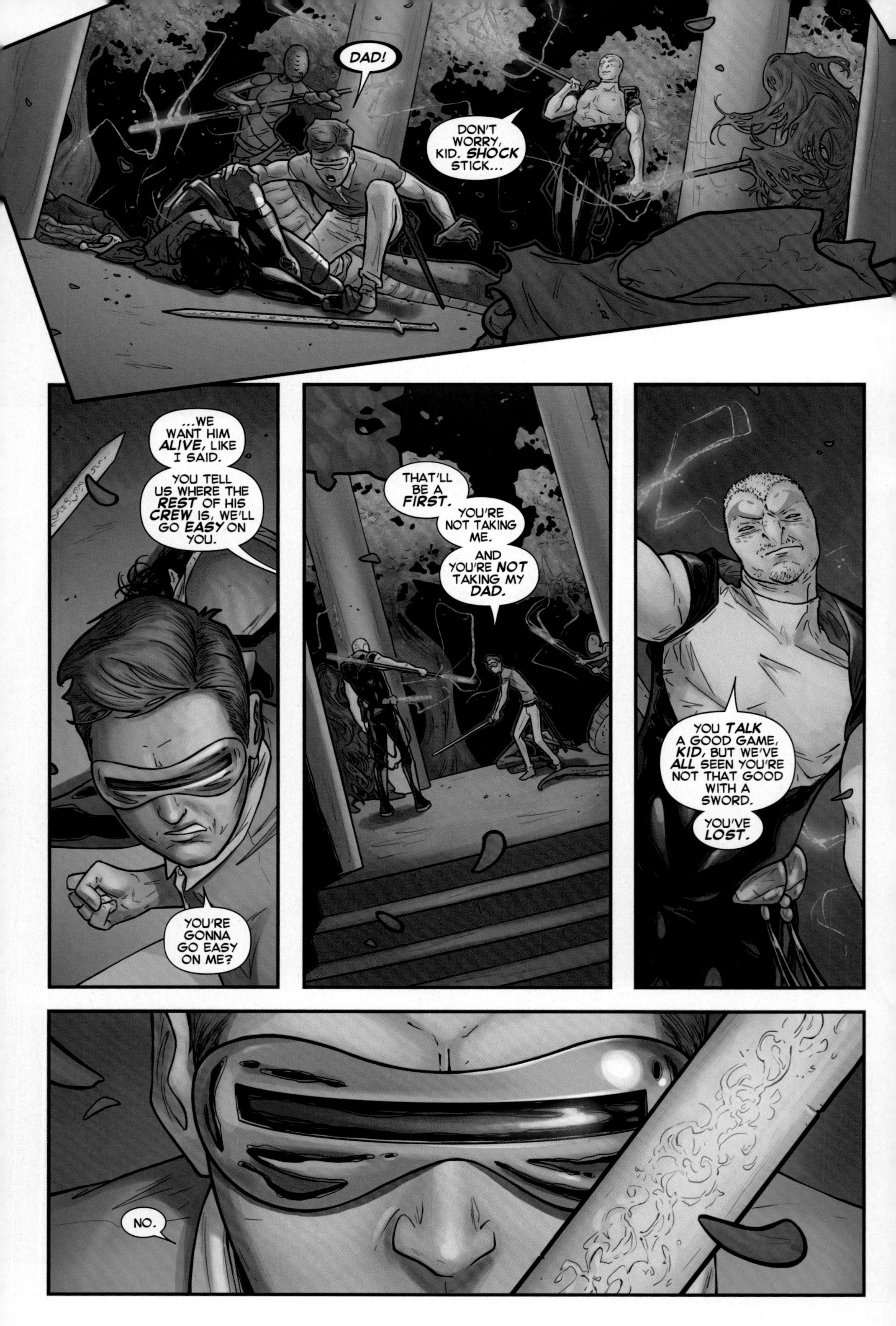
DAD!
DON'T WORRY, KID. SHOCK STICK...
...WE WANT HIM ALIVE, LIKE I SAID.
YOU TELL US WHERE THE REST OF HIS CREW IS, WE'LL GO EASY ON YOU.
YOU'RE GONNA GO EASY ON ME?
THAT'LL BE A FIRST.
YOU'RE NOT TAKING ME.
AND YOU'RE NOT TAKING MY DAD.
YOU TALK A GOOD GAME, KID, BUT WE'VE ALL SEEN YOU'RE NOT THAT GOOD WITH A SWORD.
YOU'VE LOST.
NO.

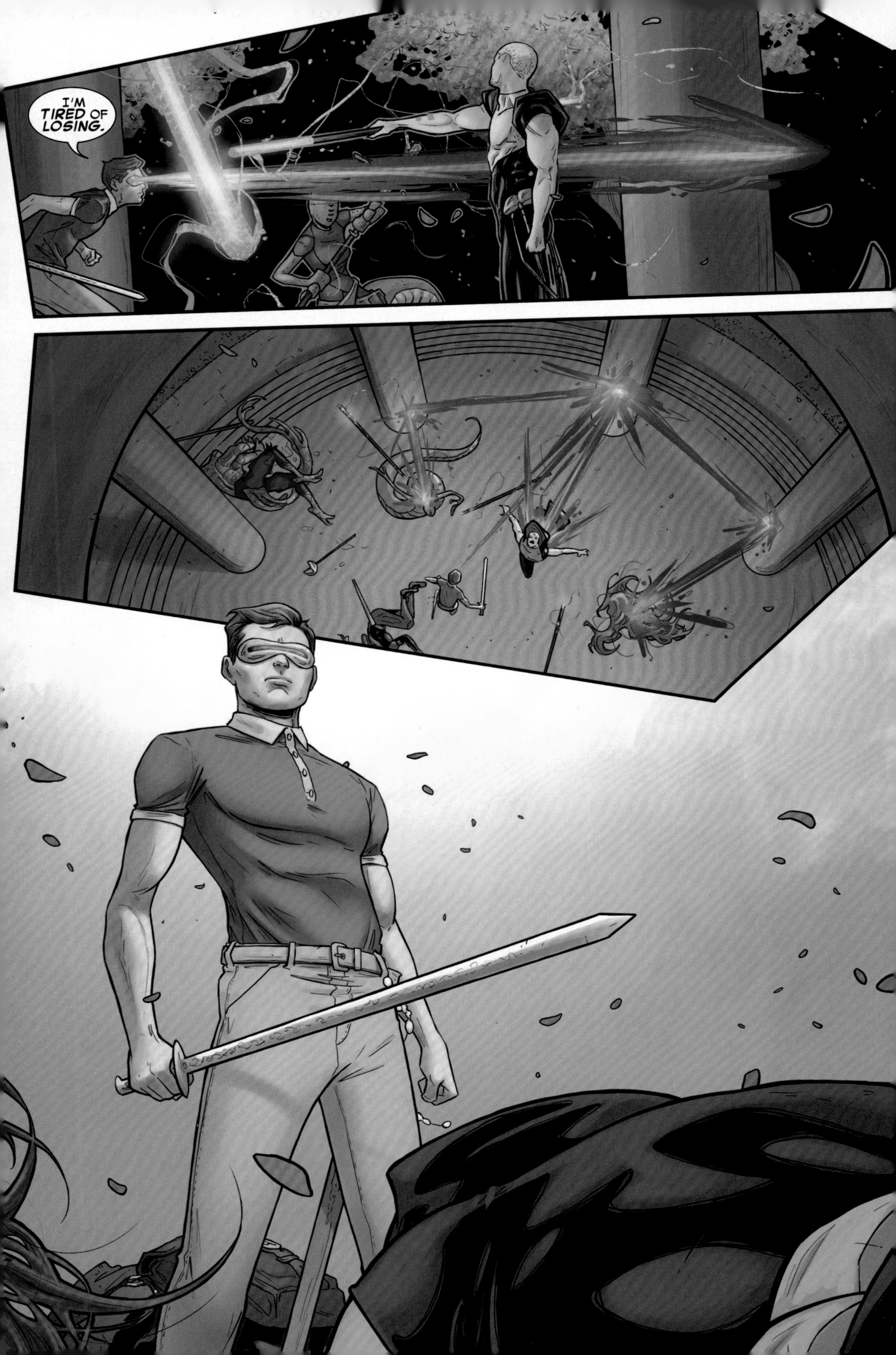
I'M TIRED OF LOSING.

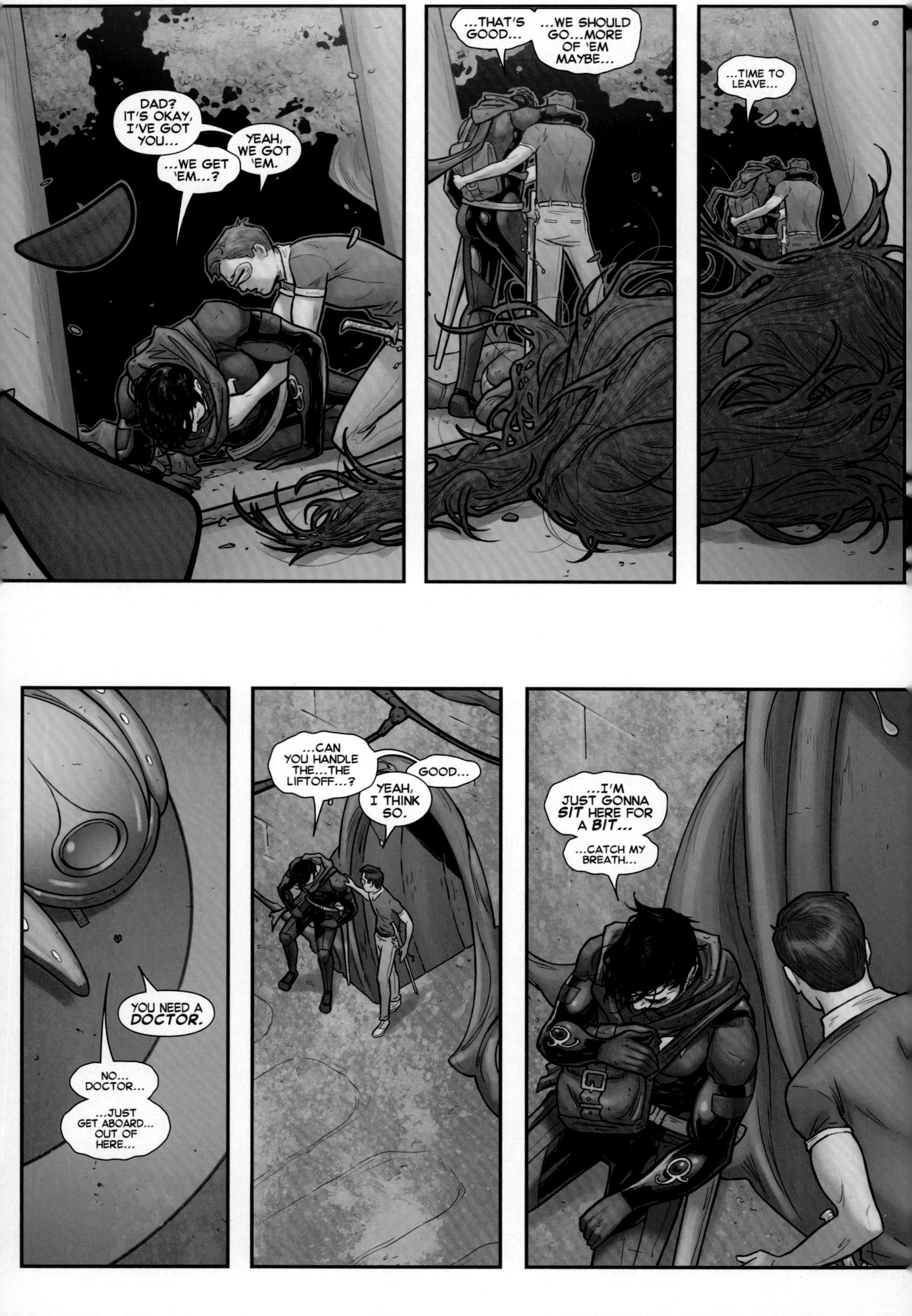
DAD? IT'S OKAY, I'VE GOT YOU...
...WE GET 'EM...?
YEAH, WE GOT 'EM.
...THAT'S GOOD...
...WE SHOULD GO...MORE OF 'EM MAYBE...
...TIME TO LEAVE...
YOU NEED A DOCTOR.
NO... DOCTOR...
...JUST GET ABOARD... OUT OF HERE...
...CAN YOU HANDLE THE...THE LIFTOFF...?
YEAH, I THINK SO.
GOOD...
...I'M JUST GONNA SIT HERE FOR A BIT...
...CATCH MY BREATH...

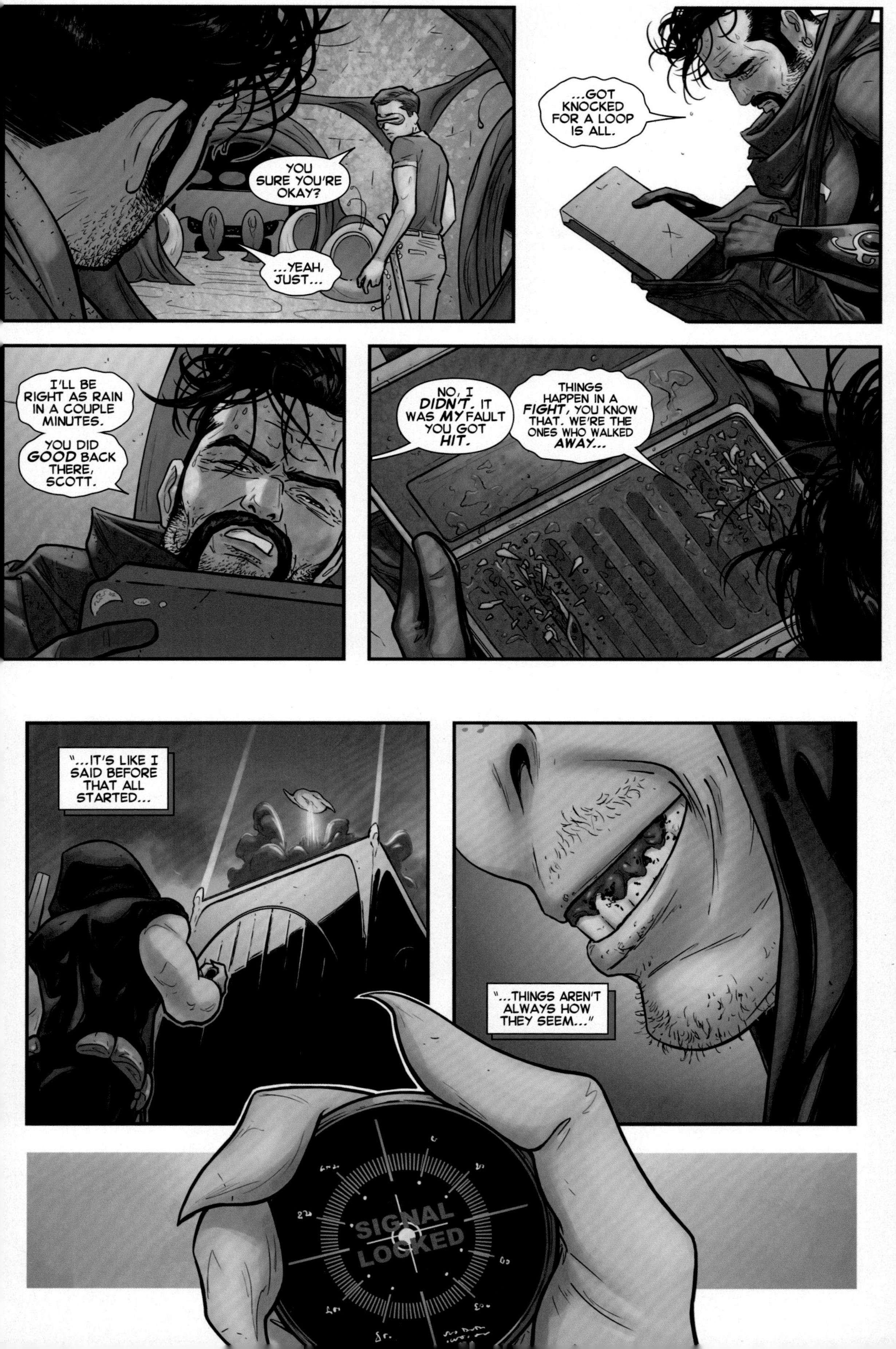
YOU SURE YOU'RE OKAY?
...YEAH, JUST...
...GOT KNOCKED FOR A LOOP IS ALL.
I'LL BE RIGHT AS RAIN IN A COUPLE MINUTES.
YOU DID GOOD BACK THERE, SCOTT.
NO, I DIDN'T. IT WAS MY FAULT YOU GOT HIT.
THINGS HAPPEN IN A FIGHT, YOU KNOW THAT. WE'RE THE ONES WHO WALKED AWAY...
"...IT'S LIKE I SAID BEFORE THAT ALL STARTED...
"...THINGS AREN'T ALWAYS HOW THEY SEEM..."
SIGNAL LOCKED

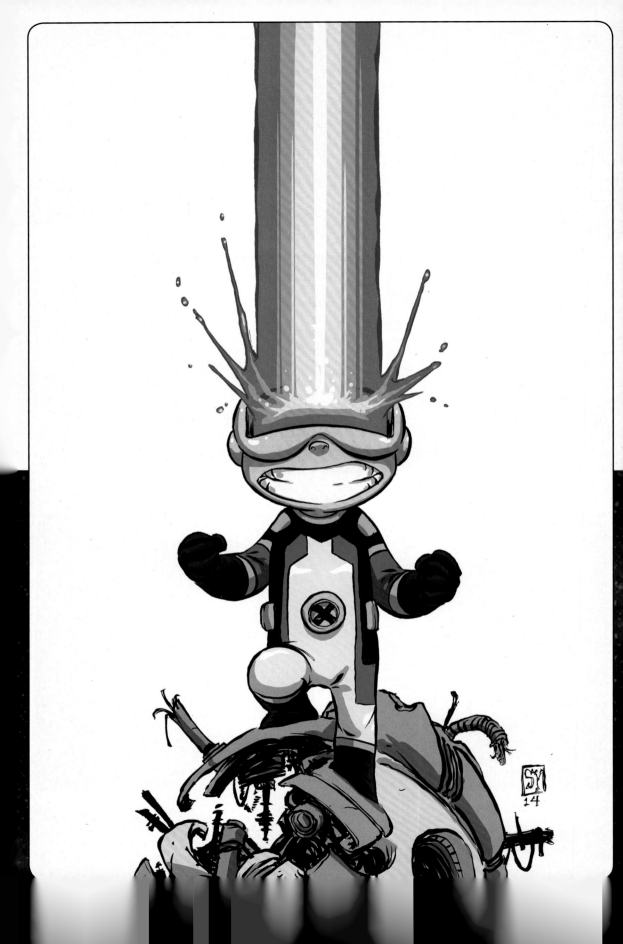

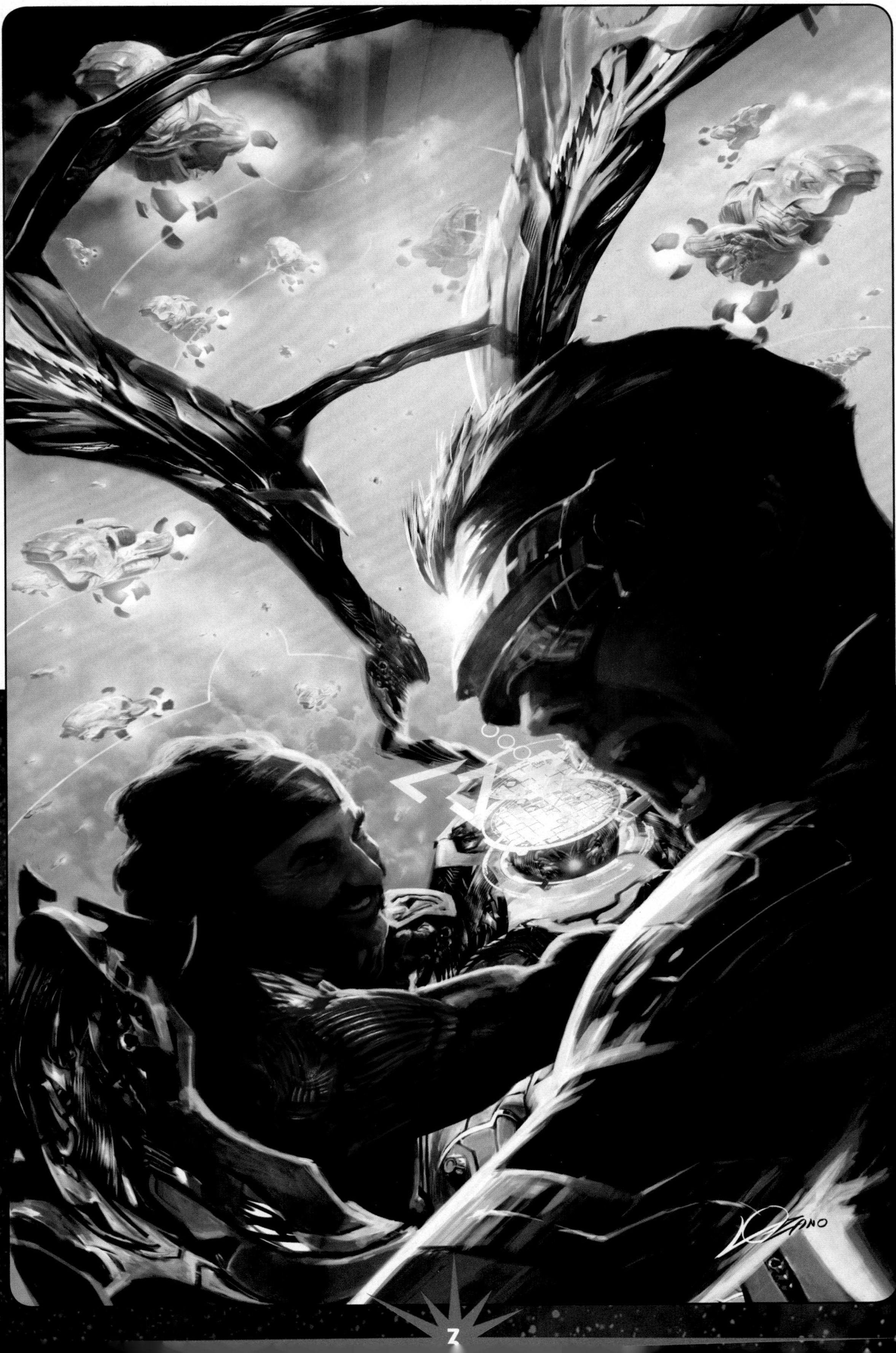

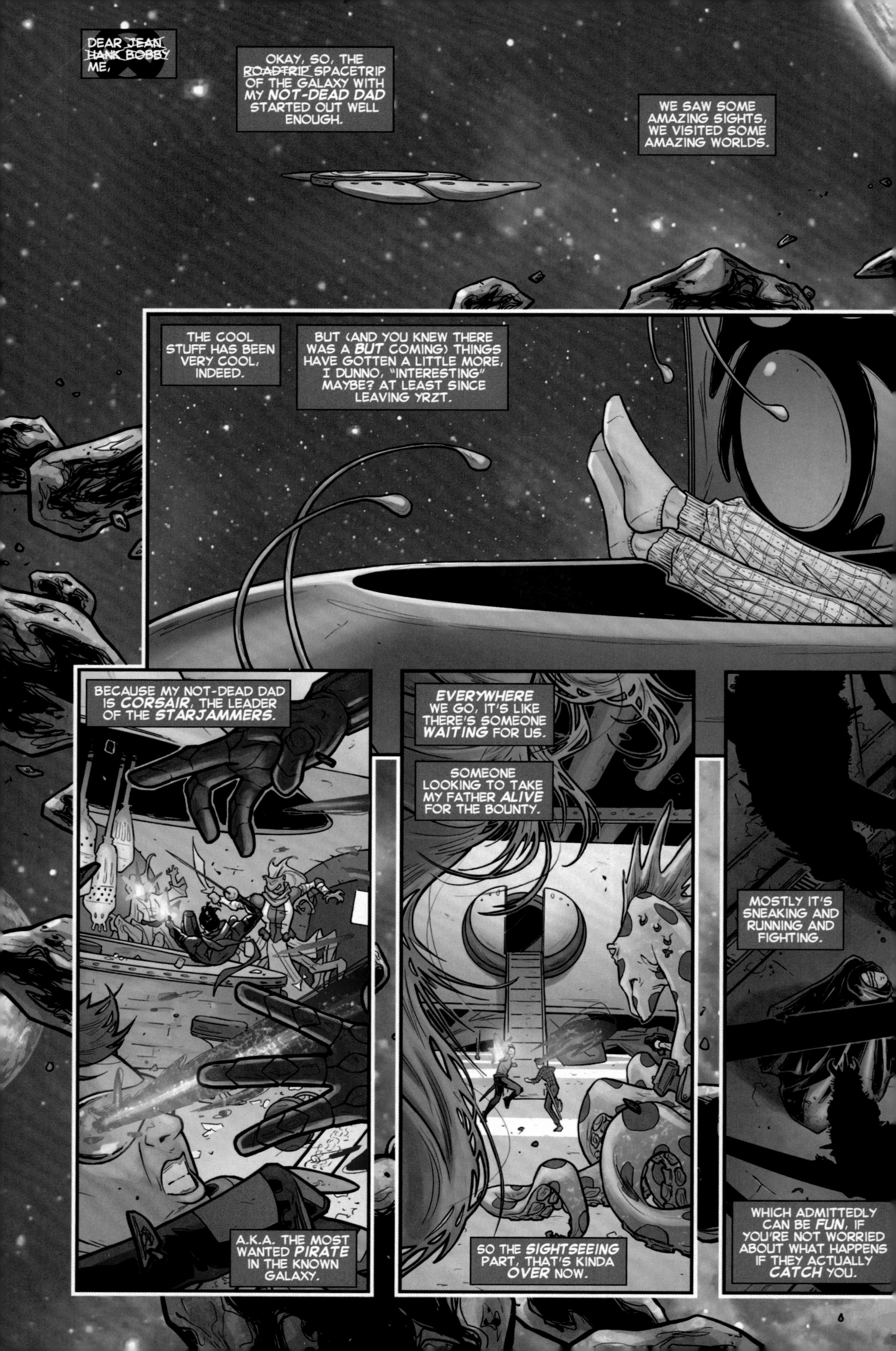
DEAR ~~JEAN~~ ~~HANK~~ ~~BOBBY~~ ME,
OKAY, SO, THE ~~ROADTRIP~~ SPACETRIP OF THE GALAXY WITH MY *NOT-DEAD DAD* STARTED OUT WELL ENOUGH.
WE SAW SOME AMAZING SIGHTS, WE VISITED SOME AMAZING WORLDS.
THE COOL STUFF HAS BEEN VERY COOL, INDEED.
BUT (AND YOU KNEW THERE WAS A *BUT* COMING) THINGS HAVE GOTTEN A LITTLE MORE, I DUNNO, "INTERESTING" MAYBE? AT LEAST SINCE LEAVING *YRZT*.
BECAUSE MY NOT-DEAD DAD IS *CORSAIR*, THE LEADER OF THE *STARJAMMERS*.
A.K.A. THE MOST WANTED *PIRATE* IN THE KNOWN GALAXY.
EVERYWHERE WE GO, IT'S LIKE THERE'S SOMEONE *WAITING* FOR US.
SOMEONE LOOKING TO TAKE MY FATHER *ALIVE* FOR THE BOUNTY.
SO THE *SIGHTSEEING* PART, THAT'S KINDA *OVER* NOW.
MOSTLY IT'S SNEAKING AND RUNNING AND FIGHTING.
WHICH ADMITTEDLY CAN BE *FUN*, IF YOU'RE NOT WORRIED ABOUT WHAT HAPPENS IF THEY ACTUALLY *CATCH* YOU.

I HAVE PERSONALLY SEEN MORE ALIENS THAN ARE IN ALL THE *STAR WARS* MOVIES COMBINED AT THIS POINT.

AND THE *REASON* IT'S BECOME "INTERESTING?"

OH, THERE'S ONE MORE THING.

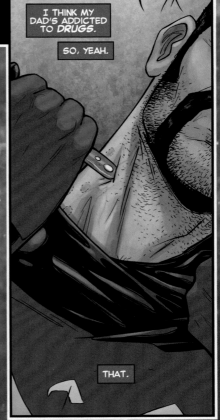

I THINK MY DAD'S ADDICTED TO *DRUGS*.

SO, YEAH.

THAT.

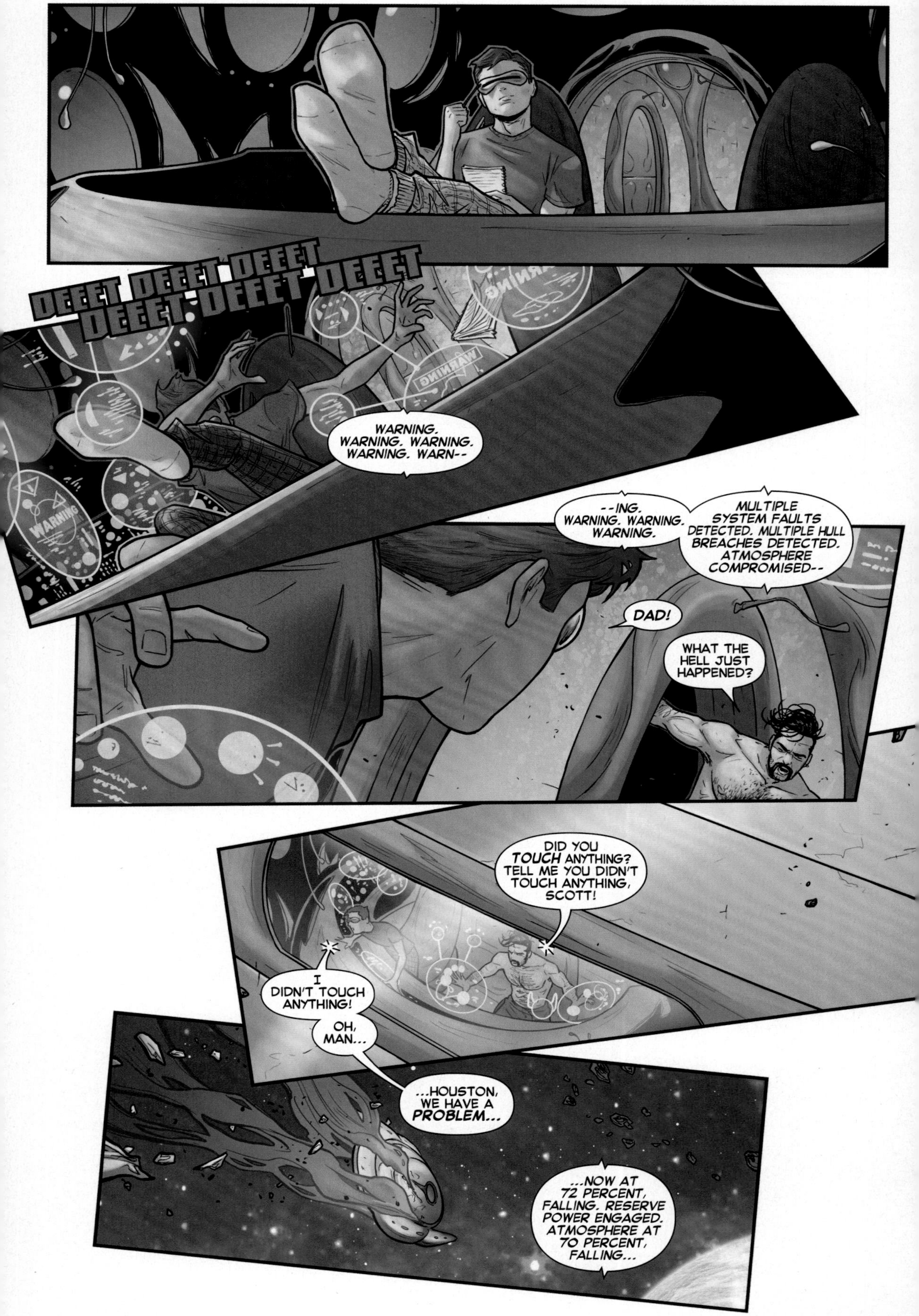
DEEET DEEET DEEET
DEEET DEEET DEEET
WARNING.
WARNING. WARNING. WARNING. WARNING. WARN--
--ING. WARNING. WARNING. WARNING.
MULTIPLE SYSTEM FAULTS DETECTED. MULTIPLE HULL BREACHES DETECTED. ATMOSPHERE COMPROMISED--
DAD!
WHAT THE HELL JUST HAPPENED?
DID YOU TOUCH ANYTHING? TELL ME YOU DIDN'T TOUCH ANYTHING, SCOTT!
I DIDN'T TOUCH ANYTHING!
OH, MAN...
...HOUSTON, WE HAVE A PROBLEM...
...NOW AT 72 PERCENT, FALLING. RESERVE POWER ENGAGED. ATMOSPHERE AT 70 PERCENT, FALLING...

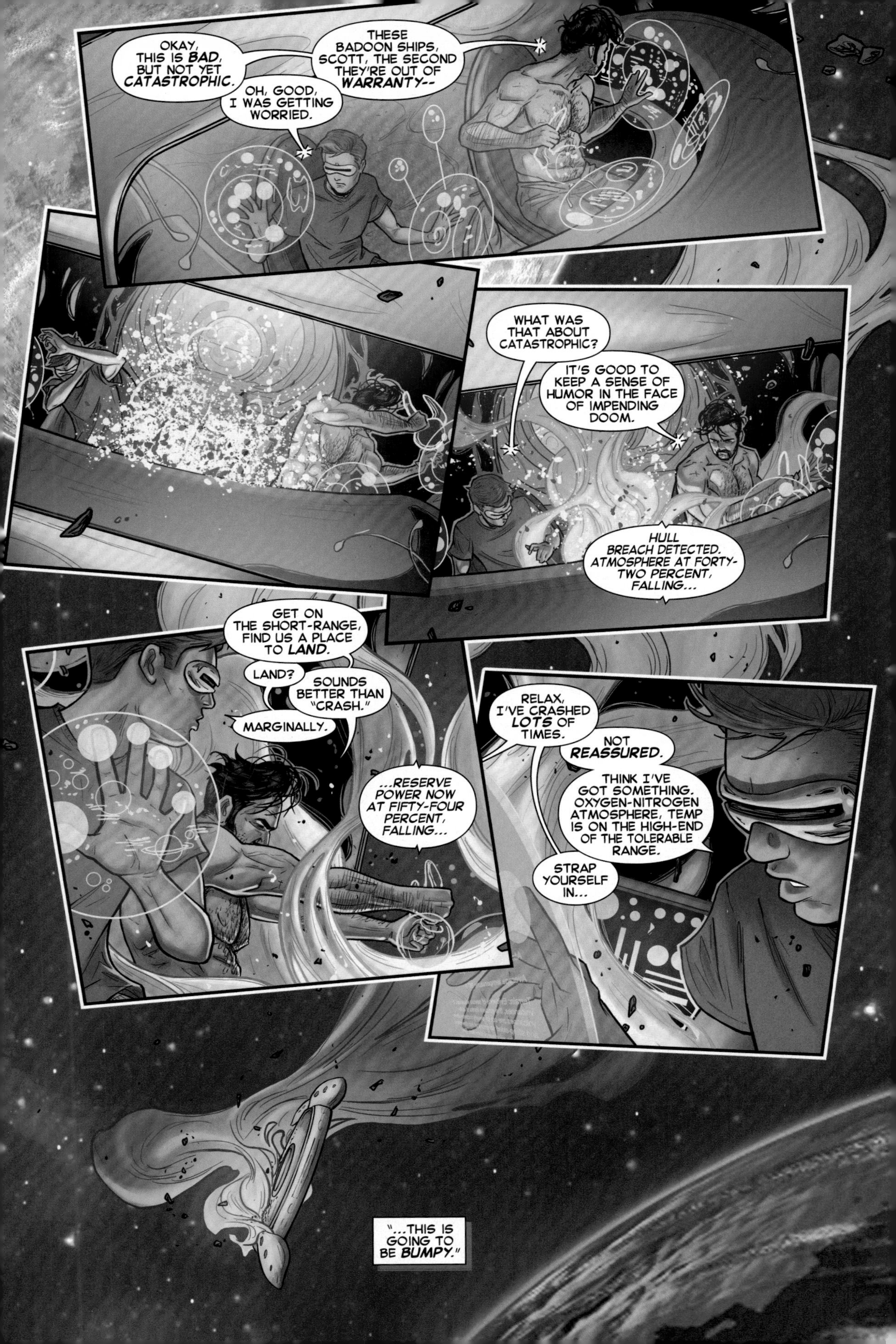

OKAY, THIS IS BAD, BUT NOT YET CATASTROPHIC.
THESE BADOON SHIPS, SCOTT, THE SECOND THEY'RE OUT OF WARRANTY--
OH, GOOD, I WAS GETTING WORRIED.
WHAT WAS THAT ABOUT CATASTROPHIC?
IT'S GOOD TO KEEP A SENSE OF HUMOR IN THE FACE OF IMPENDING DOOM.
HULL BREACH DETECTED. ATMOSPHERE AT FORTY-TWO PERCENT, FALLING...
GET ON THE SHORT-RANGE, FIND US A PLACE TO LAND.
LAND?
SOUNDS BETTER THAN "CRASH."
MARGINALLY.
...RESERVE POWER NOW AT FIFTY-FOUR PERCENT, FALLING...
RELAX, I'VE CRASHED LOTS OF TIMES.
NOT REASSURED.
THINK I'VE GOT SOMETHING. OXYGEN-NITROGEN ATMOSPHERE, TEMP IS ON THE HIGH-END OF THE TOLERABLE RANGE.
STRAP YOURSELF IN...
"...THIS IS GOING TO BE BUMPY."

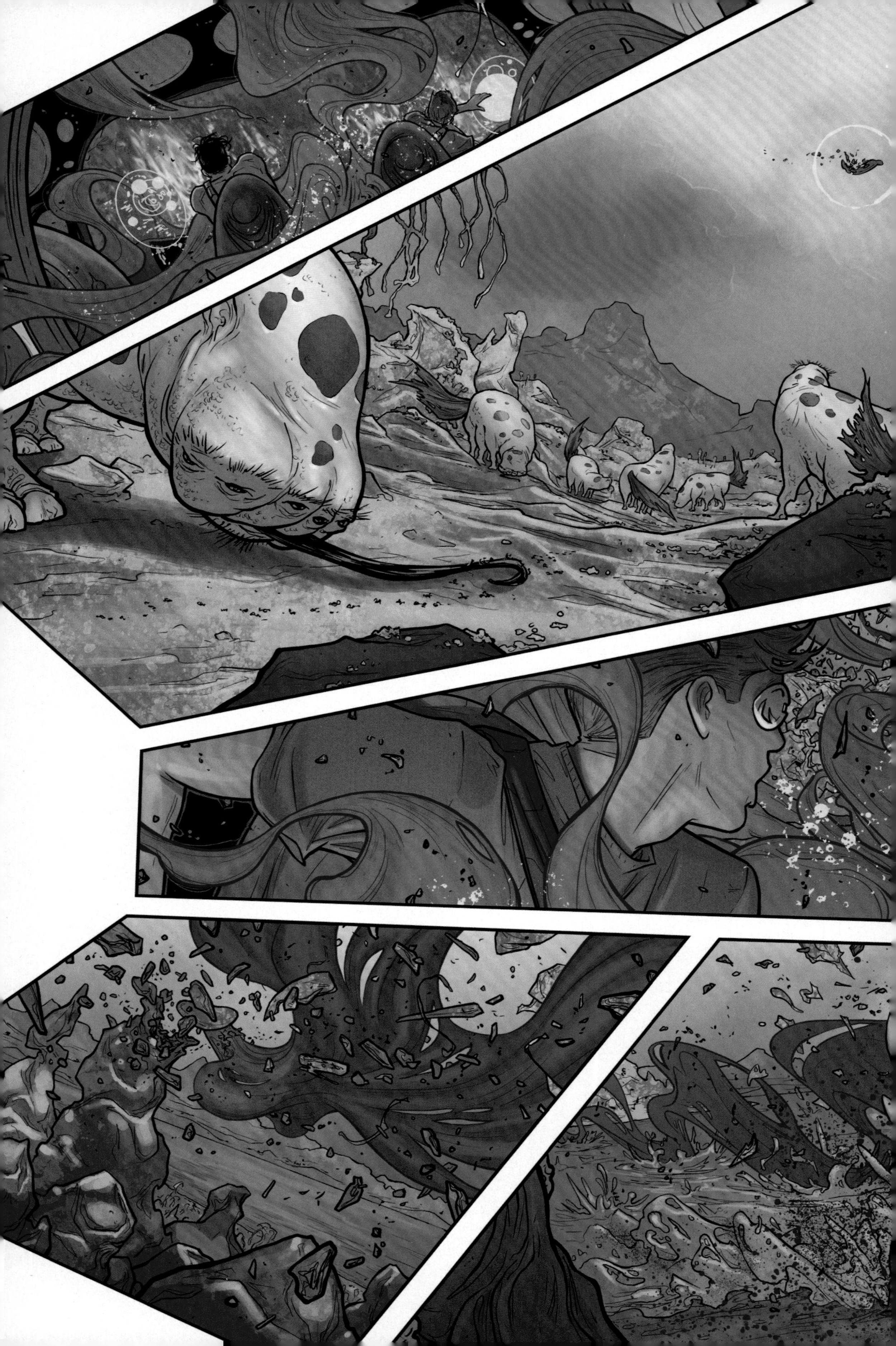

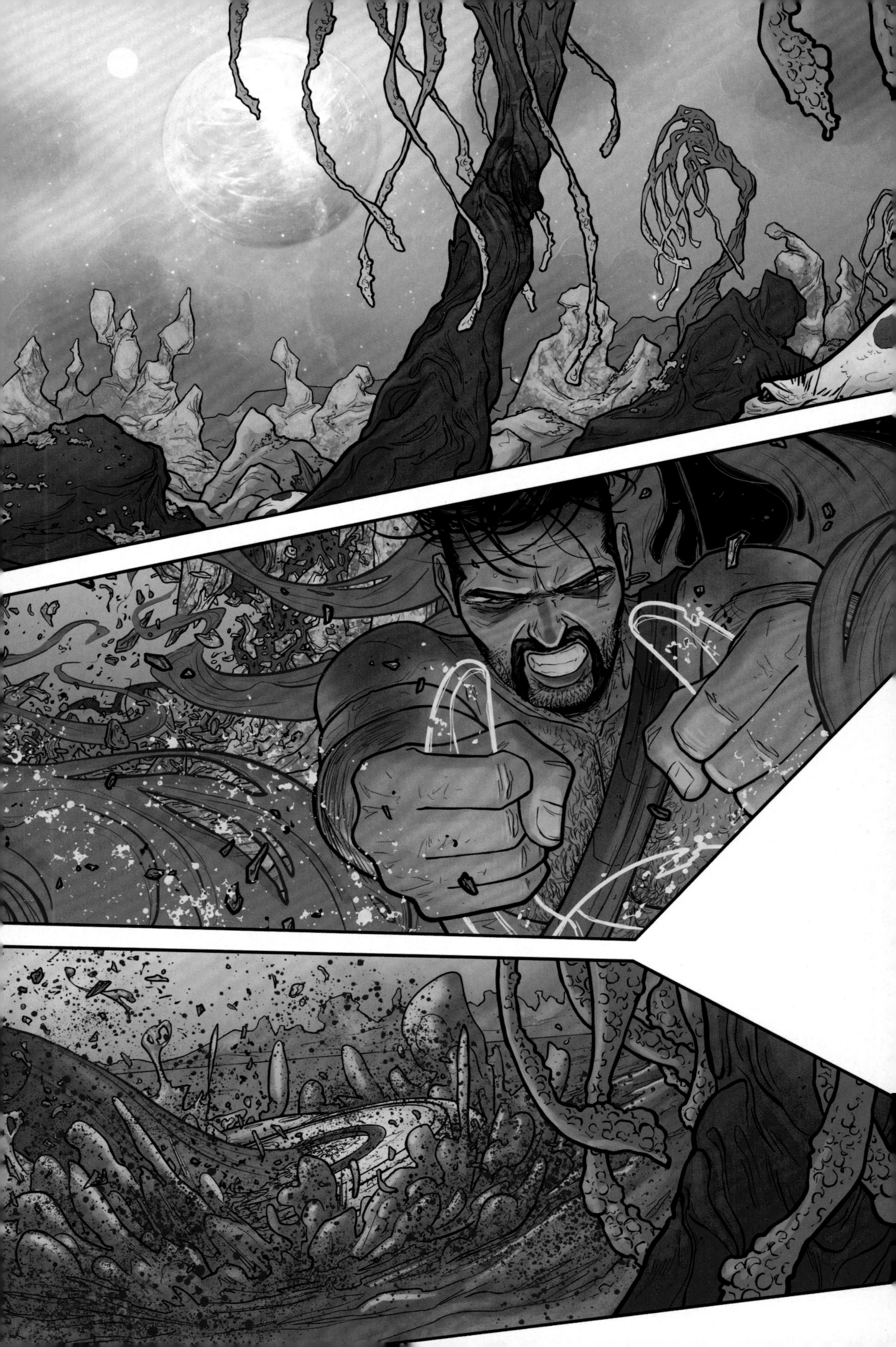

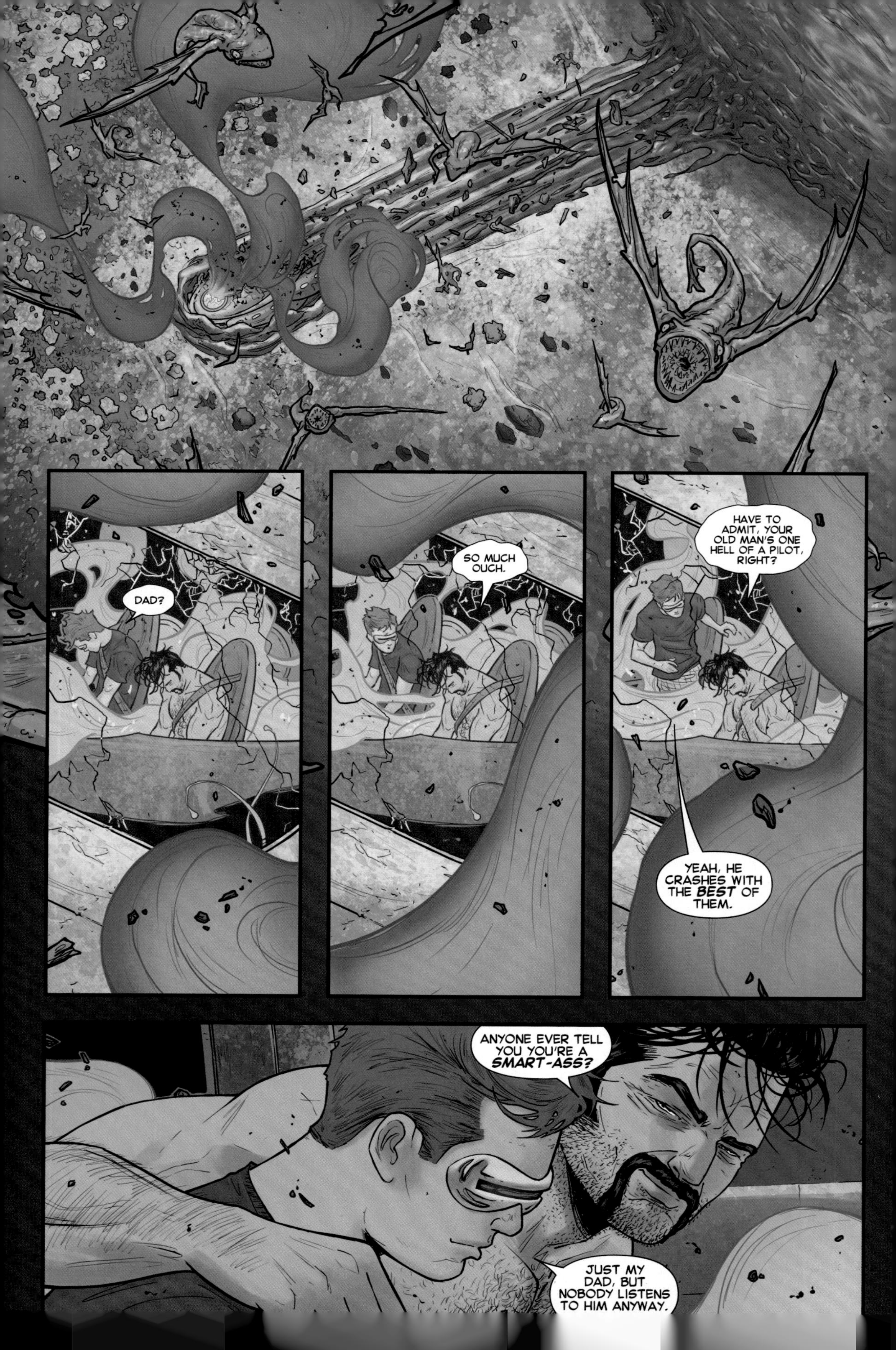
DAD?
SO MUCH OUCH.
HAVE TO ADMIT, YOUR OLD MAN'S ONE HELL OF A PILOT, RIGHT?
YEAH, HE CRASHES WITH THE BEST OF THEM.
ANYONE EVER TELL YOU YOU'RE A SMART-ASS?
JUST MY DAD, BUT NOBODY LISTENS TO HIM ANYWAY.

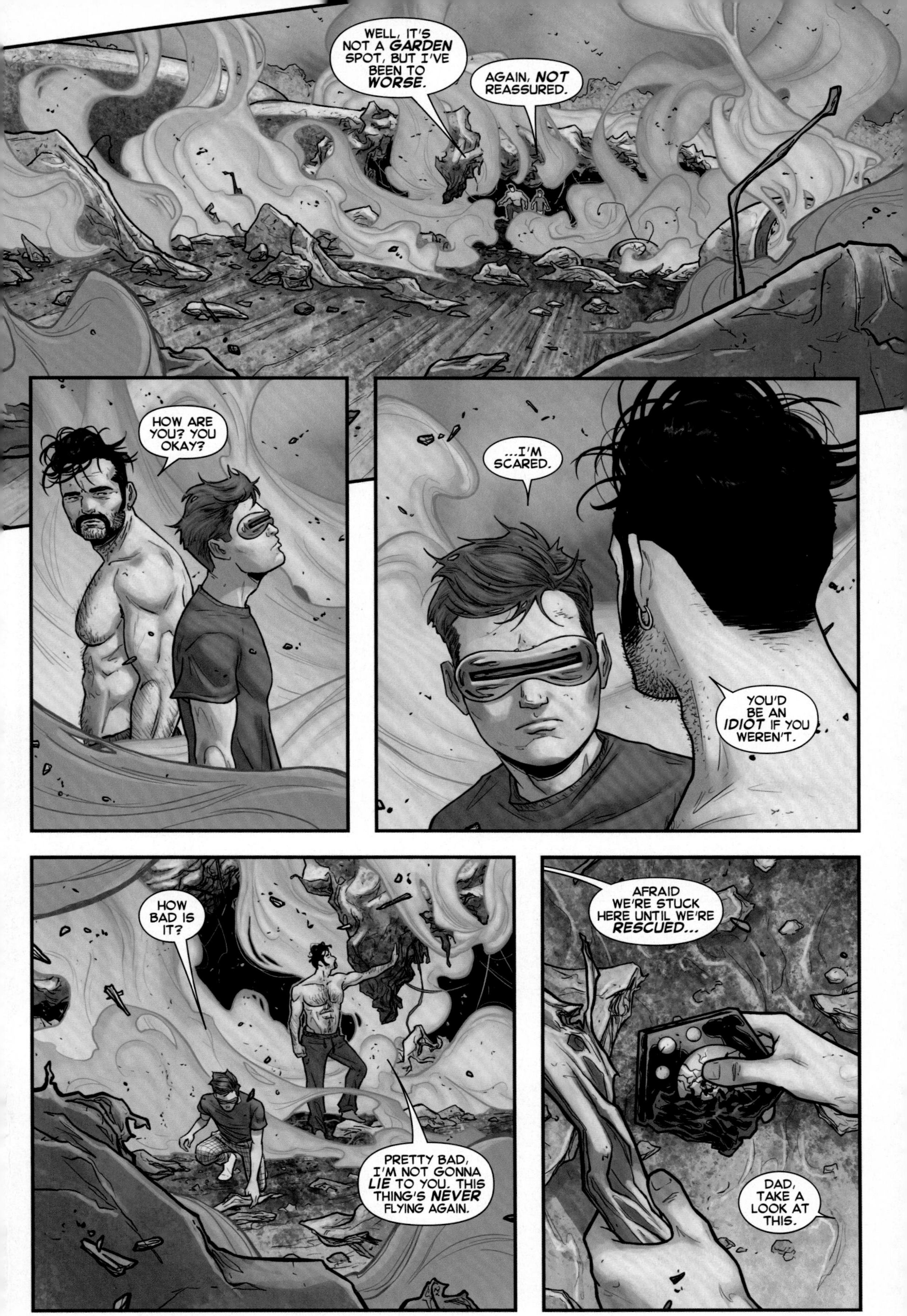
WELL, IT'S NOT A GARDEN SPOT, BUT I'VE BEEN TO WORSE.
AGAIN, NOT REASSURED.
HOW ARE YOU? YOU OKAY?
...I'M SCARED.
YOU'D BE AN IDIOT IF YOU WEREN'T.
HOW BAD IS IT?
PRETTY BAD, I'M NOT GONNA LIE TO YOU. THIS THING'S NEVER FLYING AGAIN.
AFRAID WE'RE STUCK HERE UNTIL WE'RE RESCUED...
DAD, TAKE A LOOK AT THIS.

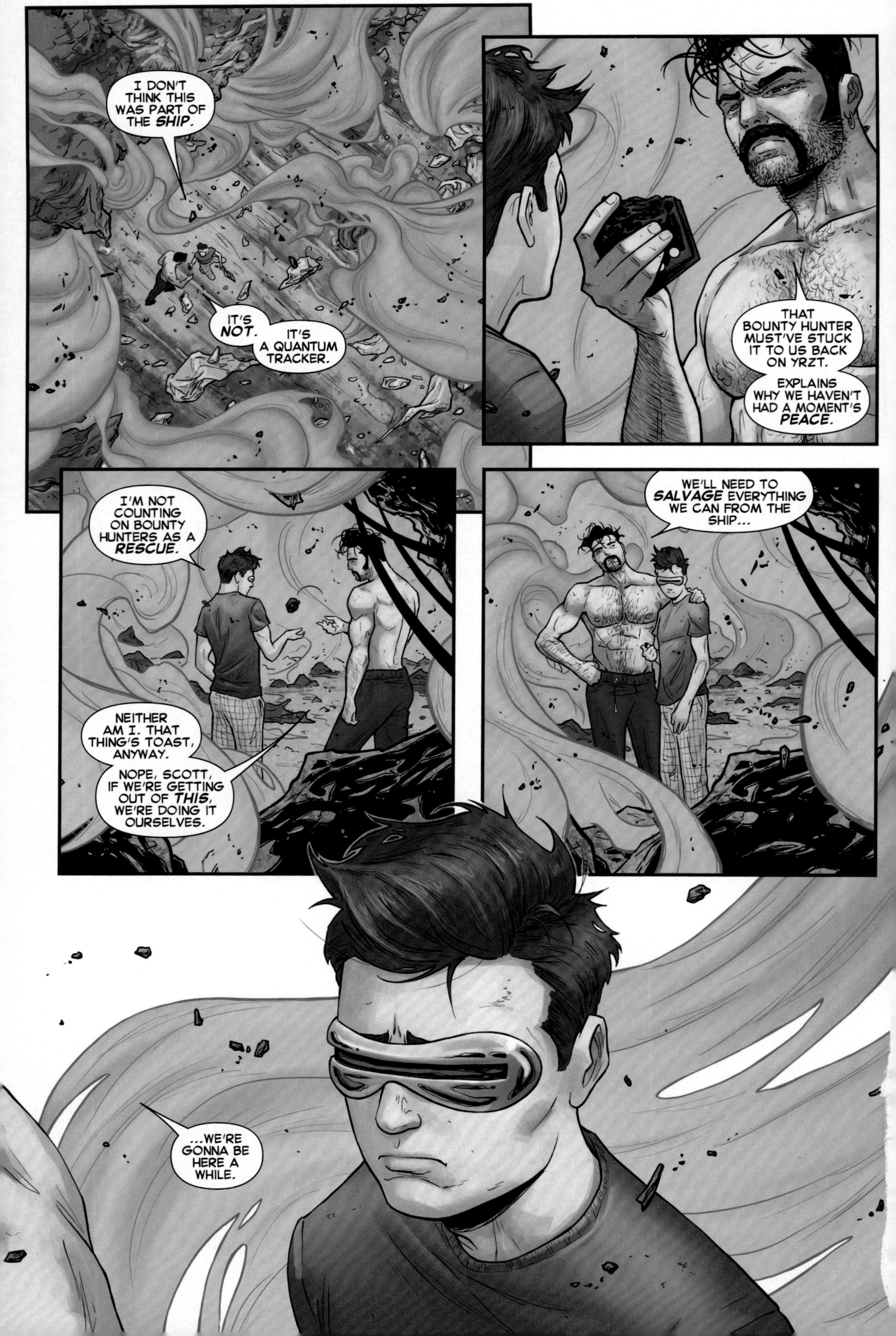
I DON'T THINK THIS WAS PART OF THE SHIP.
IT'S NOT.
IT'S A QUANTUM TRACKER.
THAT BOUNTY HUNTER MUST'VE STUCK IT TO US BACK ON YRZT.
EXPLAINS WHY WE HAVEN'T HAD A MOMENT'S PEACE.
I'M NOT COUNTING ON BOUNTY HUNTERS AS A RESCUE.
NEITHER AM I. THAT THING'S TOAST, ANYWAY.
NOPE, SCOTT, IF WE'RE GETTING OUT OF THIS, WE'RE DOING IT OURSELVES.
WE'LL NEED TO SALVAGE EVERYTHING WE CAN FROM THE SHIP...
...WE'RE GONNA BE HERE A WHILE.

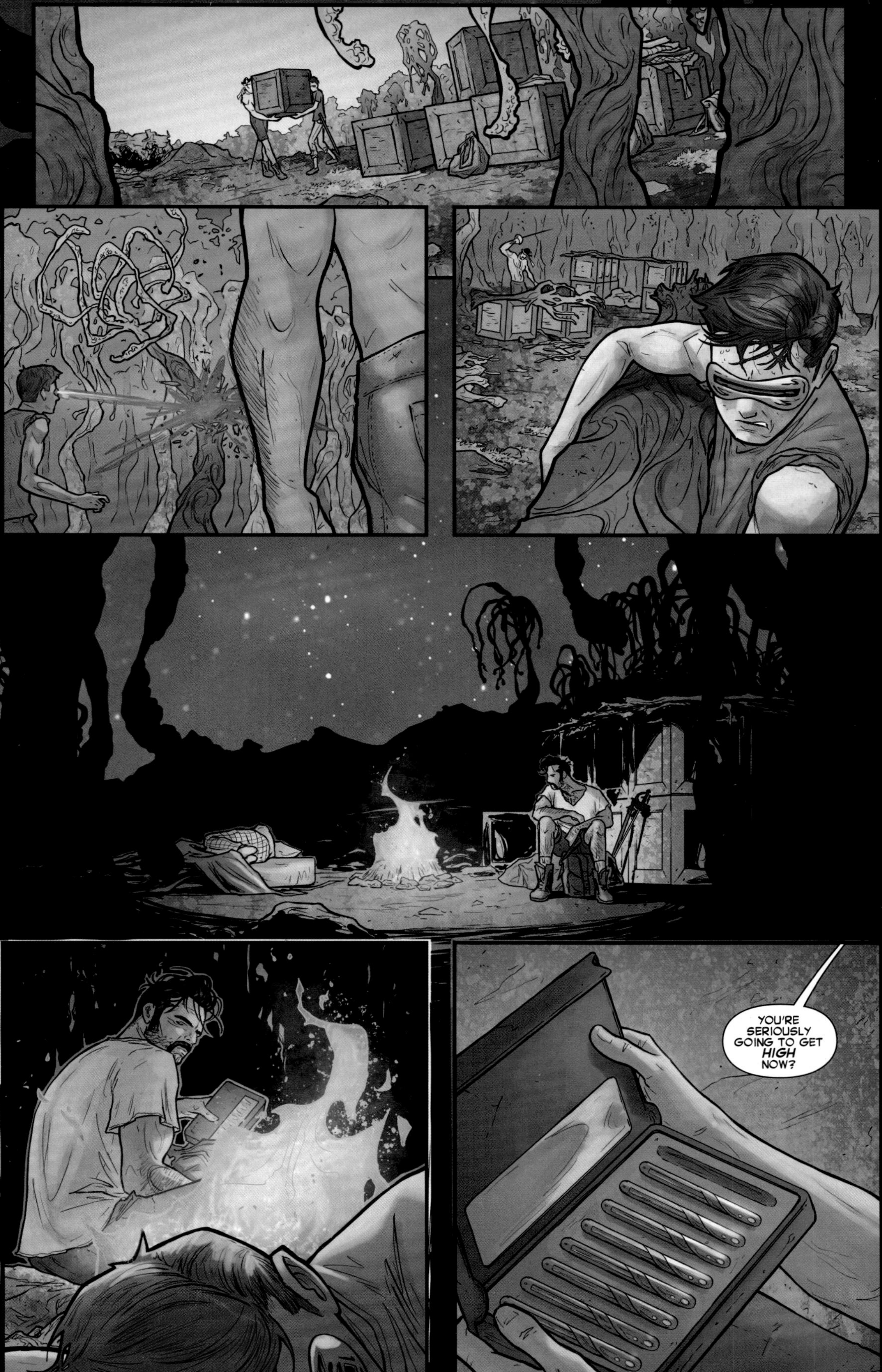
YOU'RE SERIOUSLY GOING TO GET HIGH NOW?

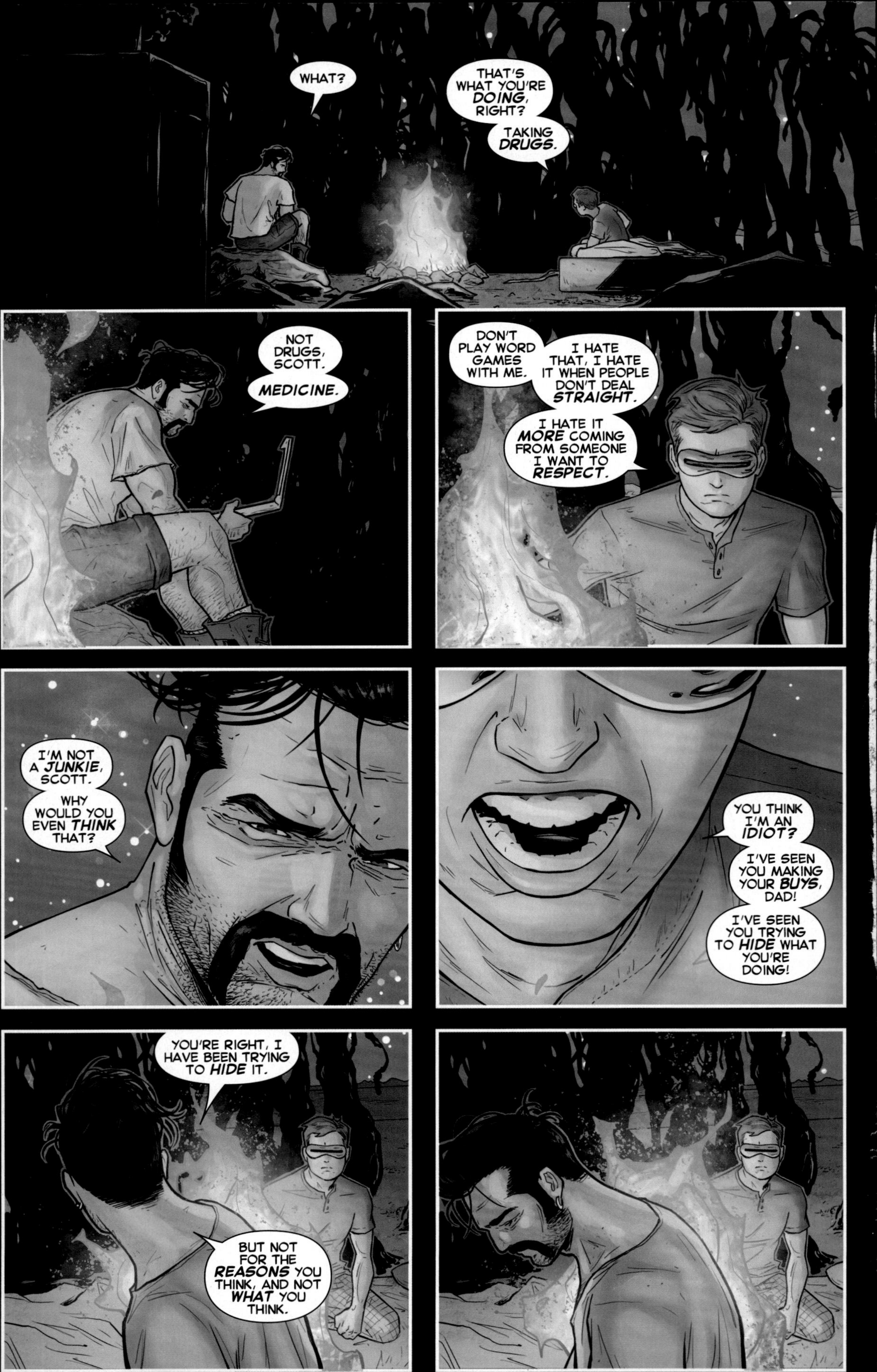
WHAT?
THAT'S WHAT YOU'RE DOING, RIGHT?
TAKING DRUGS.
NOT DRUGS, SCOTT.
MEDICINE.
DON'T PLAY WORD GAMES WITH ME.
I HATE THAT, I HATE IT WHEN PEOPLE DON'T DEAL STRAIGHT.
I HATE IT MORE COMING FROM SOMEONE I WANT TO RESPECT.
I'M NOT A JUNKIE, SCOTT.
WHY WOULD YOU EVEN THINK THAT?
YOU THINK I'M AN IDIOT?
I'VE SEEN YOU MAKING YOUR BUYS, DAD!
I'VE SEEN YOU TRYING TO HIDE WHAT YOU'RE DOING!
YOU'RE RIGHT, I HAVE BEEN TRYING TO HIDE IT.
BUT NOT FOR THE REASONS YOU THINK, AND NOT WHAT YOU THINK.

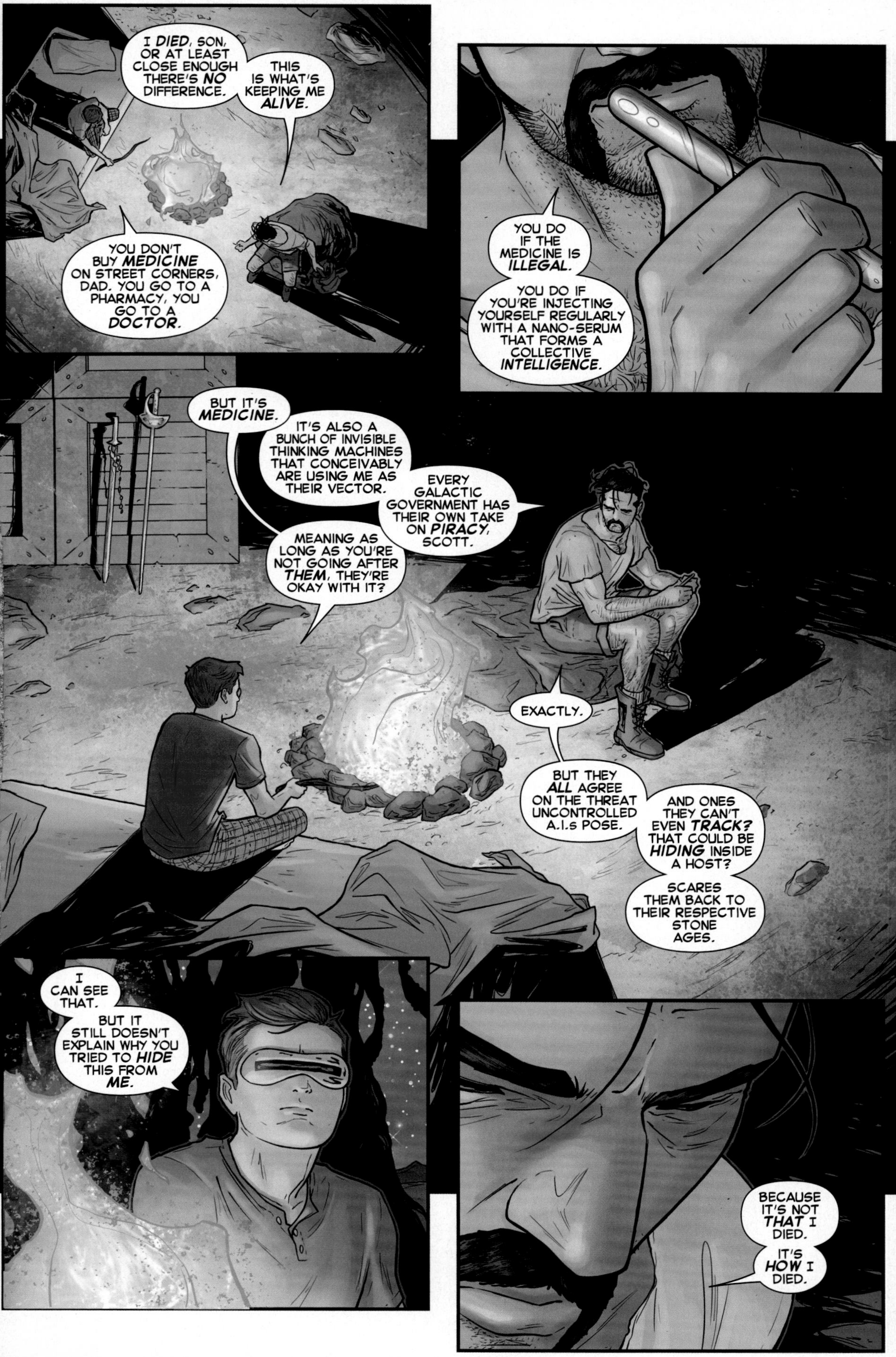
I DIED, SON, OR AT LEAST CLOSE ENOUGH THERE'S NO DIFFERENCE.
THIS IS WHAT'S KEEPING ME ALIVE.
YOU DON'T BUY MEDICINE ON STREET CORNERS, DAD. YOU GO TO A PHARMACY, YOU GO TO A DOCTOR.
YOU DO IF THE MEDICINE IS ILLEGAL.
YOU DO IF YOU'RE INJECTING YOURSELF REGULARLY WITH A NANO-SERUM THAT FORMS A COLLECTIVE INTELLIGENCE.
BUT IT'S MEDICINE.
IT'S ALSO A BUNCH OF INVISIBLE THINKING MACHINES THAT CONCEIVABLY ARE USING ME AS THEIR VECTOR.
EVERY GALACTIC GOVERNMENT HAS THEIR OWN TAKE ON PIRACY, SCOTT.
MEANING AS LONG AS YOU'RE NOT GOING AFTER THEM, THEY'RE OKAY WITH IT?
EXACTLY.
BUT THEY ALL AGREE ON THE THREAT UNCONTROLLED A.I.s POSE.
AND ONES THEY CAN'T EVEN TRACK? THAT COULD BE HIDING INSIDE A HOST?
SCARES THEM BACK TO THEIR RESPECTIVE STONE AGES.
I CAN SEE THAT.
BUT IT STILL DOESN'T EXPLAIN WHY YOU TRIED TO HIDE THIS FROM ME.
BECAUSE IT'S NOT THAT I DIED.
IT'S HOW I DIED.

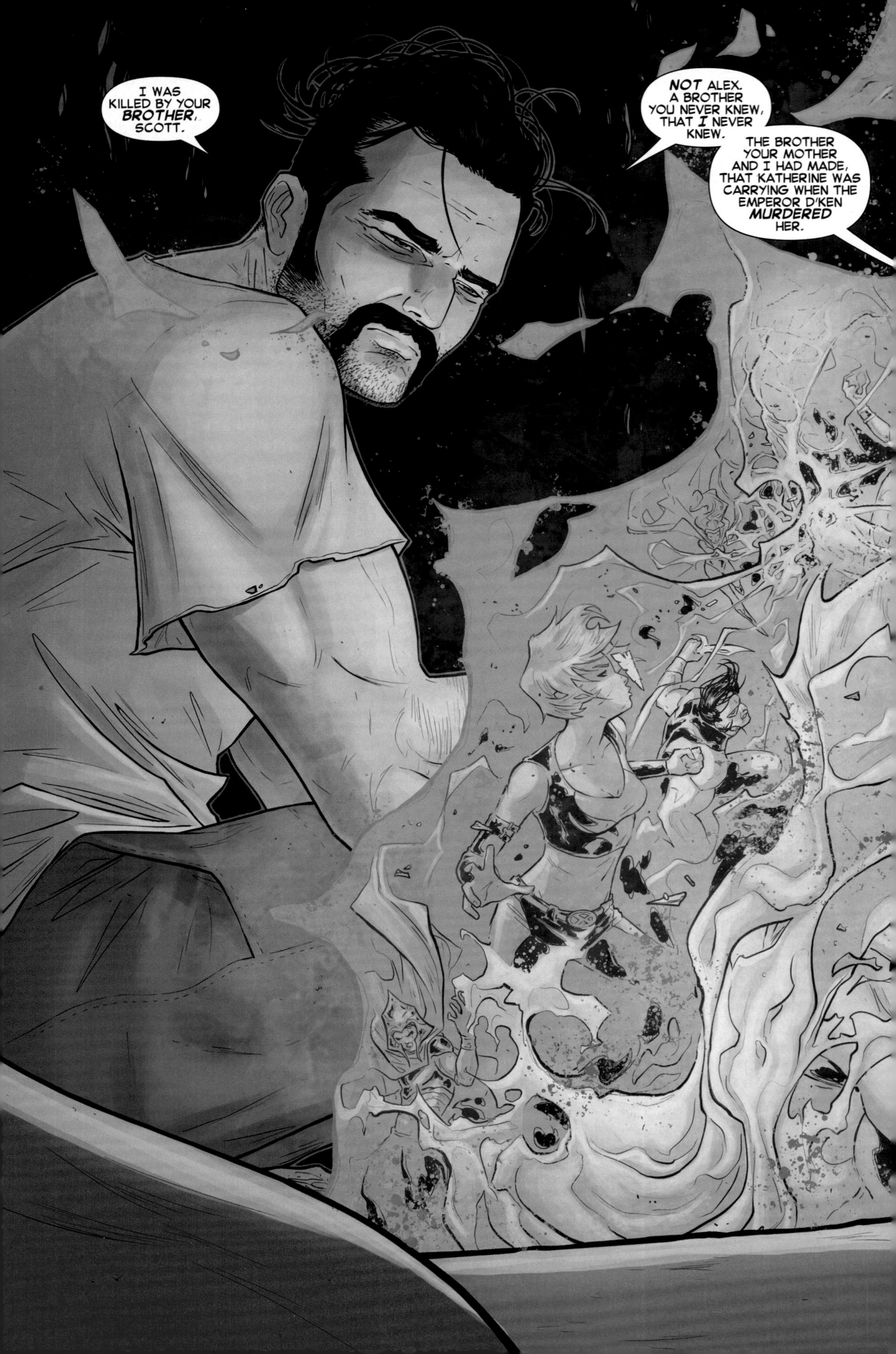
I WAS KILLED BY YOUR BROTHER, SCOTT.
NOT ALEX. A BROTHER YOU NEVER KNEW, THAT I NEVER KNEW.
THE BROTHER YOUR MOTHER AND I HAD MADE, THAT KATHERINE WAS CARRYING WHEN THE EMPEROR D'KEN MURDERED HER.

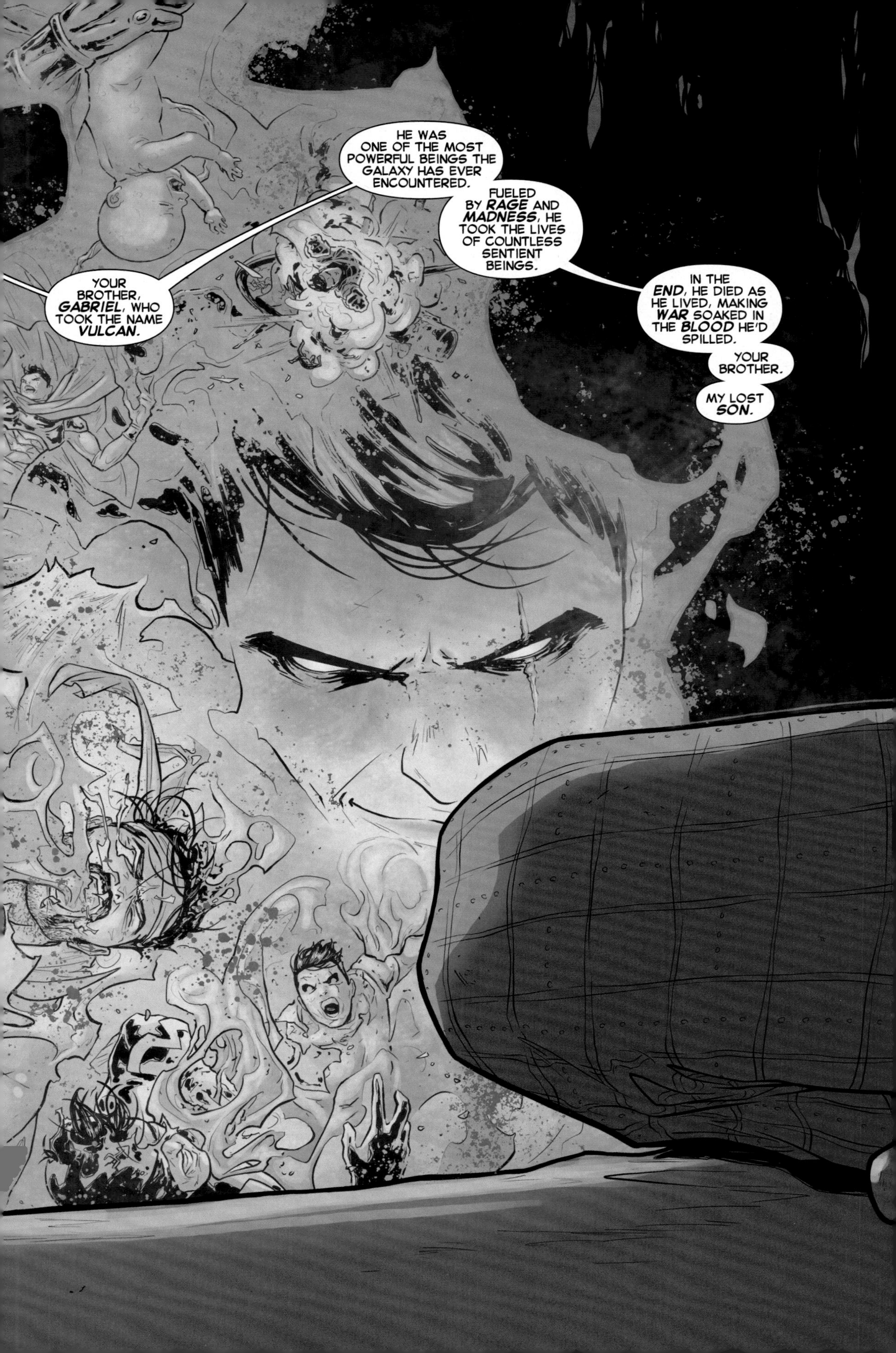
HE WAS ONE OF THE MOST POWERFUL BEINGS THE GALAXY HAS EVER ENCOUNTERED.
YOUR BROTHER, GABRIEL, WHO TOOK THE NAME VULCAN.
FUELED BY RAGE AND MADNESS, HE TOOK THE LIVES OF COUNTLESS SENTIENT BEINGS.
IN THE END, HE DIED AS HE LIVED, MAKING WAR SOAKED IN THE BLOOD HE'D SPILLED.
YOUR BROTHER.
MY LOST SON.

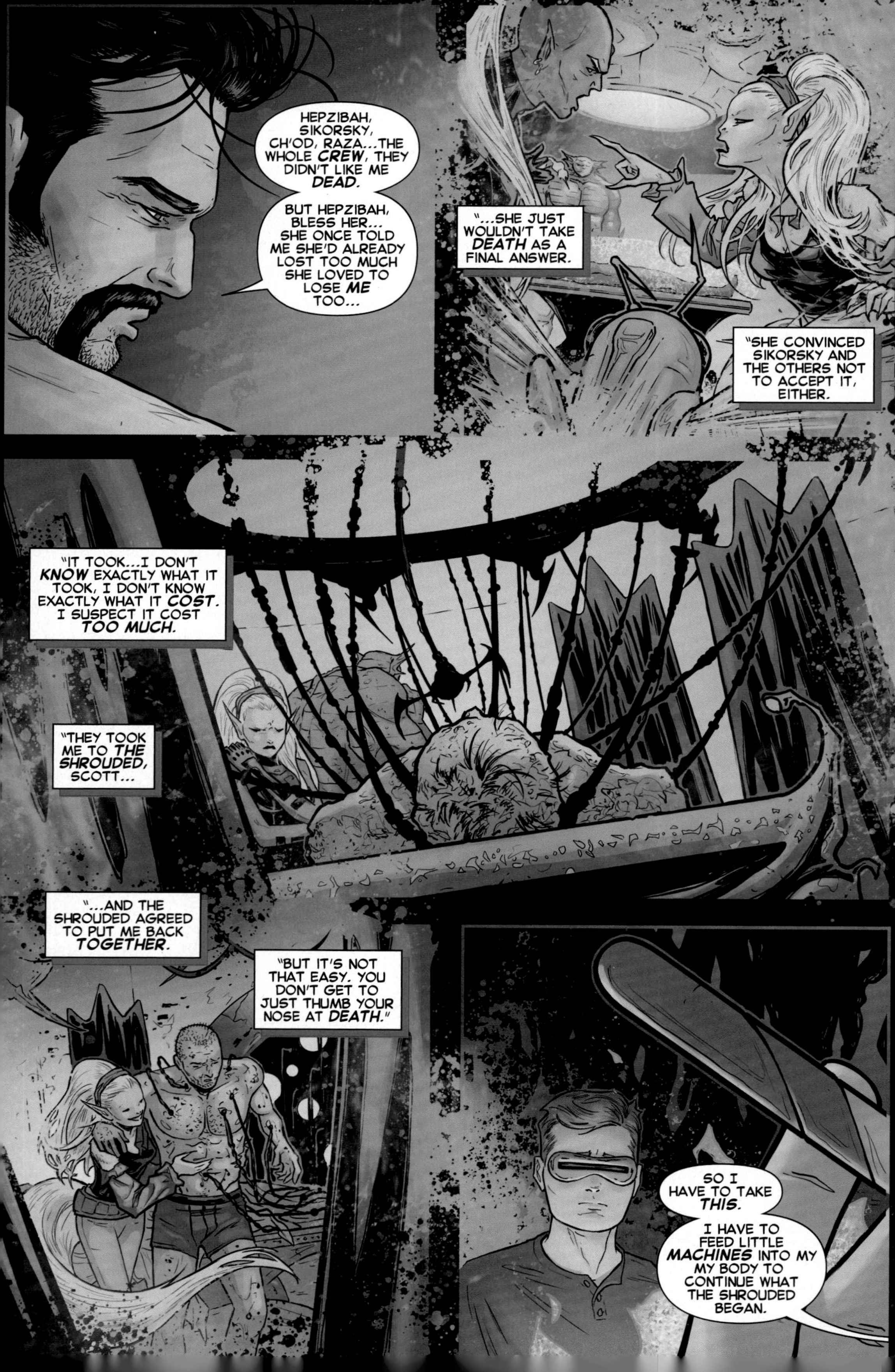
HEPZIBAH, SIKORSKY, CH'OD, RAZA...THE WHOLE CREW, THEY DIDN'T LIKE ME DEAD.
BUT HEPZIBAH, BLESS HER... SHE ONCE TOLD ME SHE'D ALREADY LOST TOO MUCH SHE LOVED TO LOSE ME TOO...
"...SHE JUST WOULDN'T TAKE DEATH AS A FINAL ANSWER.
"SHE CONVINCED SIKORSKY AND THE OTHERS NOT TO ACCEPT IT, EITHER.
"IT TOOK...I DON'T KNOW EXACTLY WHAT IT TOOK, I DON'T KNOW EXACTLY WHAT IT COST. I SUSPECT IT COST TOO MUCH.
"THEY TOOK ME TO THE SHROUDED, SCOTT...
"...AND THE SHROUDED AGREED TO PUT ME BACK TOGETHER.
"BUT IT'S NOT THAT EASY. YOU DON'T GET TO JUST THUMB YOUR NOSE AT DEATH."
SO I HAVE TO TAKE THIS.
I HAVE TO FEED LITTLE MACHINES INTO MY MY BODY TO CONTINUE WHAT THE SHROUDED BEGAN.

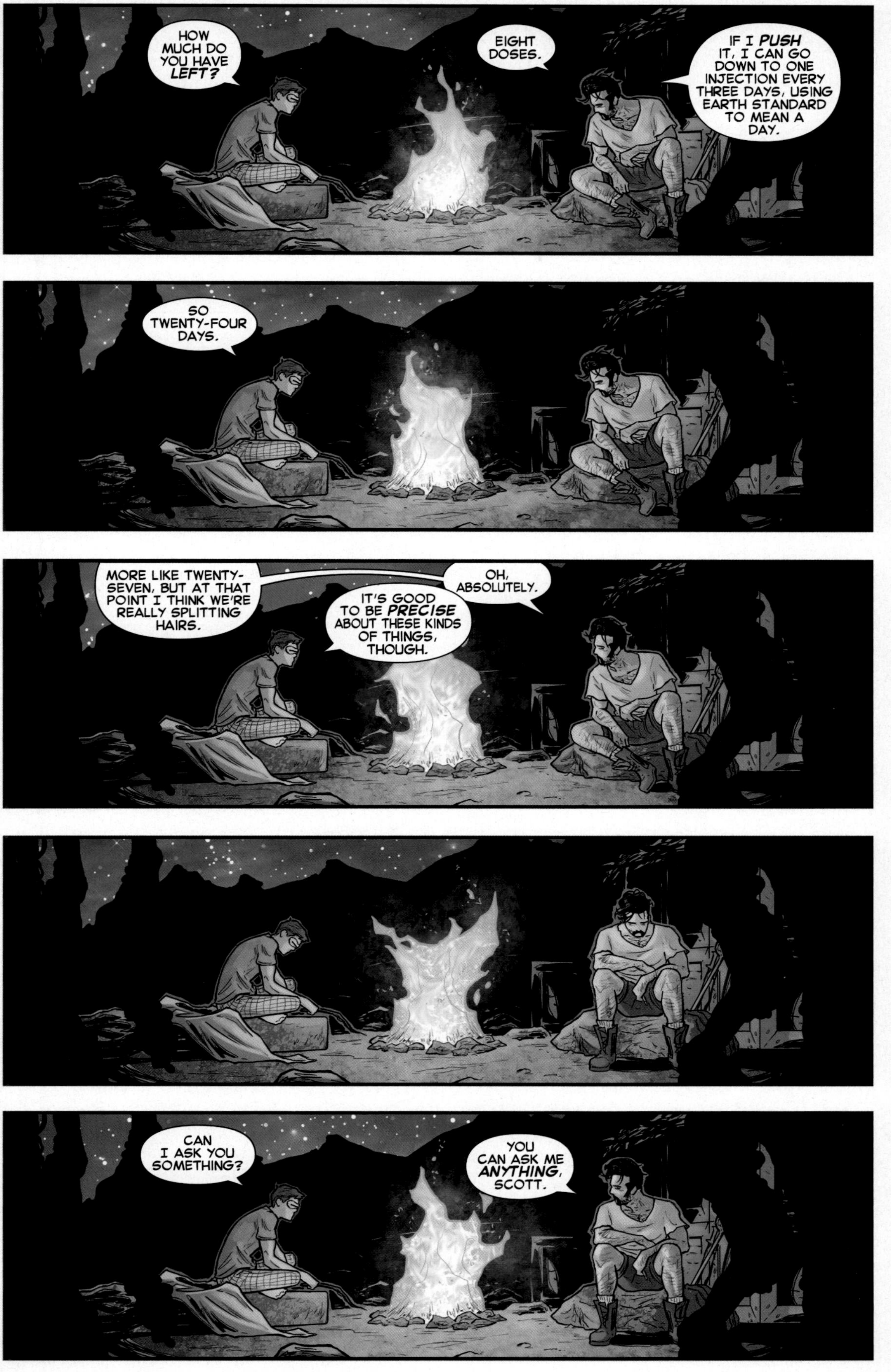
HOW MUCH DO YOU HAVE *LEFT?*
EIGHT DOSES.
IF I *PUSH* IT, I CAN GO DOWN TO ONE INJECTION EVERY THREE DAYS, USING EARTH STANDARD TO MEAN A DAY.
SO TWENTY-FOUR DAYS.
MORE LIKE TWENTY-SEVEN, BUT AT THAT POINT I THINK WE'RE REALLY SPLITTING HAIRS.
IT'S GOOD TO BE *PRECISE* ABOUT THESE KINDS OF THINGS, THOUGH.
OH, ABSOLUTELY.
CAN I ASK YOU SOMETHING?
YOU CAN ASK ME *ANYTHING*, SCOTT.

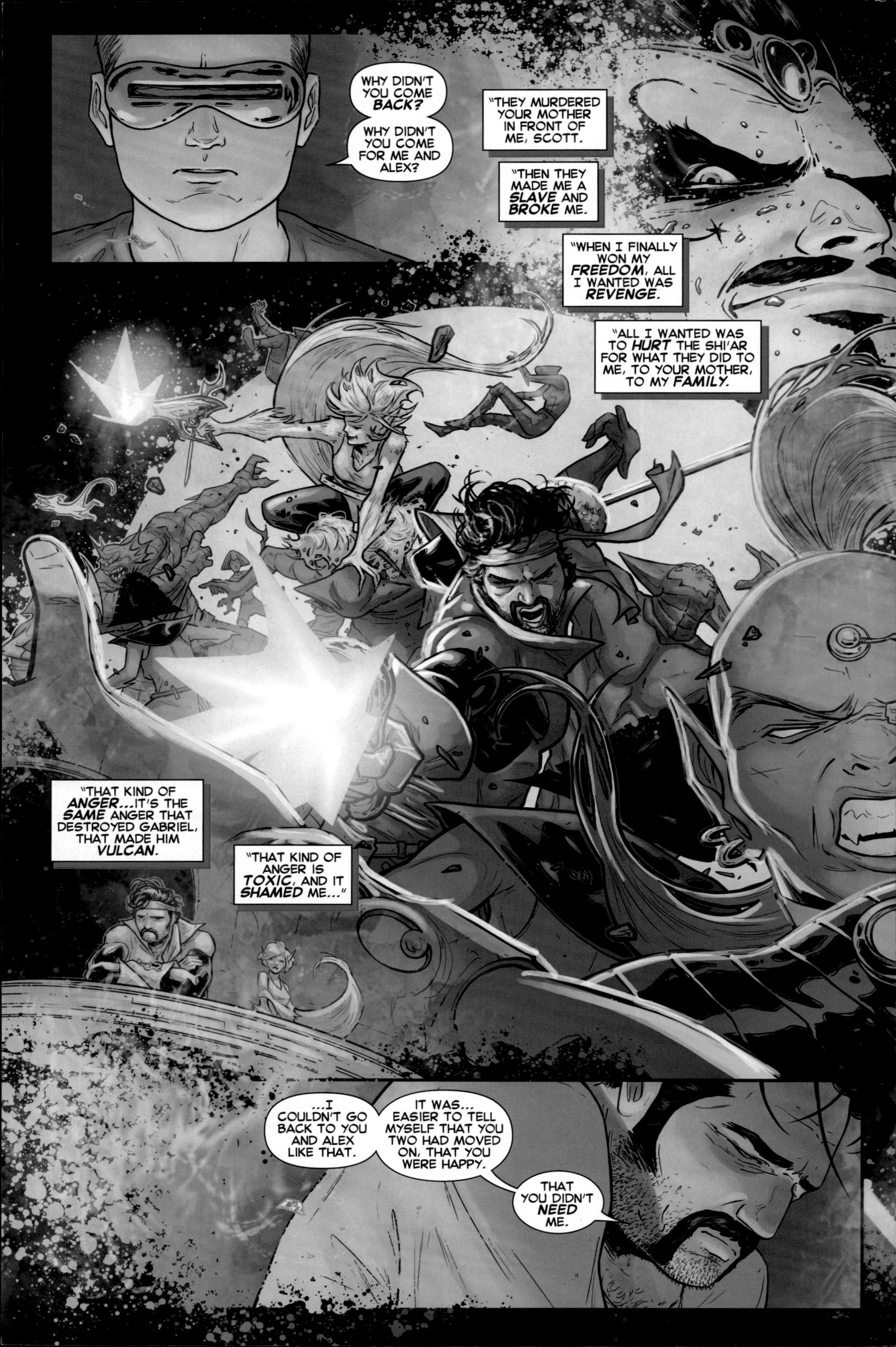
WHY DIDN'T YOU COME BACK?
WHY DIDN'T YOU COME FOR ME AND ALEX?
"THEY MURDERED YOUR MOTHER IN FRONT OF ME, SCOTT.
"THEN THEY MADE ME A SLAVE AND BROKE ME.
"WHEN I FINALLY WON MY FREEDOM, ALL I WANTED WAS REVENGE.
"ALL I WANTED WAS TO HURT THE SHI'AR FOR WHAT THEY DID TO ME, TO YOUR MOTHER, TO MY FAMILY.
"THAT KIND OF ANGER... IT'S THE SAME ANGER THAT DESTROYED GABRIEL, THAT MADE HIM VULCAN.
"THAT KIND OF ANGER IS TOXIC, AND IT SHAMED ME..."
...I COULDN'T GO BACK TO YOU AND ALEX LIKE THAT.
IT WAS... EASIER TO TELL MYSELF THAT YOU TWO HAD MOVED ON, THAT YOU WERE HAPPY.
THAT YOU DIDN'T NEED ME.

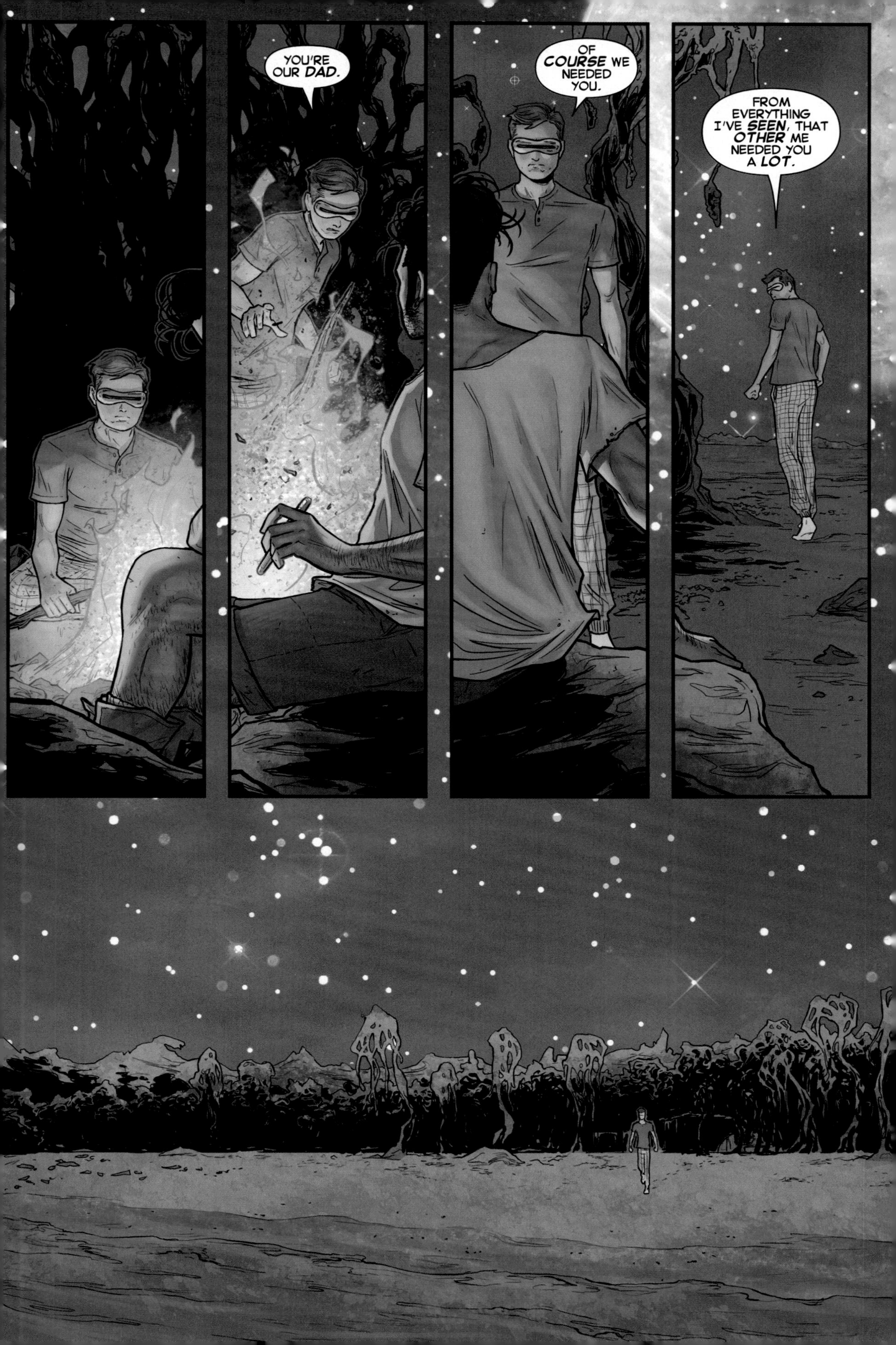
YOU'RE OUR DAD.
OF COURSE WE NEEDED YOU.
FROM EVERYTHING I'VE SEEN, THAT OTHER ME NEEDED YOU A LOT.

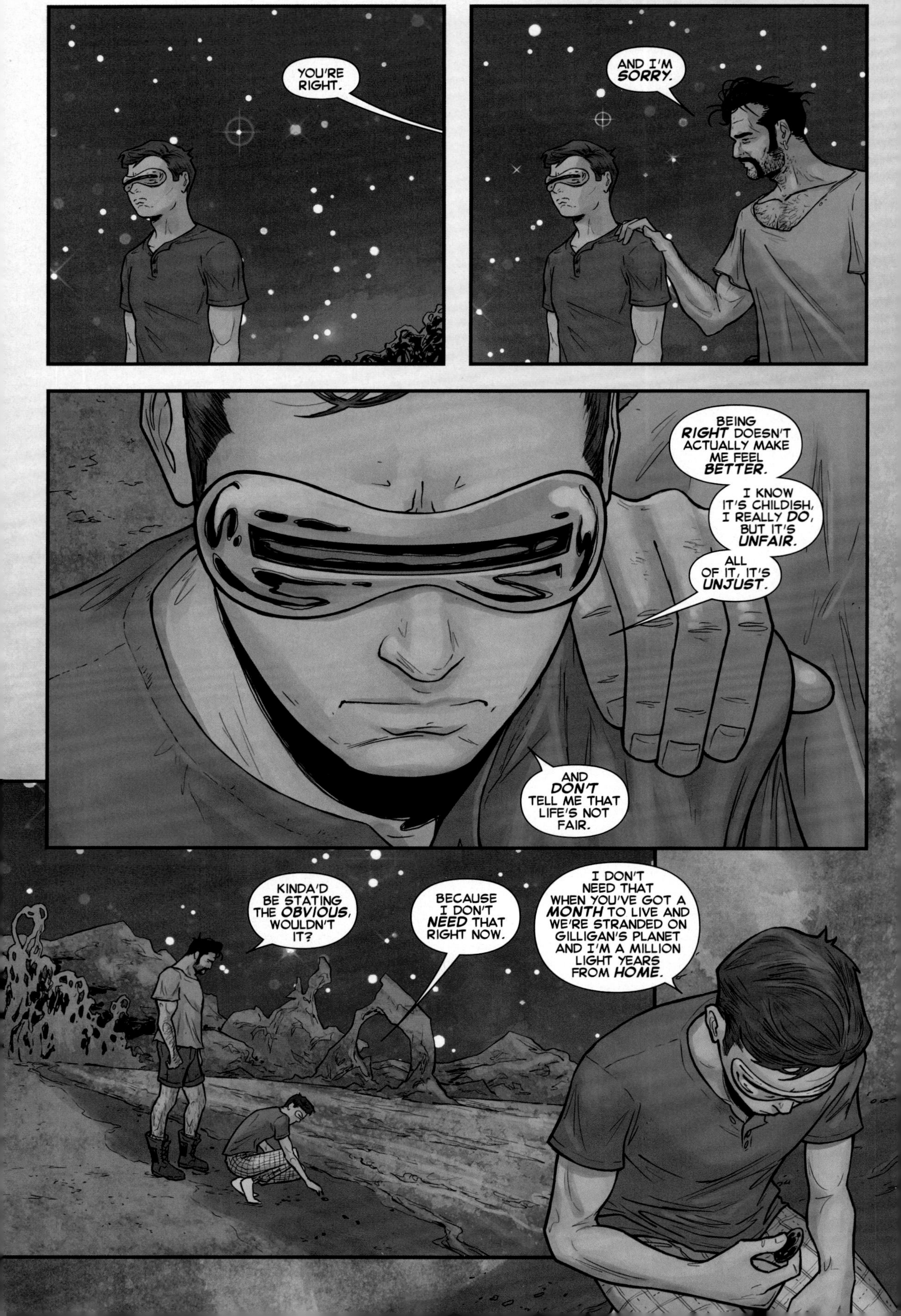
YOU'RE RIGHT.
AND I'M SORRY.
BEING RIGHT DOESN'T ACTUALLY MAKE ME FEEL BETTER.
I KNOW IT'S CHILDISH, I REALLY DO, BUT IT'S UNFAIR.
ALL OF IT, IT'S UNJUST.
AND DON'T TELL ME THAT LIFE'S NOT FAIR.
KINDA'D BE STATING THE OBVIOUS, WOULDN'T IT?
BECAUSE I DON'T NEED THAT RIGHT NOW.
I DON'T NEED THAT WHEN YOU'VE GOT A MONTH TO LIVE AND WE'RE STRANDED ON GILLIGAN'S PLANET AND I'M A MILLION LIGHT YEARS FROM HOME.

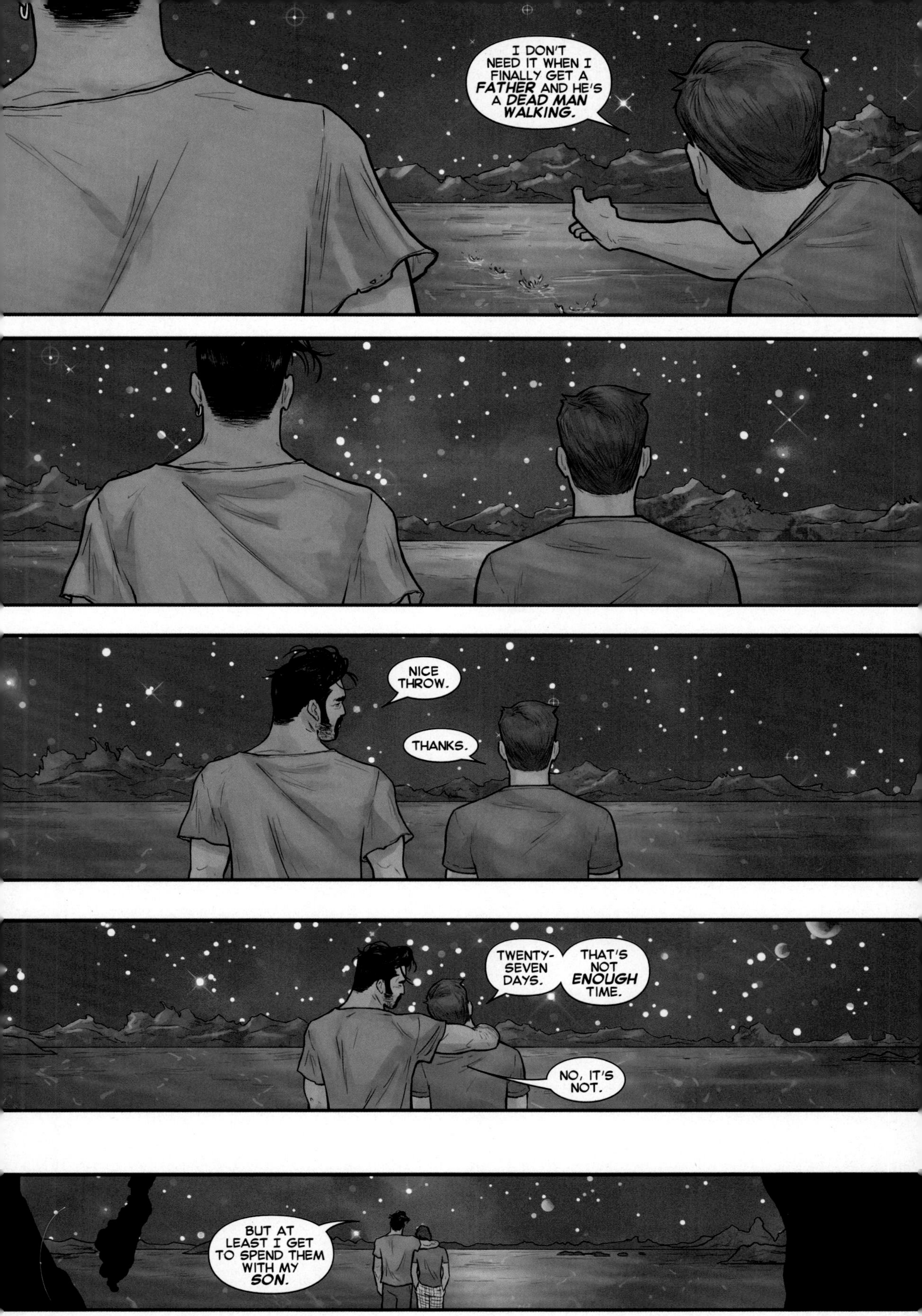
I DON'T NEED IT WHEN I FINALLY GET A FATHER AND HE'S A DEAD MAN WALKING.
NICE THROW.
THANKS.
TWENTY-SEVEN DAYS.
THAT'S NOT ENOUGH TIME.
NO, IT'S NOT.
BUT AT LEAST I GET TO SPEND THEM WITH MY SON.

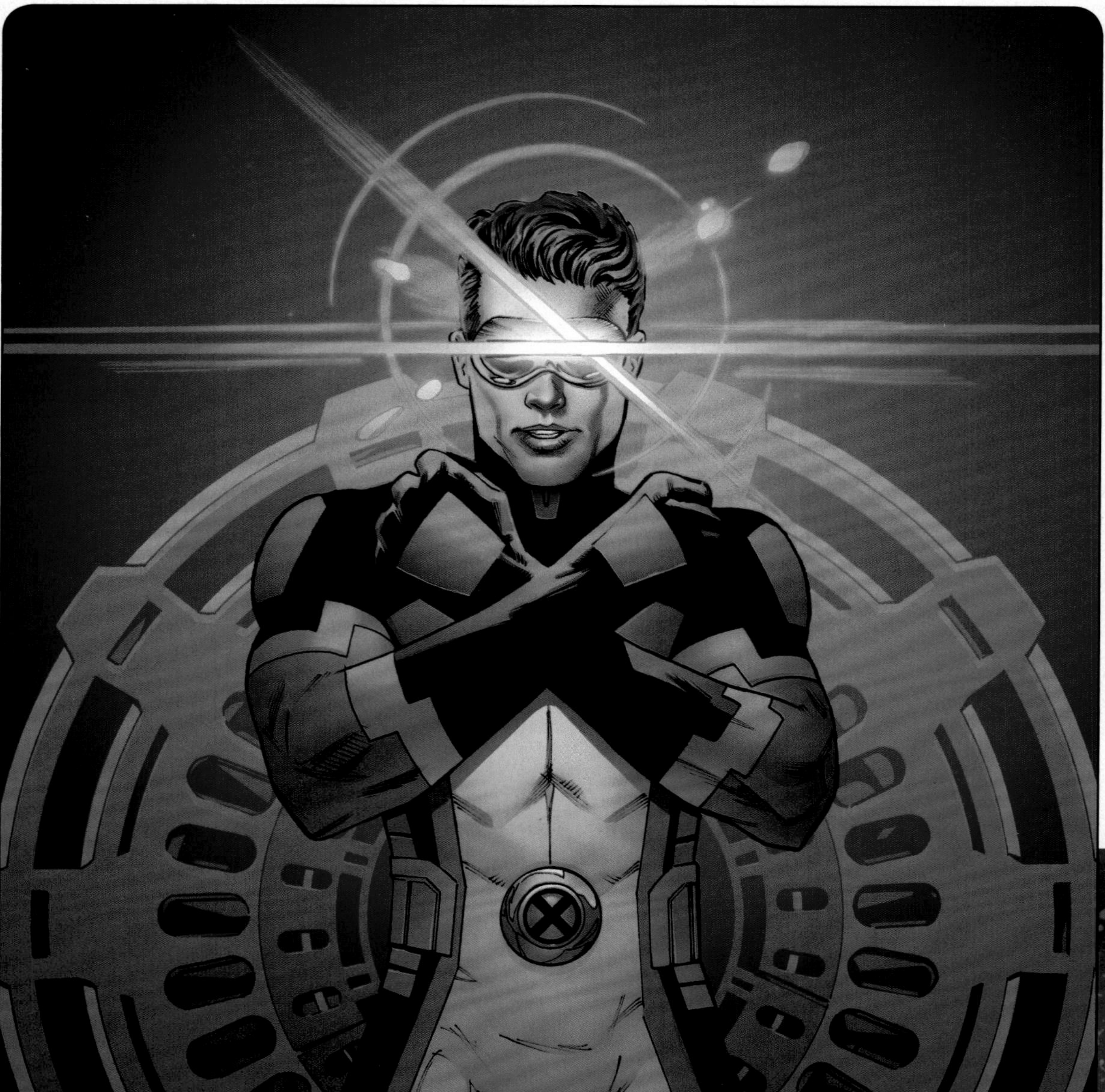

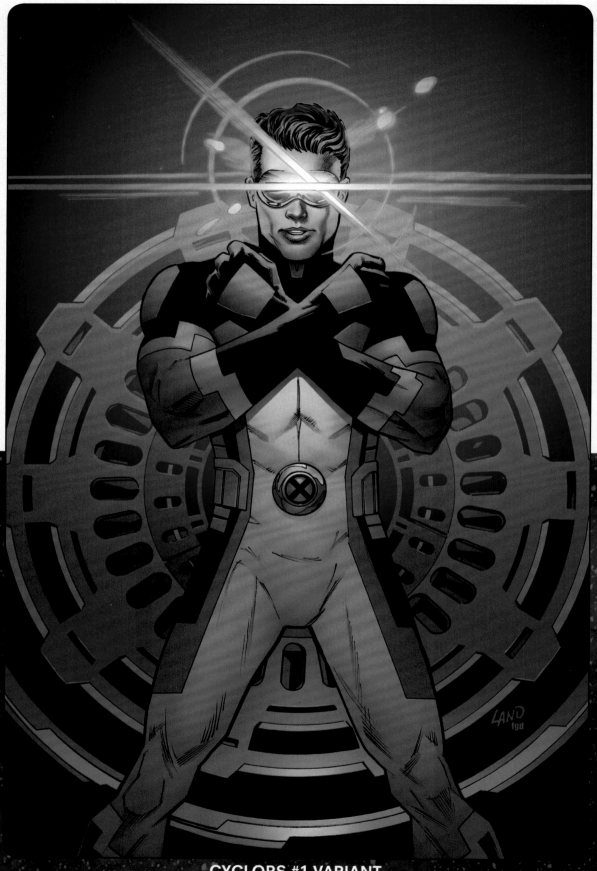

CYCLOPS #1 VARIANT
BY GREG LAND & FRANK D'ARMATA

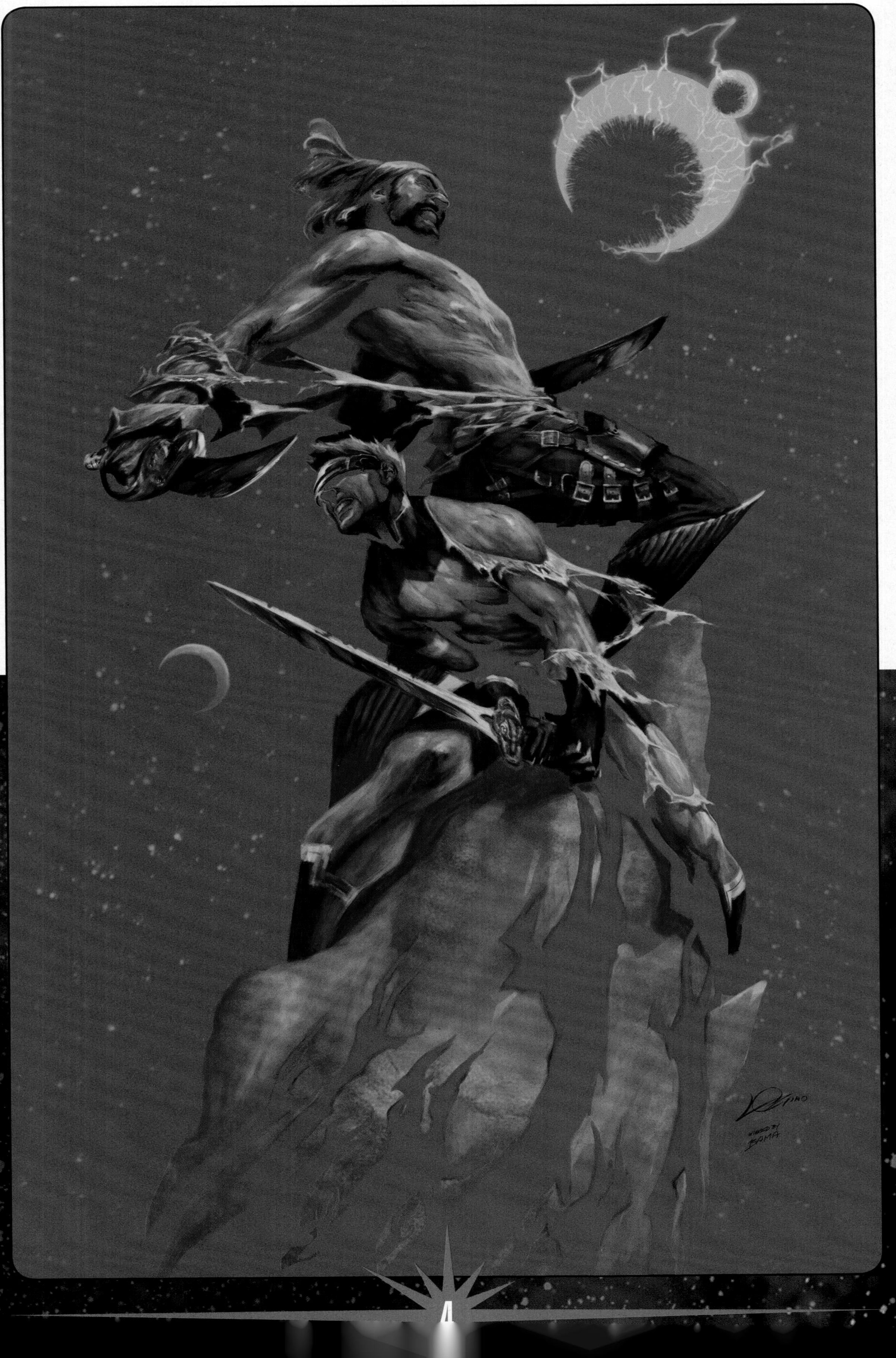
4

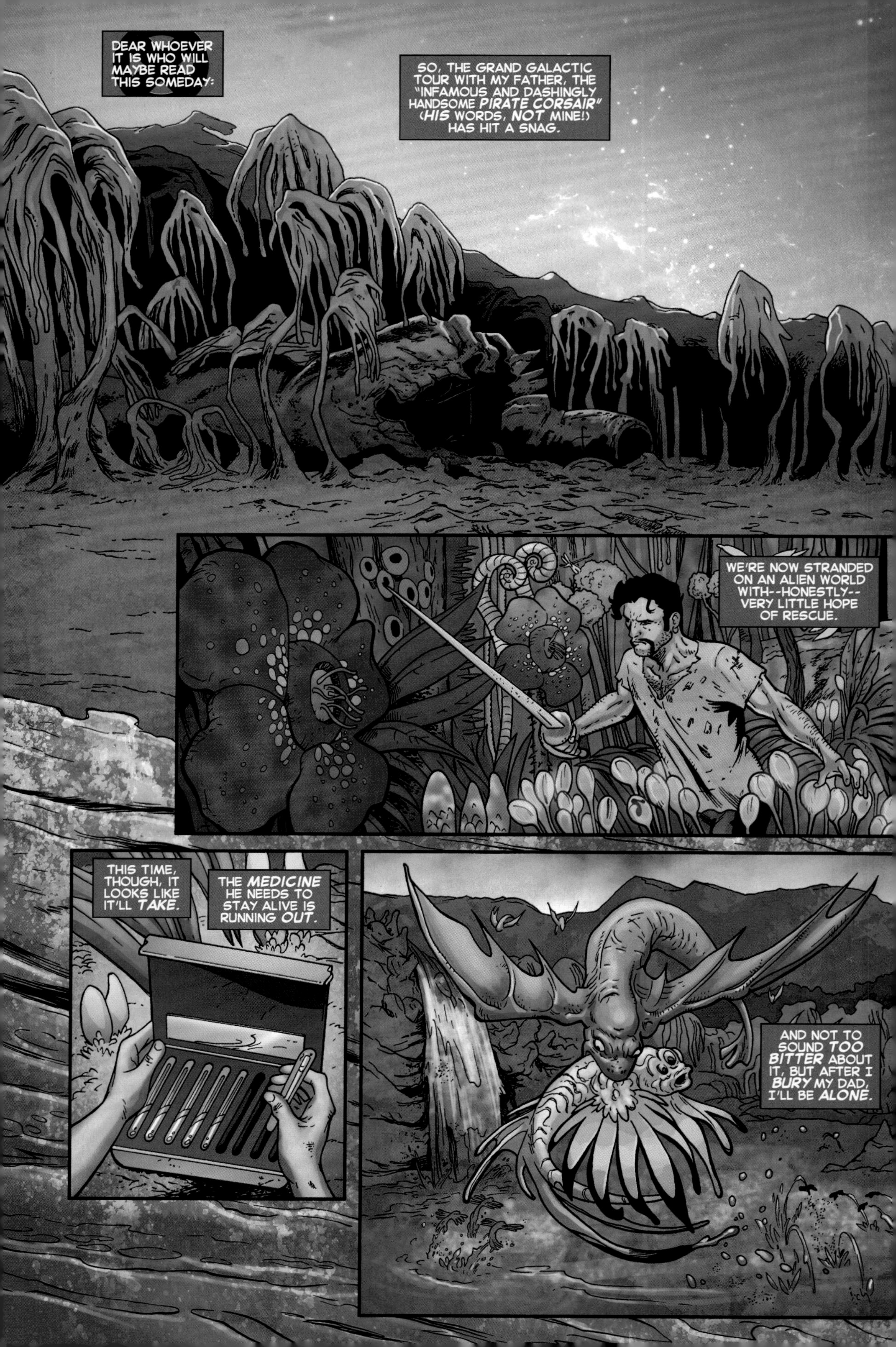
DEAR WHOEVER IT IS WHO WILL MAYBE READ THIS SOMEDAY:
SO, THE GRAND GALACTIC TOUR WITH MY FATHER, THE "INFAMOUS AND DASHINGLY HANDSOME PIRATE CORSAIR" (HIS WORDS, NOT MINE!) HAS HIT A SNAG.
WE'RE NOW STRANDED ON AN ALIEN WORLD WITH--HONESTLY--VERY LITTLE HOPE OF RESCUE.
THIS TIME, THOUGH, IT LOOKS LIKE IT'LL TAKE.
THE MEDICINE HE NEEDS TO STAY ALIVE IS RUNNING OUT.
AND NOT TO SOUND TOO BITTER ABOUT IT, BUT AFTER I BURY MY DAD, I'LL BE ALONE.

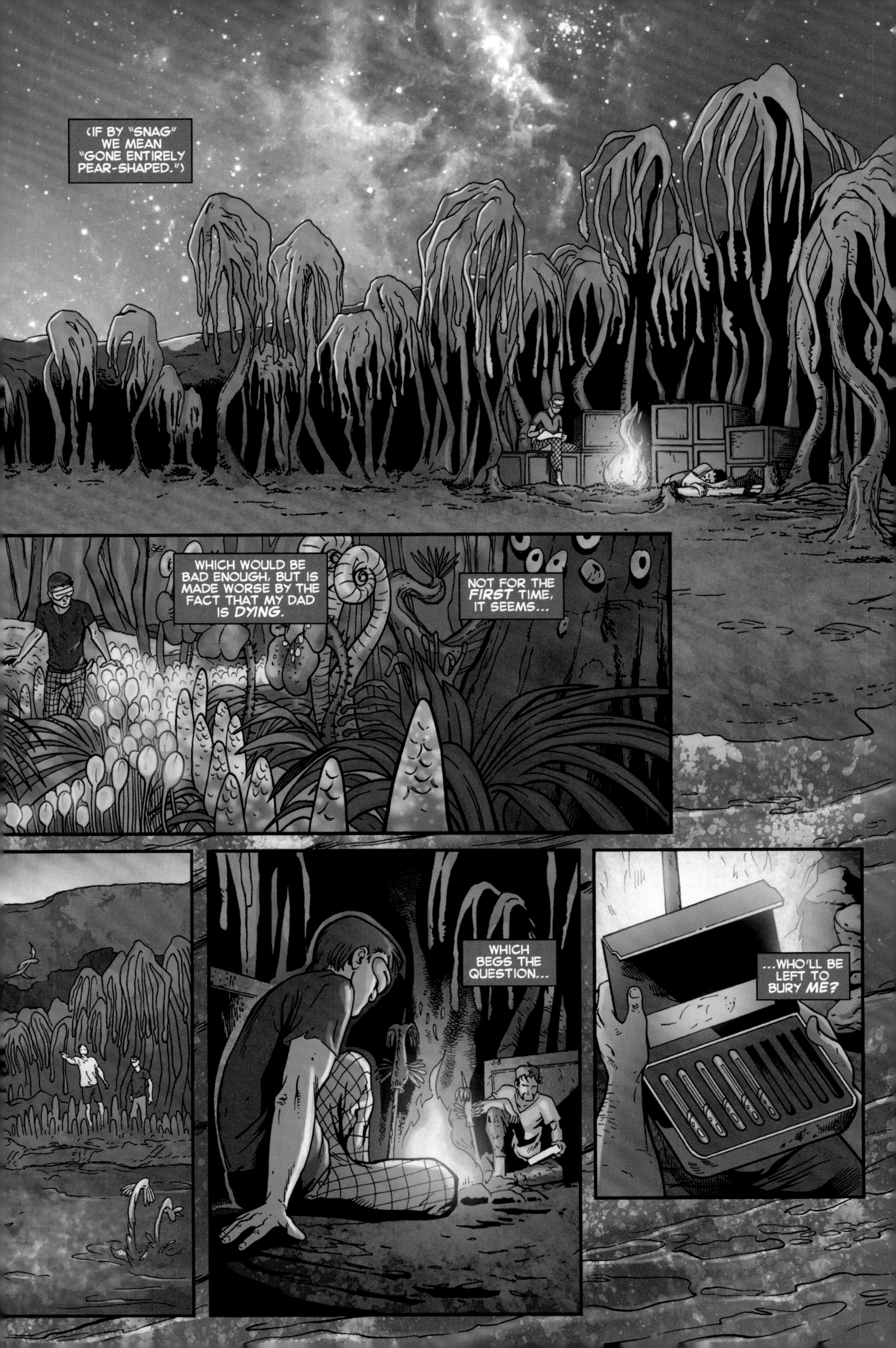
(IF BY "SNAG" WE MEAN "GONE ENTIRELY PEAR-SHAPED.")
WHICH WOULD BE BAD ENOUGH, BUT IS MADE WORSE BY THE FACT THAT MY DAD IS *DYING*.
NOT FOR THE *FIRST* TIME, IT SEEMS...
WHICH BEGS THE QUESTION...
...WHO'LL BE LEFT TO BURY *ME?*

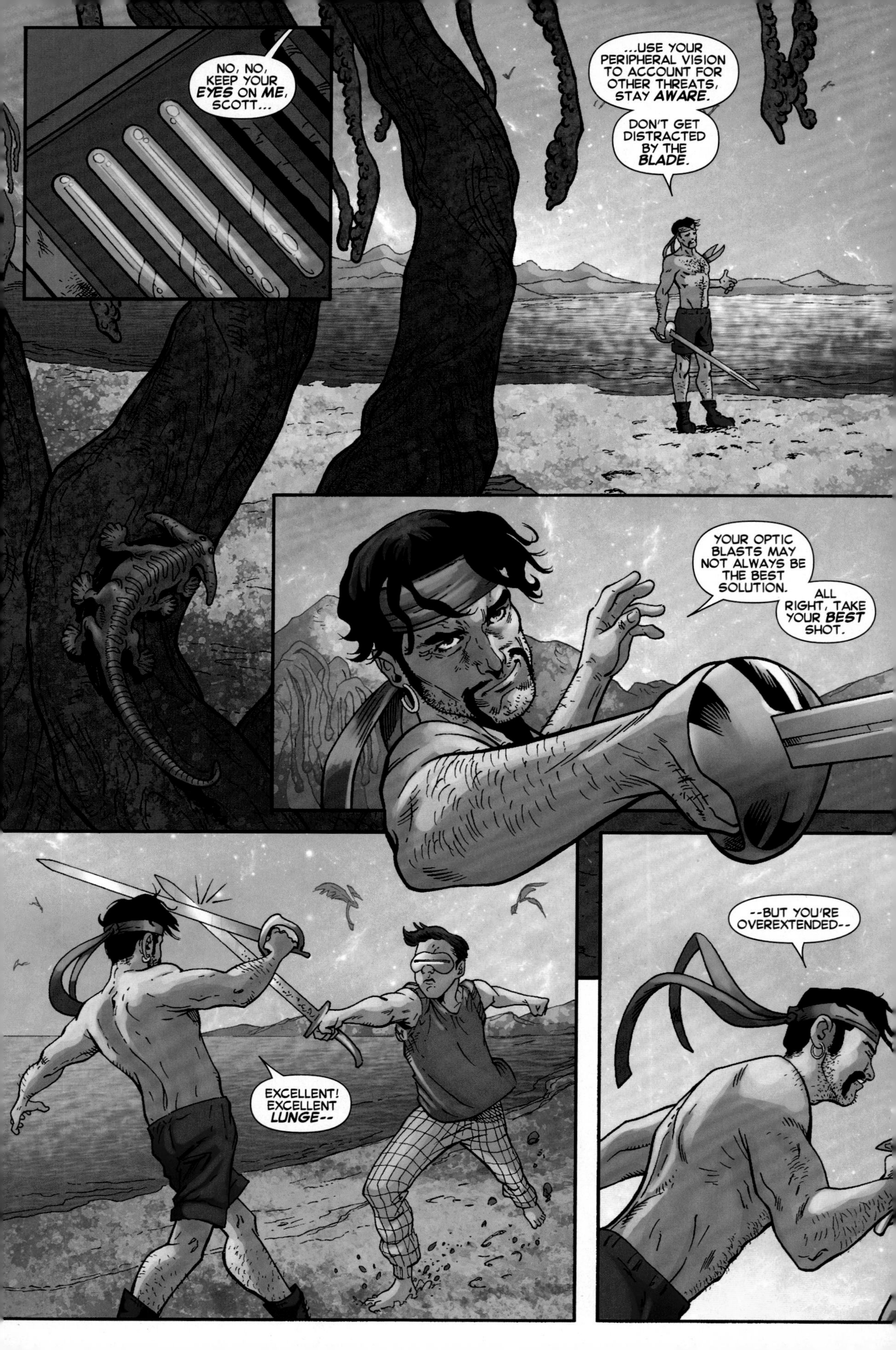
NO, NO, KEEP YOUR *EYES* ON *ME*, SCOTT...
...USE YOUR PERIPHERAL VISION TO ACCOUNT FOR OTHER THREATS, STAY *AWARE*.
DON'T GET DISTRACTED BY THE *BLADE*.
YOUR OPTIC BLASTS MAY NOT ALWAYS BE THE BEST SOLUTION.
ALL RIGHT, TAKE YOUR *BEST* SHOT.
EXCELLENT! EXCELLENT *LUNGE*--
--BUT YOU'RE OVEREXTENDED--

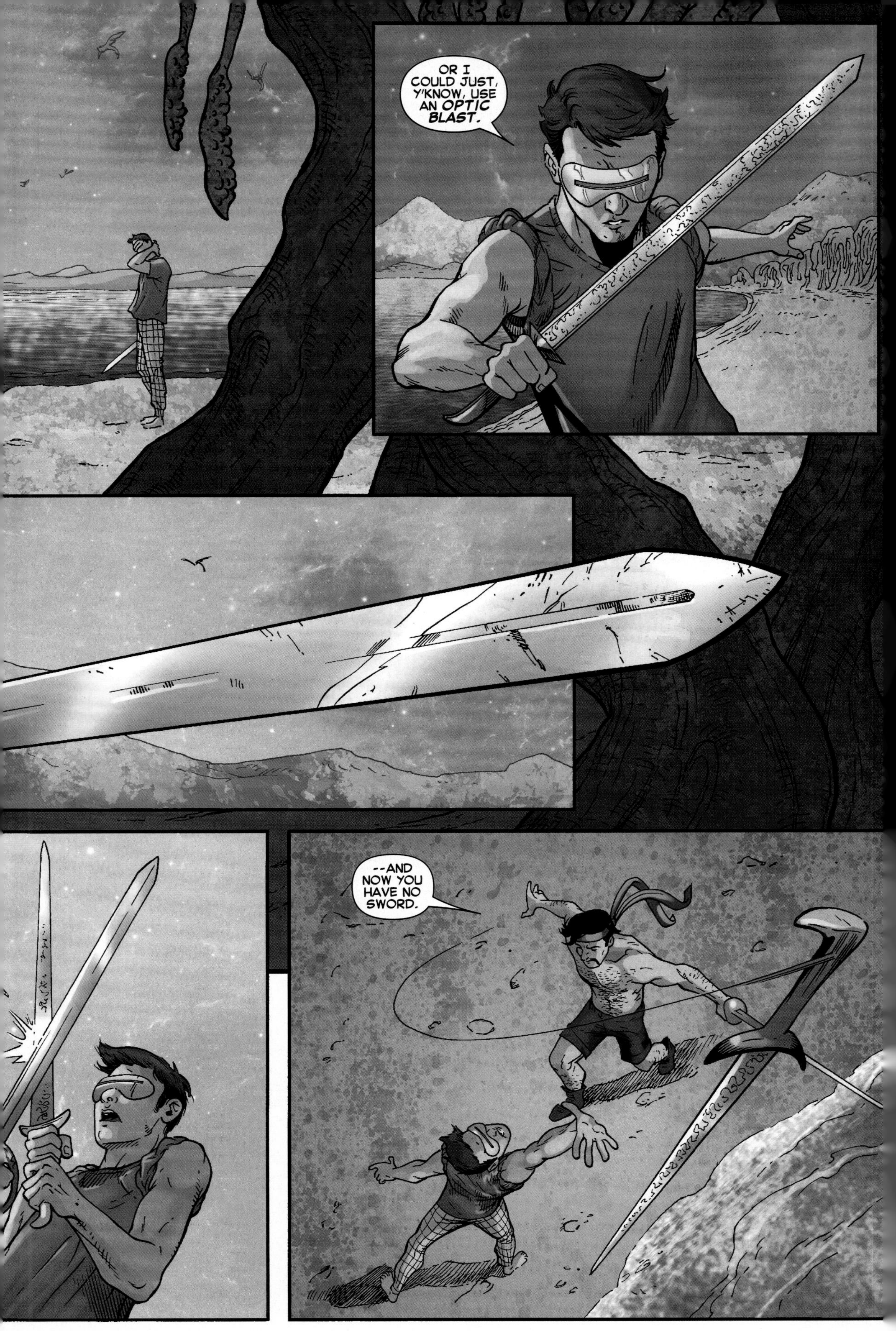
OR I COULD JUST, Y'KNOW, USE AN OPTIC BLAST.
--AND NOW YOU HAVE NO SWORD.

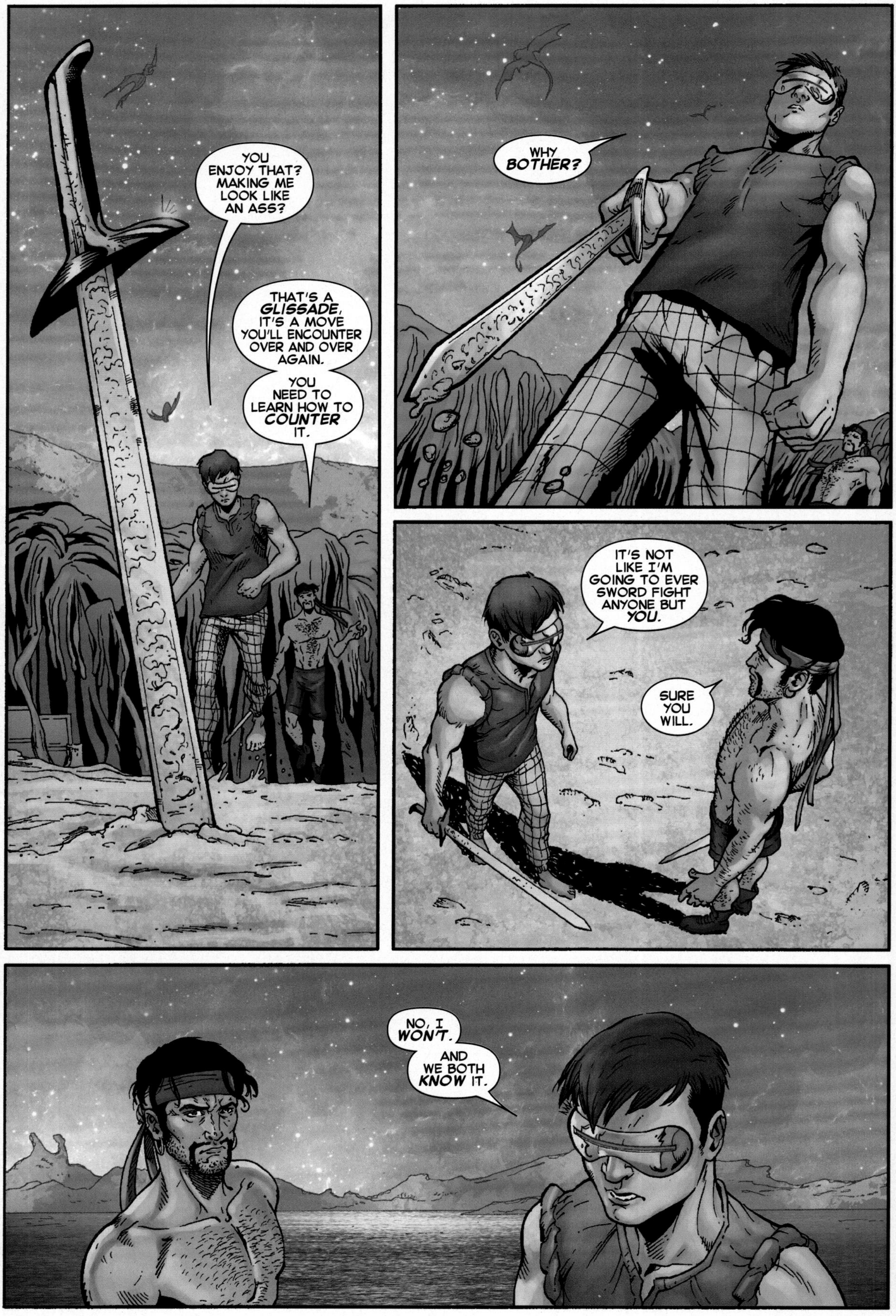
YOU ENJOY THAT? MAKING ME LOOK LIKE AN ASS?
THAT'S A GLISSADE, IT'S A MOVE YOU'LL ENCOUNTER OVER AND OVER AGAIN.
YOU NEED TO LEARN HOW TO COUNTER IT.
WHY BOTHER?
IT'S NOT LIKE I'M GOING TO EVER SWORD FIGHT ANYONE BUT YOU.
SURE YOU WILL.
NO, I WON'T.
AND WE BOTH KNOW IT.

ANOTHER ONE?

YEAH. BIDING THEIR TIME, I THINK.

I BET THEY TASTE LIKE *CHICKEN.*

ONE, *GROSS.*

TWO, NO *WAY* AM I EATING ONE OF *THOSE.* WAY TOO CREEPY-LOOKING.

AND THREE, DID I SAY *GROSS?*

YOU WANT TO EAT ONLY THE FLORA AND THE FISH, FINE, BUT SOONER OR LATER, YOU MAY HAVE TO *DIVERSIFY* YOUR DIET.

I DON'T WANT TO *TALK* ABOUT THIS, DAD.

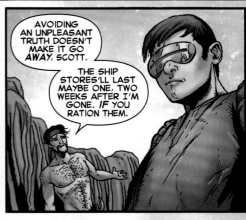

AVOIDING AN UNPLEASANT TRUTH DOESN'T MAKE IT GO *AWAY,* SCOTT.

THE SHIP STORES'LL LAST MAYBE ONE, TWO WEEKS AFTER I'M GONE. *IF* YOU RATION THEM.

BUT SOONER OR LATER, YOUR FOOD'S GONNA RUN *OUT.*

YOU'RE GONNA NEED TO *EAT* IF YOU WANT TO MAKE IT UNTIL YOU'RE *RESCUED.*

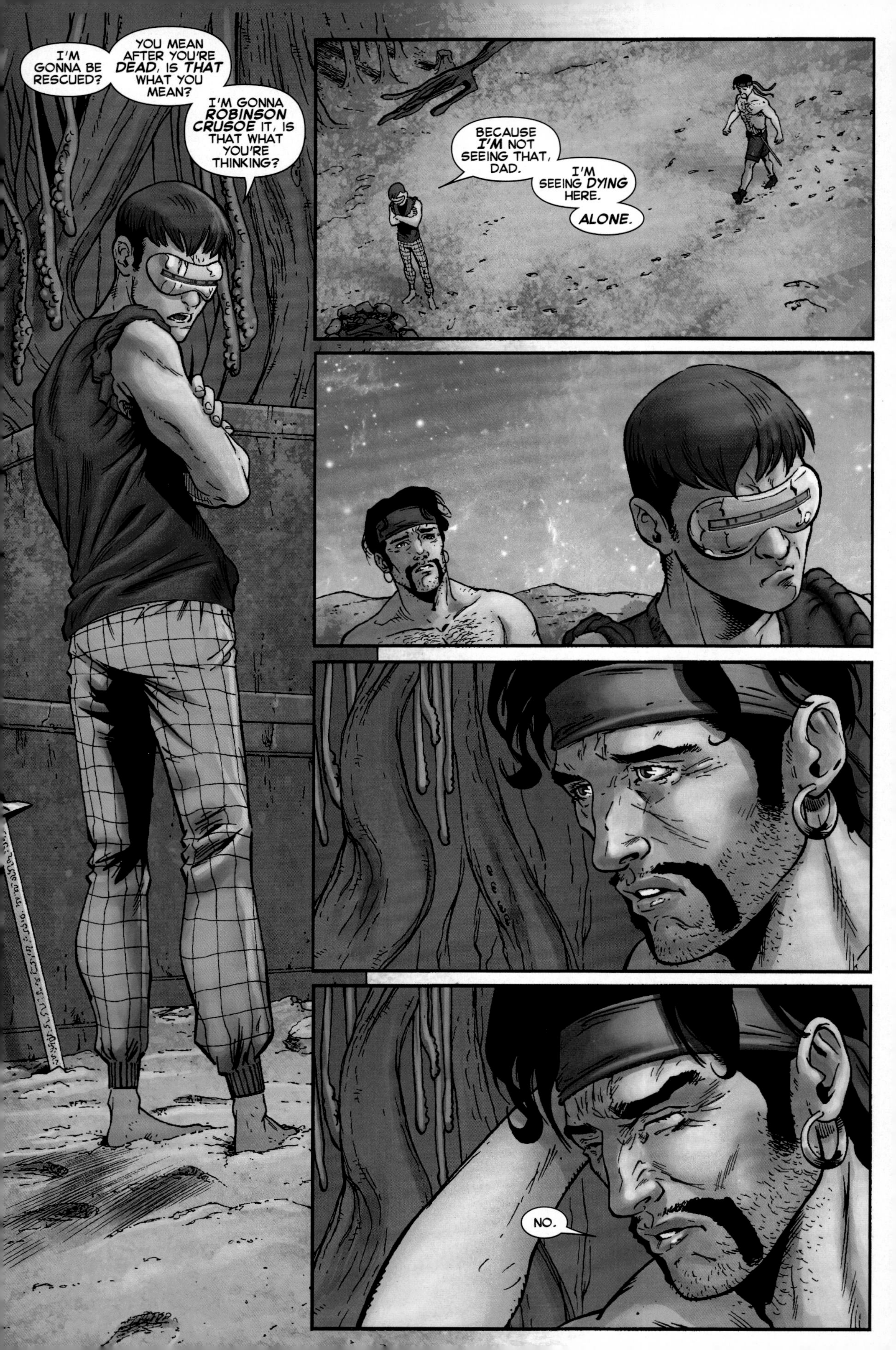
I'M GONNA BE RESCUED?
YOU MEAN AFTER YOU'RE DEAD, IS THAT WHAT YOU MEAN?
I'M GONNA ROBINSON CRUSOE IT, IS THAT WHAT YOU'RE THINKING?
BECAUSE I'M NOT SEEING THAT, DAD.
I'M SEEING DYING HERE.
ALONE.
NO.

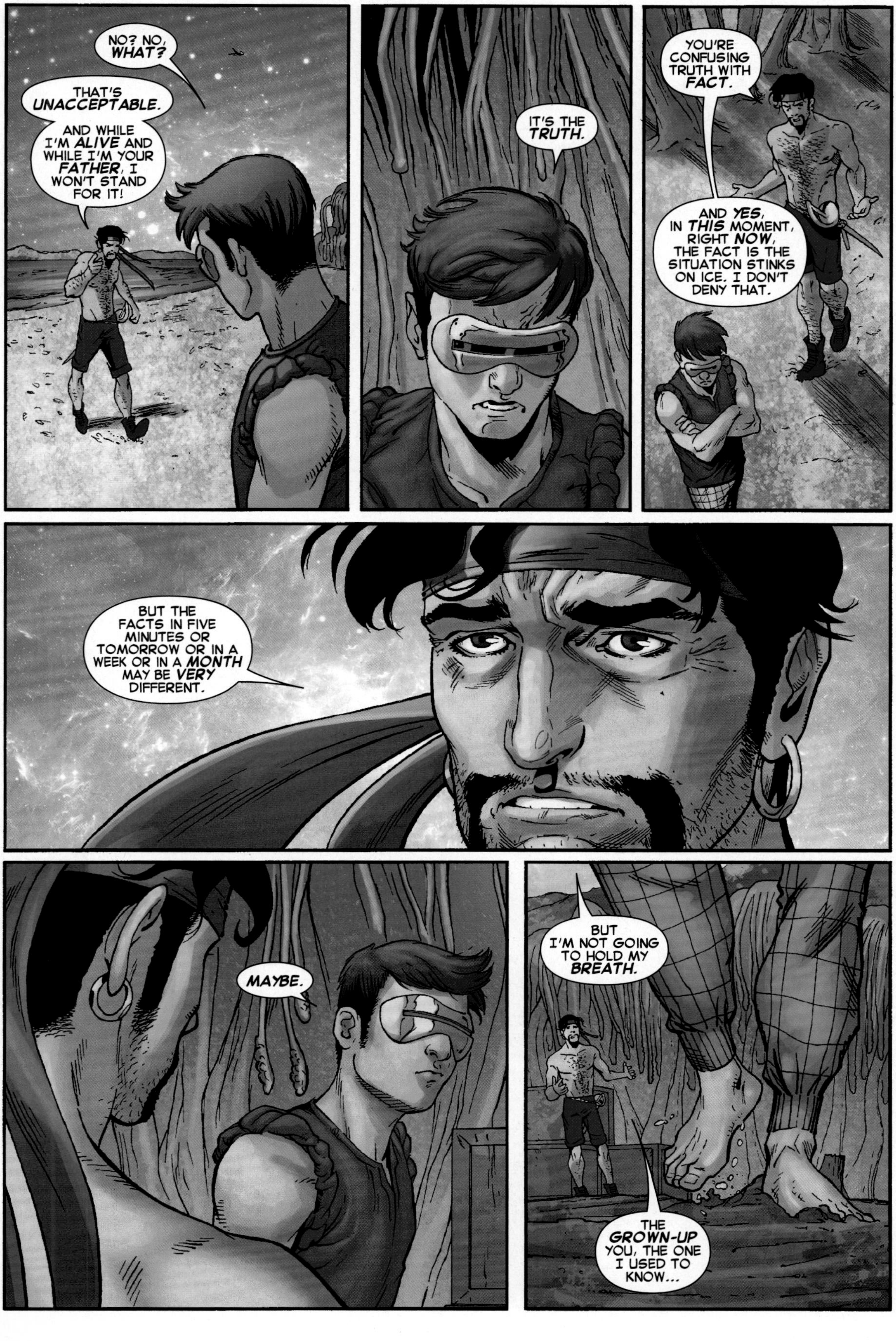
NO? NO, WHAT?
THAT'S UNACCEPTABLE.
AND WHILE I'M ALIVE AND WHILE I'M YOUR FATHER, I WON'T STAND FOR IT!
IT'S THE TRUTH.
YOU'RE CONFUSING TRUTH WITH FACT.
AND YES, IN THIS MOMENT, RIGHT NOW, THE FACT IS THE SITUATION STINKS ON ICE. I DON'T DENY THAT.
BUT THE FACTS IN FIVE MINUTES OR TOMORROW OR IN A WEEK OR IN A MONTH MAY BE VERY DIFFERENT.
MAYBE.
BUT I'M NOT GOING TO HOLD MY BREATH.
THE GROWN-UP YOU, THE ONE I USED TO KNOW...

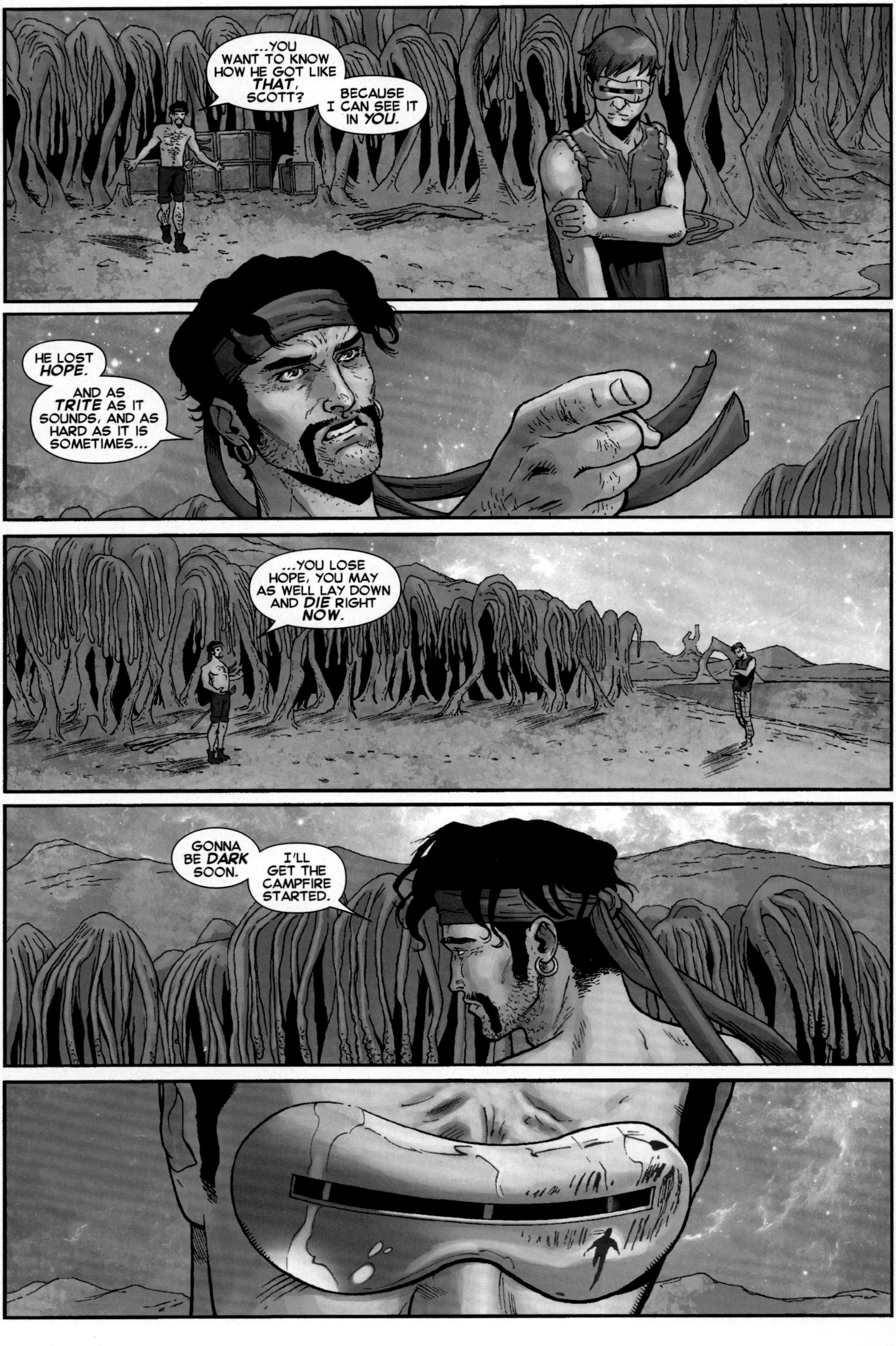
...YOU WANT TO KNOW HOW HE GOT LIKE THAT, SCOTT?
BECAUSE I CAN SEE IT IN YOU.
HE LOST HOPE.
AND AS TRITE AS IT SOUNDS, AND AS HARD AS IT IS SOMETIMES...
...YOU LOSE HOPE, YOU MAY AS WELL LAY DOWN AND DIE RIGHT NOW.
GONNA BE DARK SOON.
I'LL GET THE CAMPFIRE STARTED.

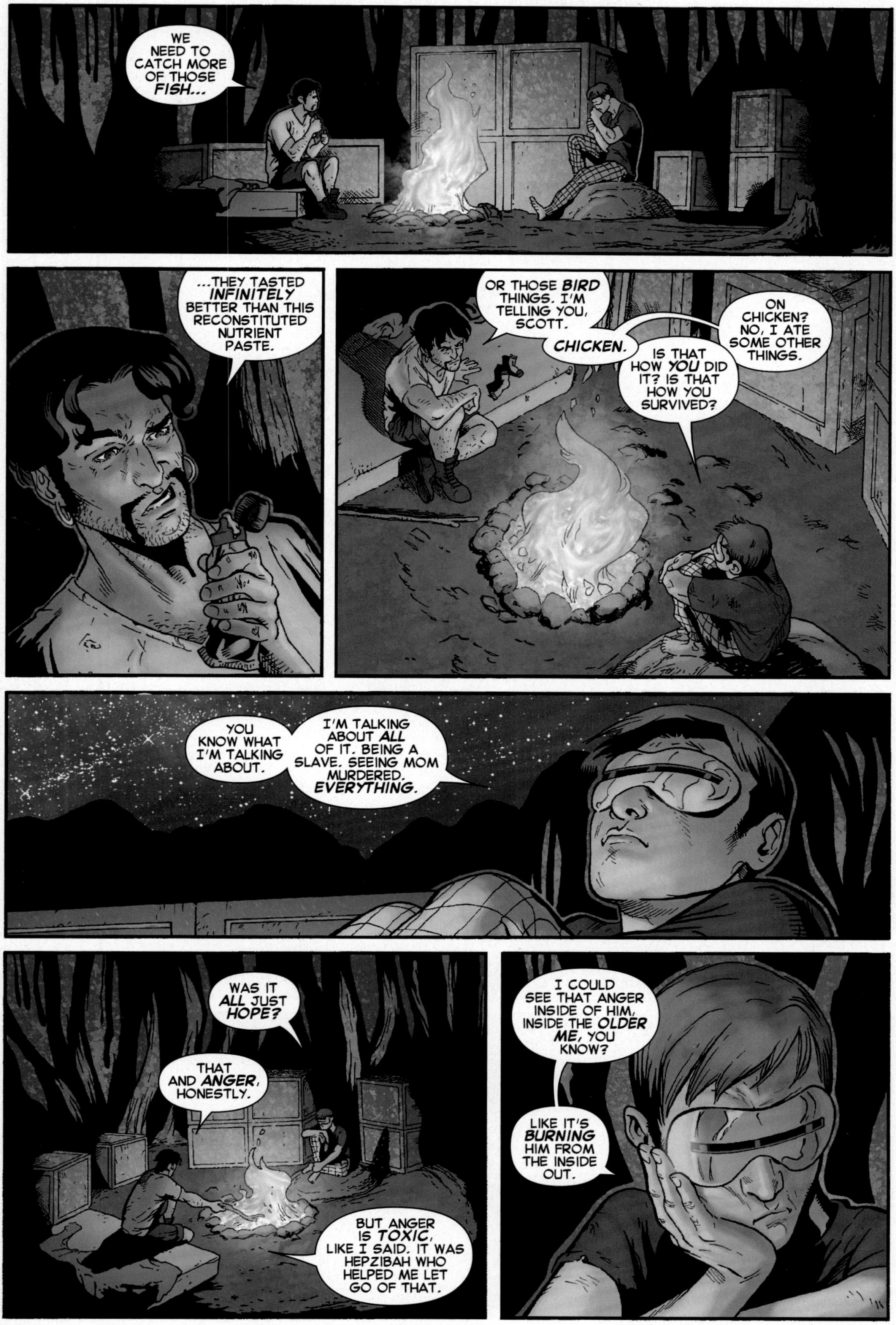

WE NEED TO CATCH MORE OF THOSE FISH...
...THEY TASTED INFINITELY BETTER THAN THIS RECONSTITUTED NUTRIENT PASTE.
OR THOSE BIRD THINGS. I'M TELLING YOU, SCOTT.
CHICKEN.
ON CHICKEN? NO, I ATE SOME OTHER THINGS.
IS THAT HOW YOU DID IT? IS THAT HOW YOU SURVIVED?
YOU KNOW WHAT I'M TALKING ABOUT.
I'M TALKING ABOUT ALL OF IT. BEING A SLAVE. SEEING MOM MURDERED. EVERYTHING.
WAS IT ALL JUST HOPE?
THAT AND ANGER, HONESTLY.
BUT ANGER IS TOXIC, LIKE I SAID. IT WAS HEPZIBAH WHO HELPED ME LET GO OF THAT.
I COULD SEE THAT ANGER INSIDE OF HIM, INSIDE THE OLDER ME, YOU KNOW?
LIKE IT'S BURNING HIM FROM THE INSIDE OUT.

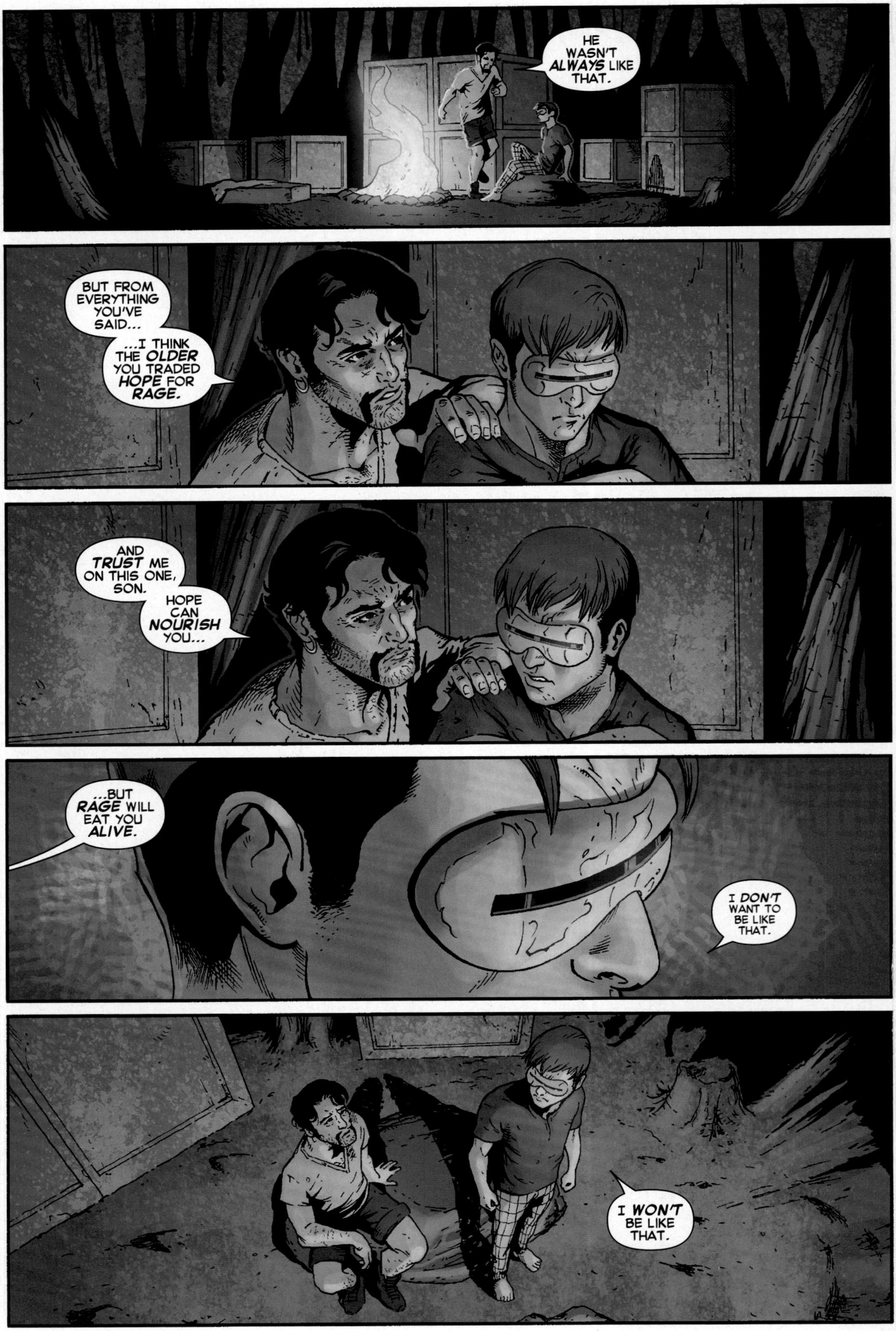
HE WASN'T ALWAYS LIKE THAT.
BUT FROM EVERYTHING YOU'VE SAID...
...I THINK THE OLDER YOU TRADED HOPE FOR RAGE.
AND TRUST ME ON THIS ONE, SON.
HOPE CAN NOURISH YOU...
...BUT RAGE WILL EAT YOU ALIVE.
I DON'T WANT TO BE LIKE THAT.
I WON'T BE LIKE THAT.

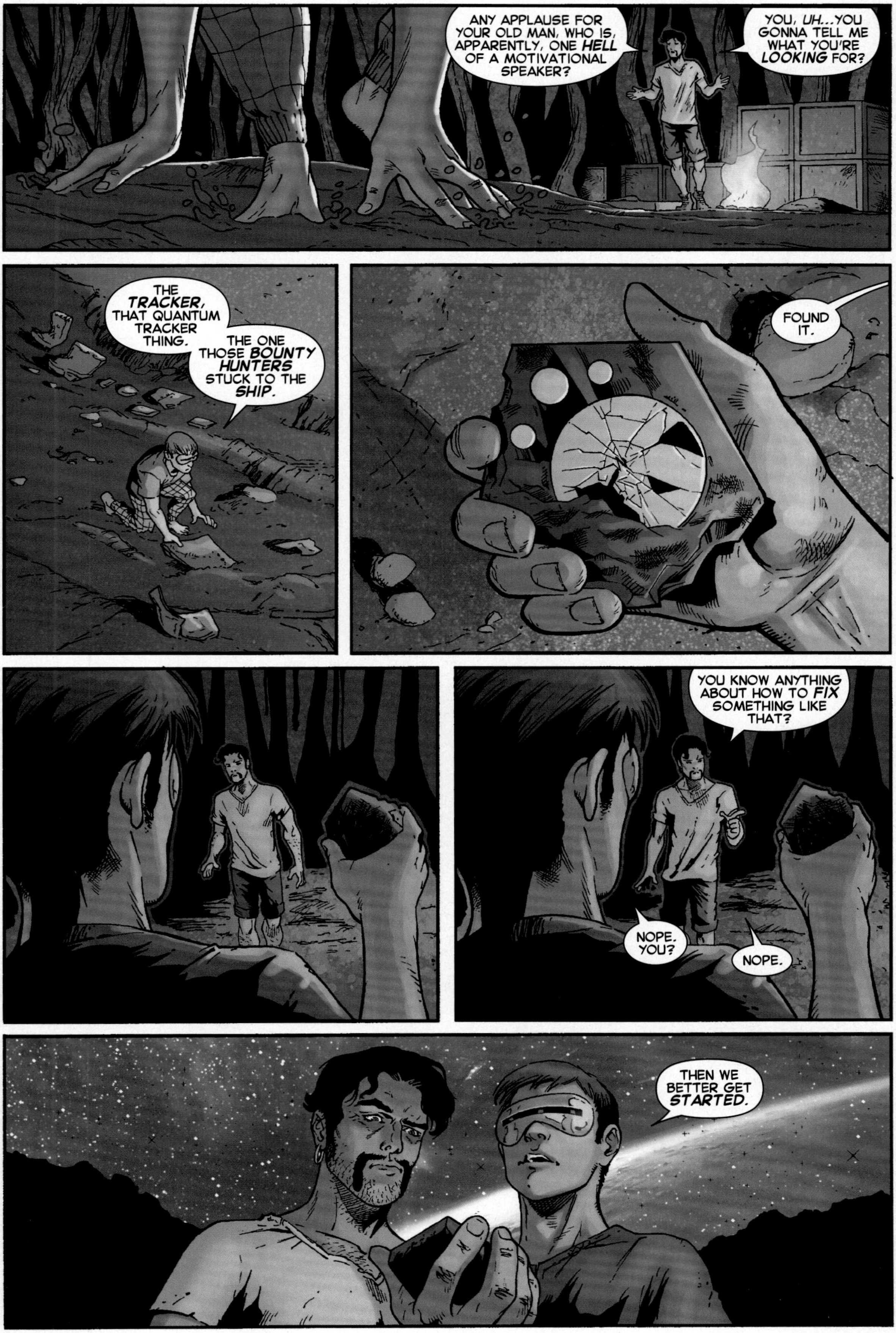
ANY APPLAUSE FOR YOUR OLD MAN, WHO IS, APPARENTLY, ONE HELL OF A MOTIVATIONAL SPEAKER?
YOU, UH...YOU GONNA TELL ME WHAT YOU'RE LOOKING FOR?
THE TRACKER, THAT QUANTUM TRACKER THING.
THE ONE THOSE BOUNTY HUNTERS STUCK TO THE SHIP.
FOUND IT.
YOU KNOW ANYTHING ABOUT HOW TO FIX SOMETHING LIKE THAT?
NOPE. YOU?
NOPE.
THEN WE BETTER GET STARTED.

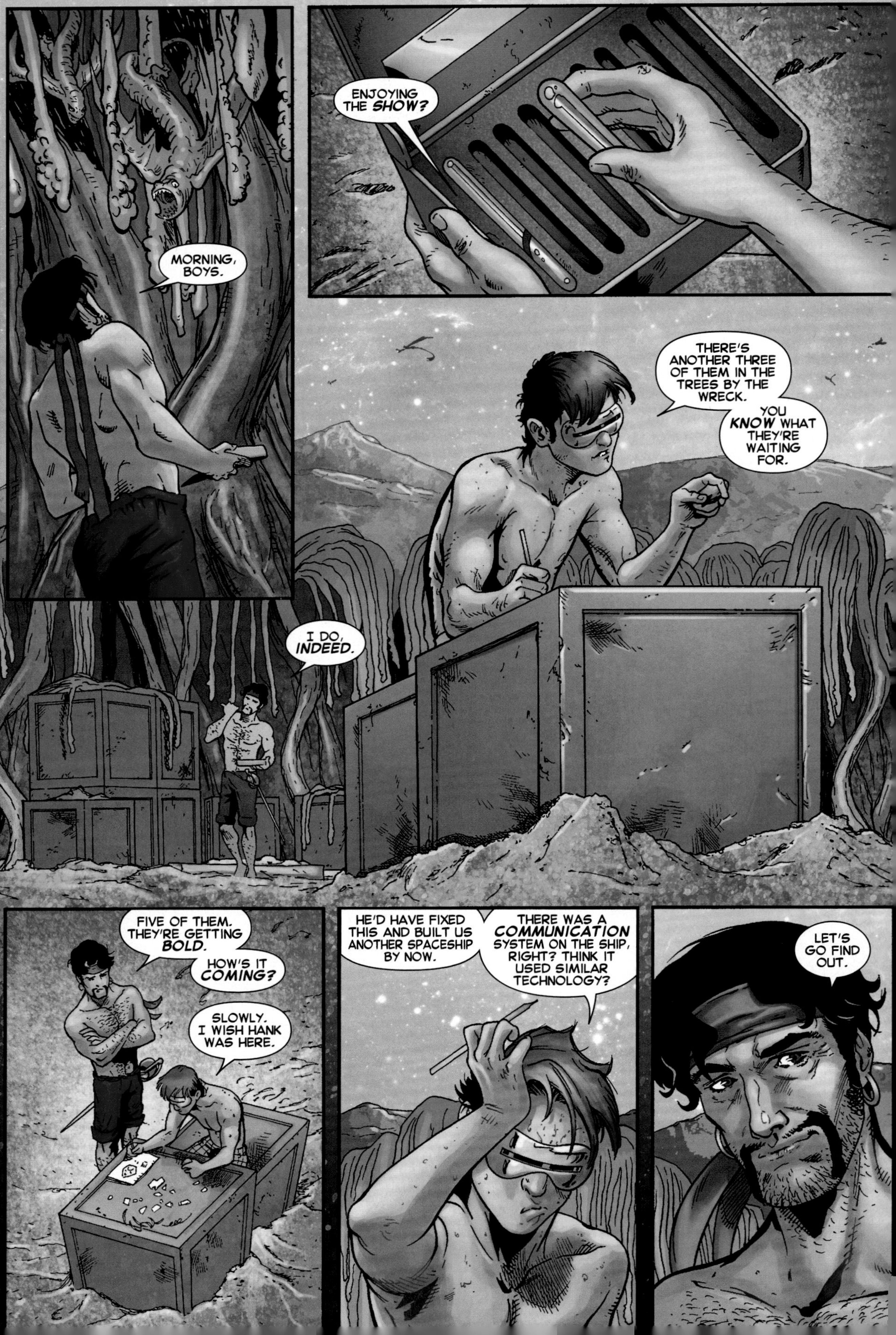
MORNING, BOYS.
ENJOYING THE SHOW?
THERE'S ANOTHER THREE OF THEM IN THE TREES BY THE WRECK.
YOU KNOW WHAT THEY'RE WAITING FOR.
I DO, INDEED.
FIVE OF THEM. THEY'RE GETTING BOLD.
HOW'S IT COMING?
SLOWLY. I WISH HANK WAS HERE.
HE'D HAVE FIXED THIS AND BUILT US ANOTHER SPACESHIP BY NOW.
THERE WAS A COMMUNICATION SYSTEM ON THE SHIP, RIGHT? THINK IT USED SIMILAR TECHNOLOGY?
LET'S GO FIND OUT.

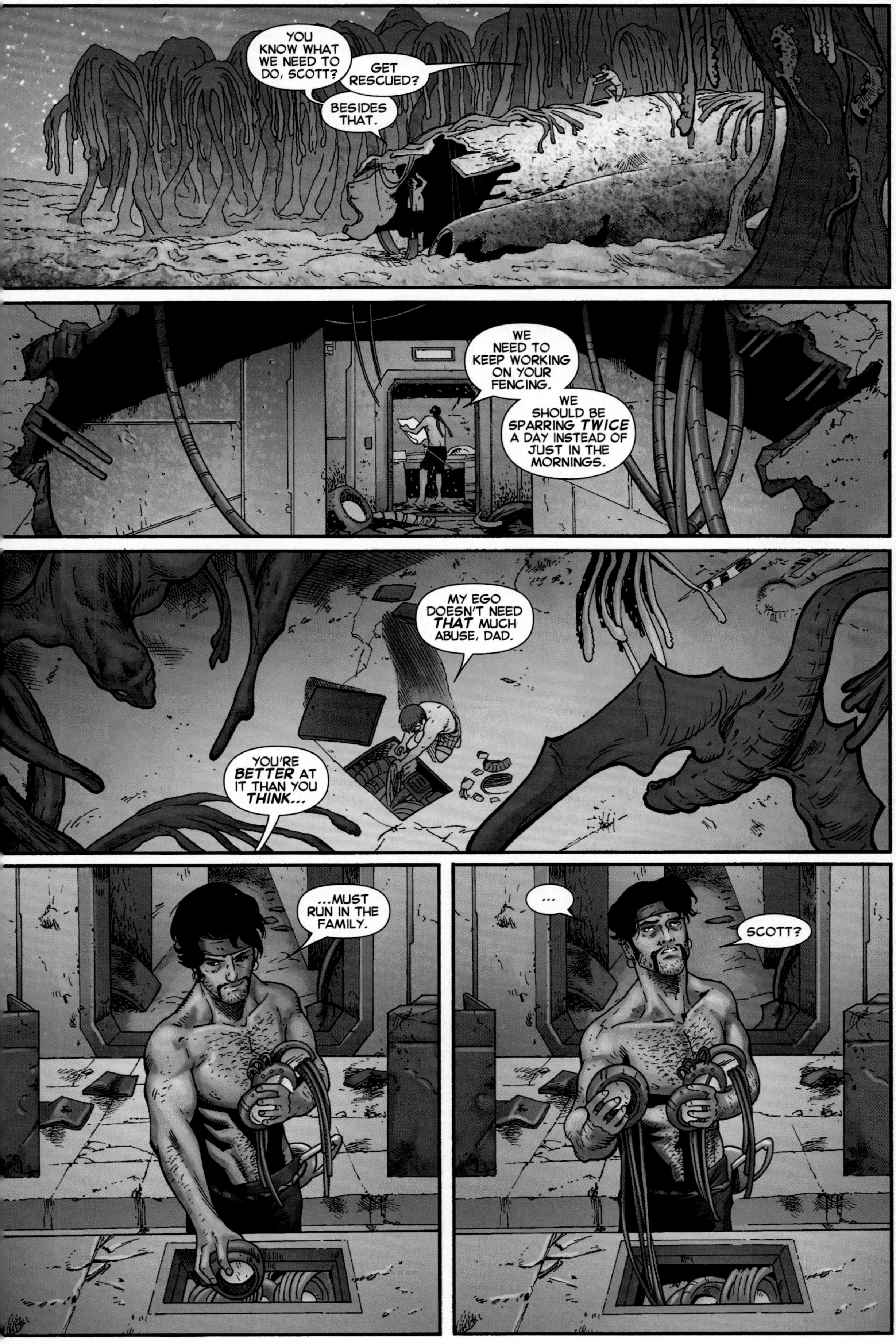
YOU KNOW WHAT WE NEED TO DO, SCOTT?
GET RESCUED?
BESIDES THAT.
WE NEED TO KEEP WORKING ON YOUR FENCING.
WE SHOULD BE SPARRING TWICE A DAY INSTEAD OF JUST IN THE MORNINGS.
MY EGO DOESN'T NEED THAT MUCH ABUSE, DAD.
YOU'RE BETTER AT IT THAN YOU THINK...
...MUST RUN IN THE FAMILY.
...
SCOTT?

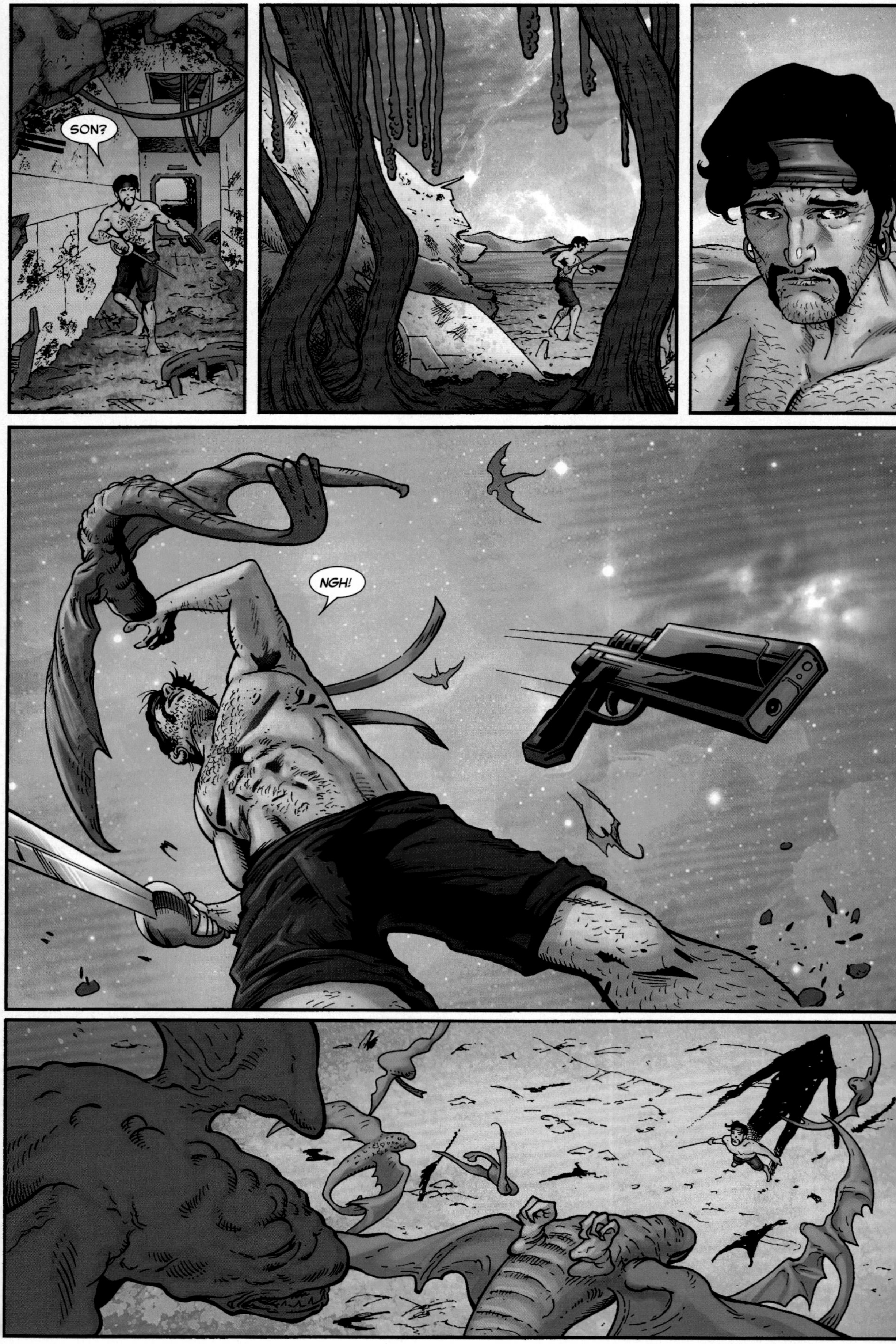
SON?
NGH!

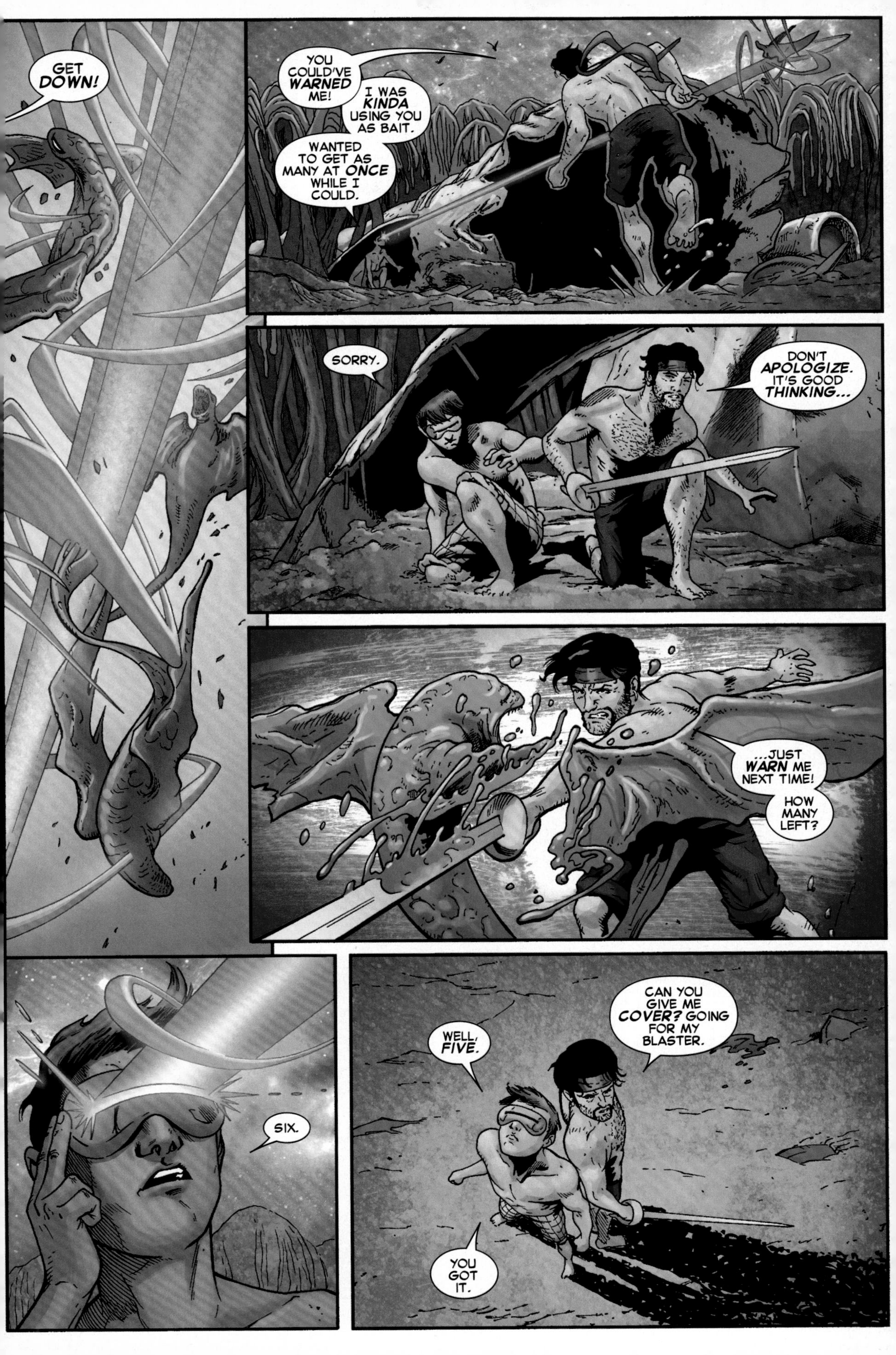

GET DOWN!
YOU COULD'VE WARNED ME!
I WAS KINDA USING YOU AS BAIT.
WANTED TO GET AS MANY AT ONCE WHILE I COULD.
SORRY.
DON'T APOLOGIZE. IT'S GOOD THINKING...
...JUST WARN ME NEXT TIME!
HOW MANY LEFT?
SIX.
WELL, FIVE.
CAN YOU GIVE ME COVER? GOING FOR MY BLASTER.
YOU GOT IT.

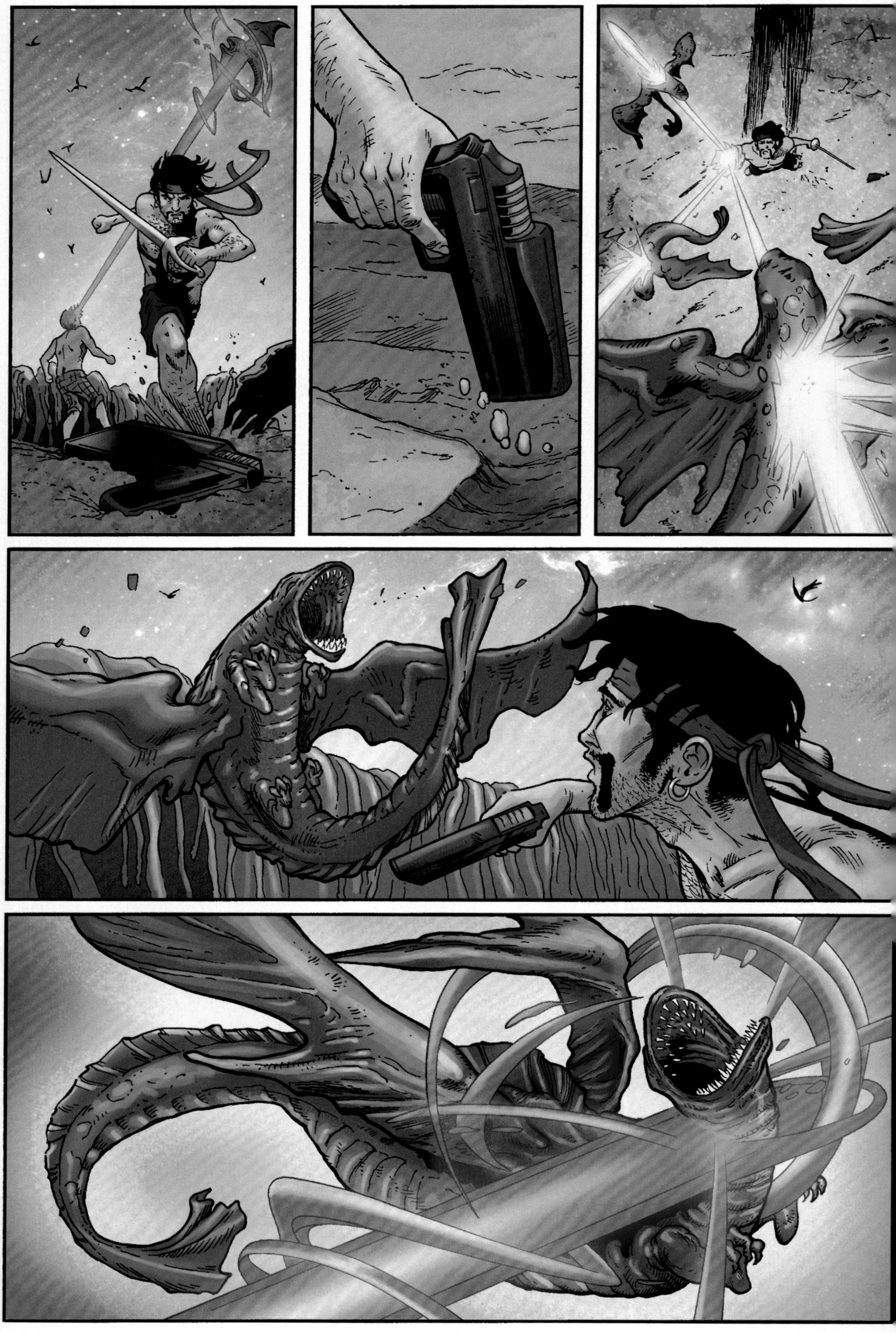

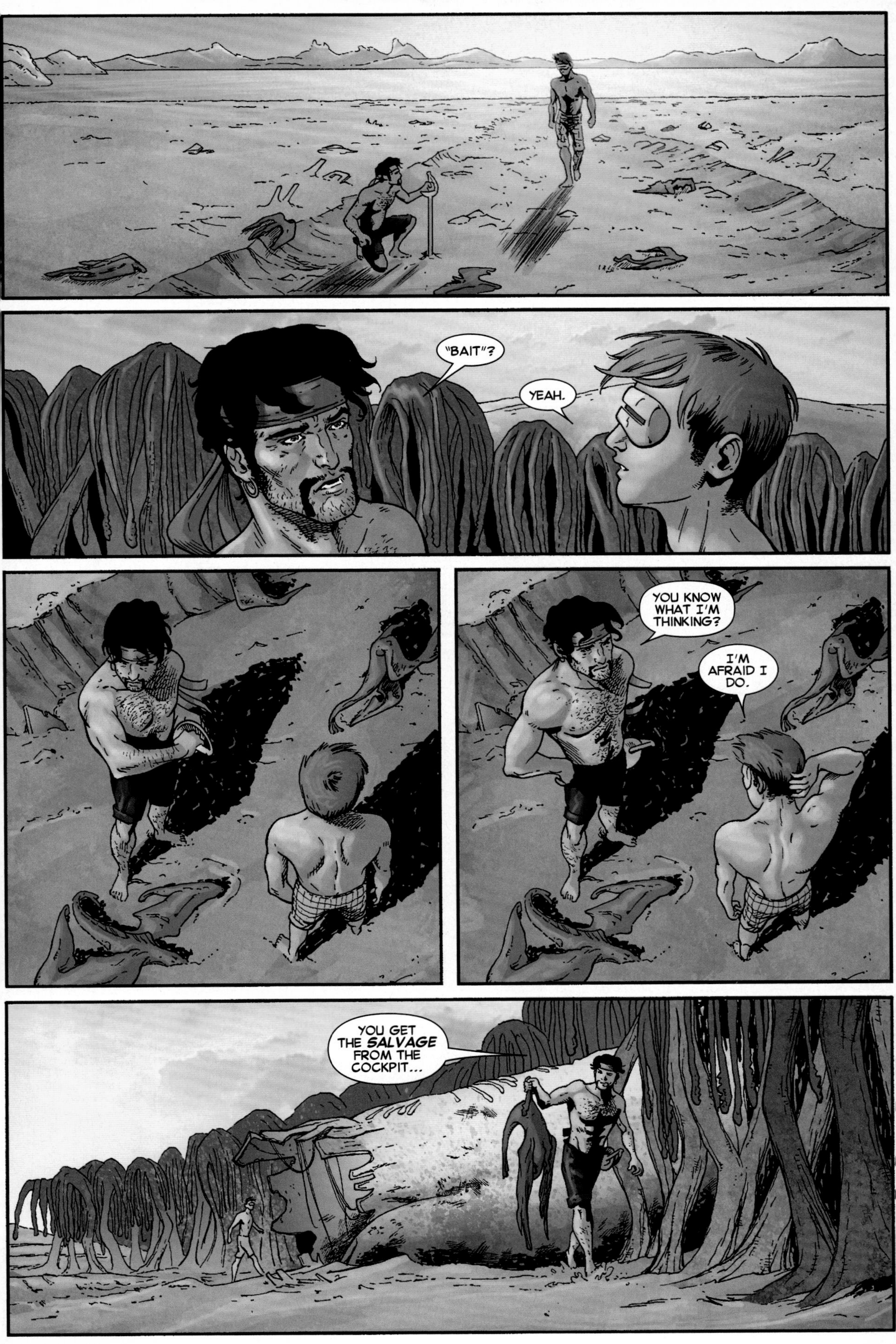
"BAIT"?
YEAH.
YOU KNOW WHAT I'M THINKING?
I'M AFRAID I DO.
YOU GET THE SALVAGE FROM THE COCKPIT...

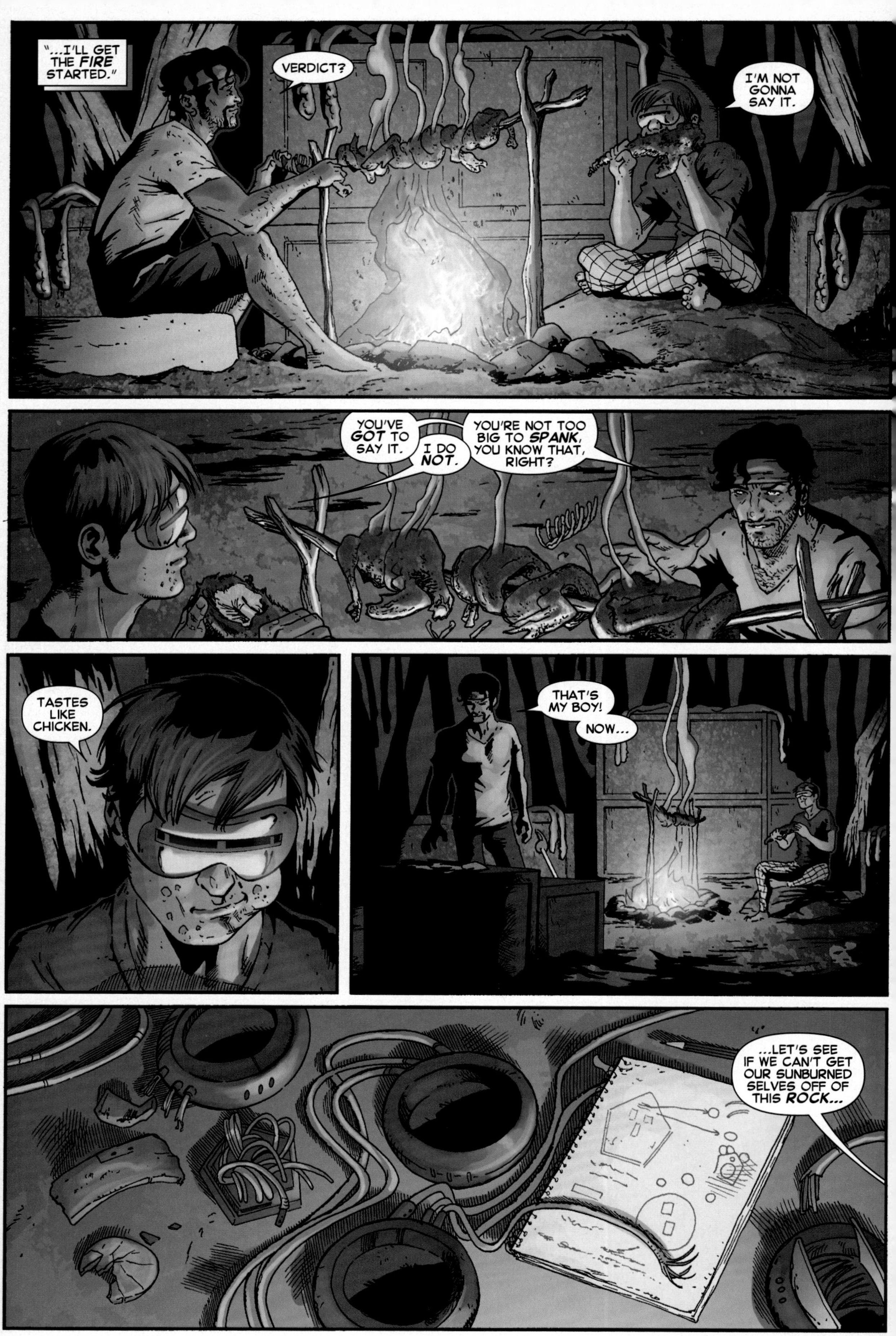
"...I'LL GET THE FIRE STARTED."
VERDICT?
I'M NOT GONNA SAY IT.
YOU'VE GOT TO SAY IT.
I DO NOT.
YOU'RE NOT TOO BIG TO SPANK, YOU KNOW THAT, RIGHT?
TASTES LIKE CHICKEN.
THAT'S MY BOY!
NOW...
...LET'S SEE IF WE CAN'T GET OUR SUNBURNED SELVES OFF OF THIS ROCK...

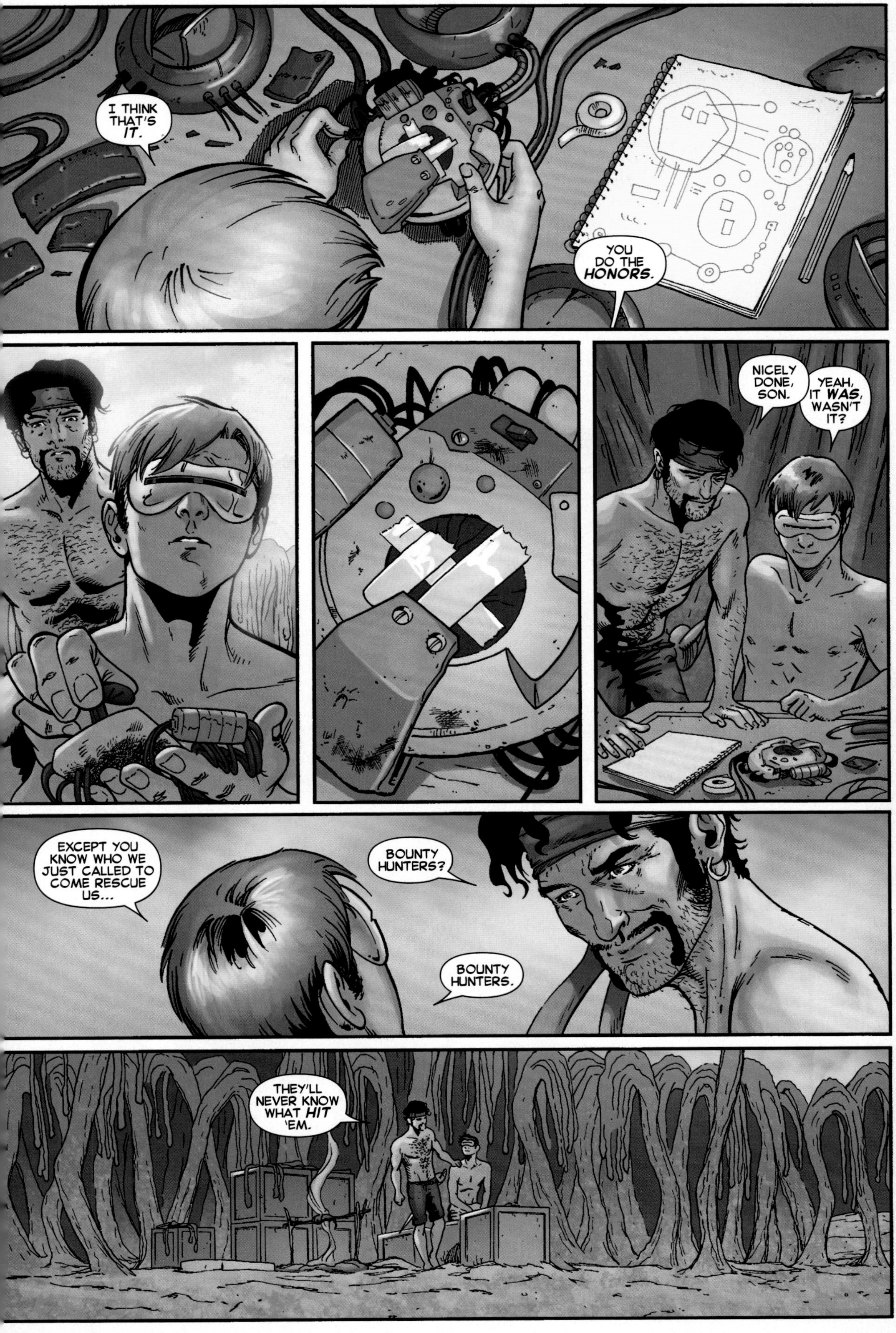

I THINK THAT'S *IT.*
YOU DO THE ***HONORS.***
NICELY DONE, SON.
YEAH, IT ***WAS,*** WASN'T IT?
EXCEPT YOU KNOW WHO WE JUST CALLED TO COME RESCUE US...
BOUNTY HUNTERS?
BOUNTY HUNTERS.
THEY'LL NEVER KNOW WHAT *HIT* 'EM.

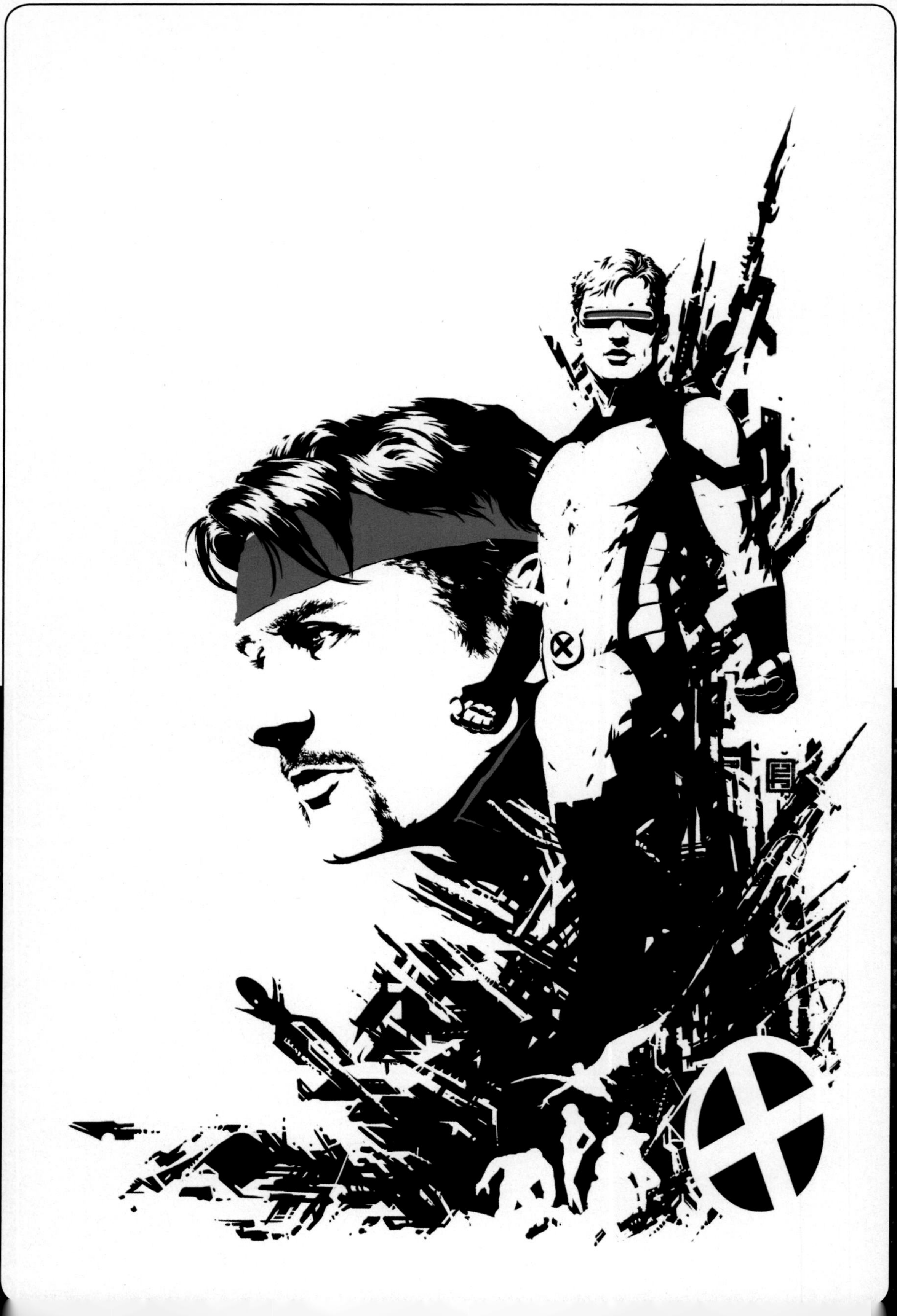

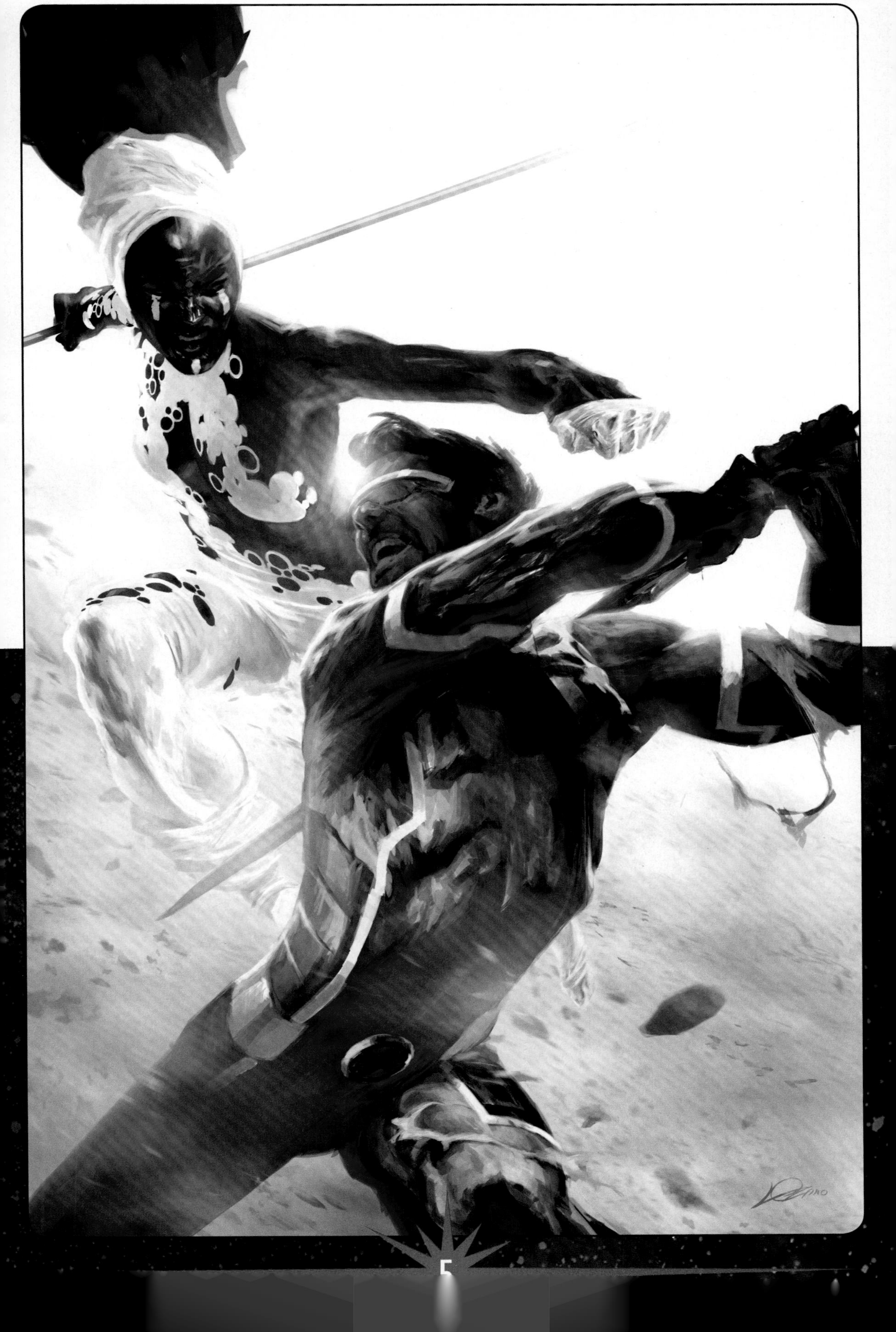

5

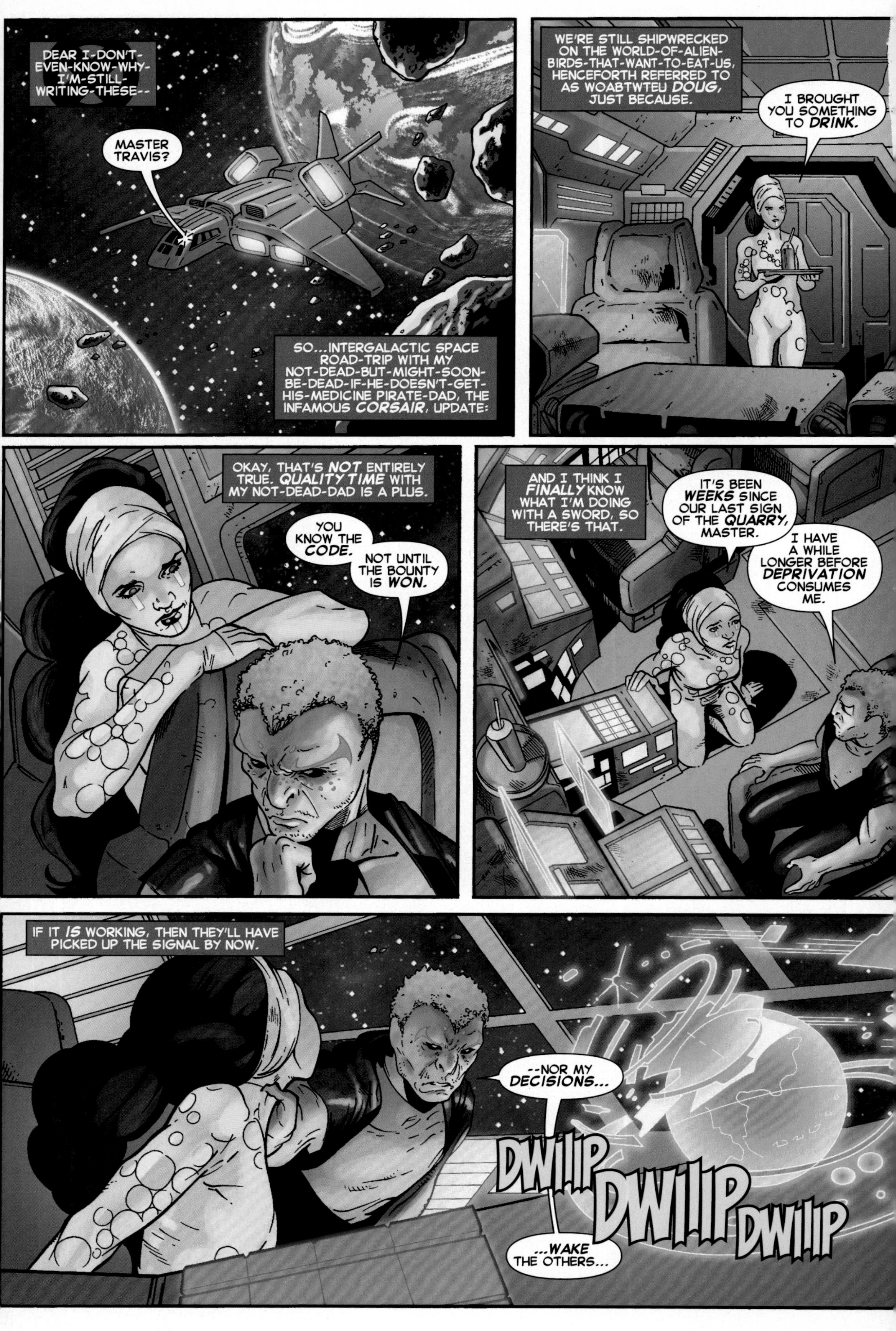
DEAR I-DON'T-EVEN-KNOW-WHY-I'M-STILL-WRITING-THESE--
MASTER TRAVIS?
SO...INTERGALACTIC SPACE ROAD-TRIP WITH MY NOT-DEAD-BUT-MIGHT-SOON-BE-DEAD-IF-HE-DOESN'T-GET-HIS-MEDICINE PIRATE-DAD, THE INFAMOUS CORSAIR, UPDATE:
WE'RE STILL SHIPWRECKED ON THE WORLD-OF-ALIEN-BIRDS-THAT-WANT-TO-EAT-US, HENCEFORTH REFERRED TO AS WOABTWTEU DOUG, JUST BECAUSE.
I BROUGHT YOU SOMETHING TO DRINK.
OKAY, THAT'S NOT ENTIRELY TRUE. QUALITY TIME WITH MY NOT-DEAD-DAD IS A PLUS.
YOU KNOW THE CODE.
NOT UNTIL THE BOUNTY IS WON.
AND I THINK I FINALLY KNOW WHAT I'M DOING WITH A SWORD, SO THERE'S THAT.
IT'S BEEN WEEKS SINCE OUR LAST SIGN OF THE QUARRY, MASTER.
I HAVE A WHILE LONGER BEFORE DEPRIVATION CONSUMES ME.
IF IT IS WORKING, THEN THEY'LL HAVE PICKED UP THE SIGNAL BY NOW.
--NOR MY DECISIONS...
DWIIIP DWIIIP DWIIIP
...WAKE THE OTHERS...

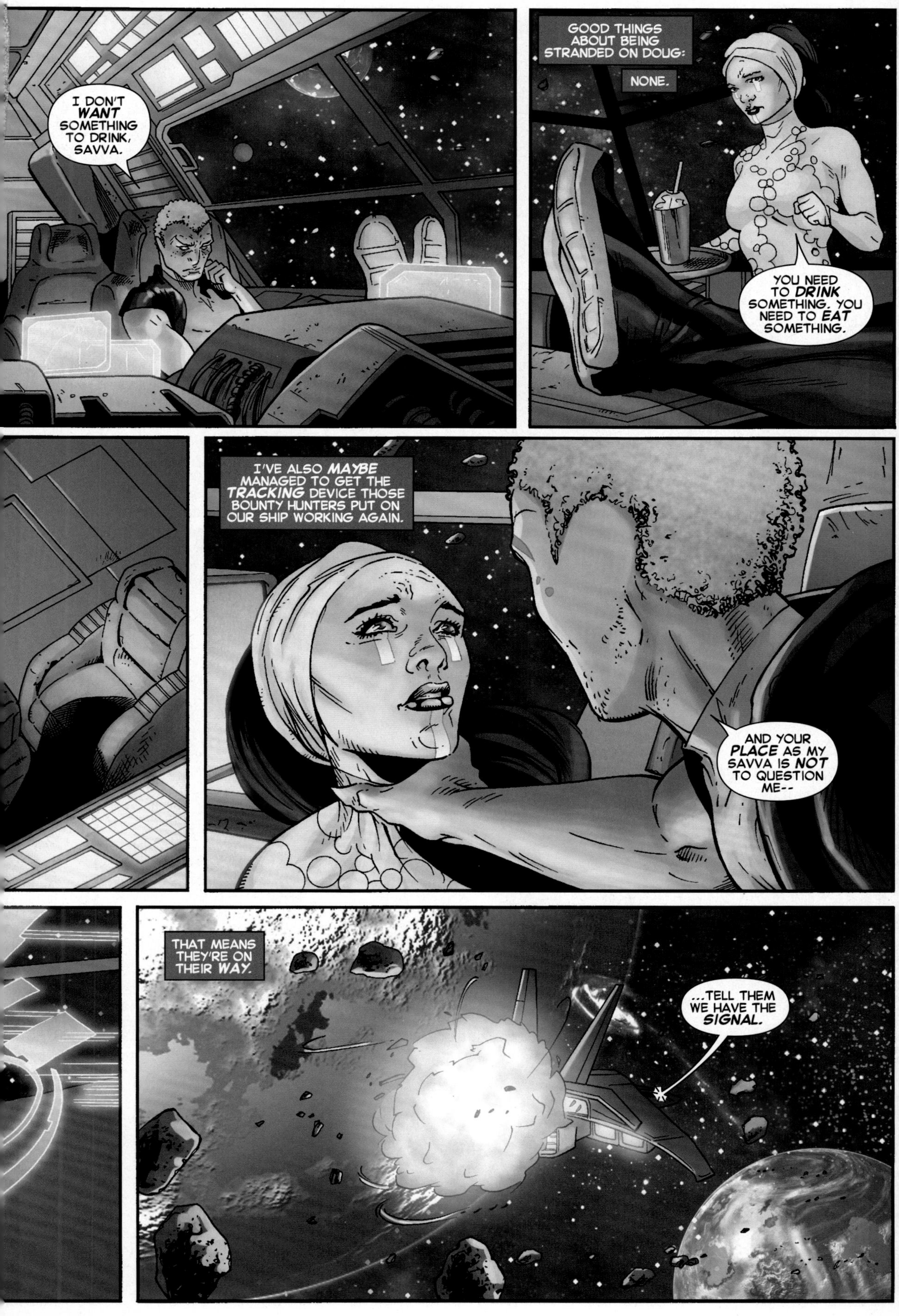

I DON'T WANT SOMETHING TO DRINK, SAVVA.
GOOD THINGS ABOUT BEING STRANDED ON DOUG:
NONE.
YOU NEED TO DRINK SOMETHING. YOU NEED TO EAT SOMETHING.
I'VE ALSO MAYBE MANAGED TO GET THE TRACKING DEVICE THOSE BOUNTY HUNTERS PUT ON OUR SHIP WORKING AGAIN.
AND YOUR PLACE AS MY SAVVA IS NOT TO QUESTION ME--
THAT MEANS THEY'RE ON THEIR WAY.
...TELL THEM WE HAVE THE SIGNAL.

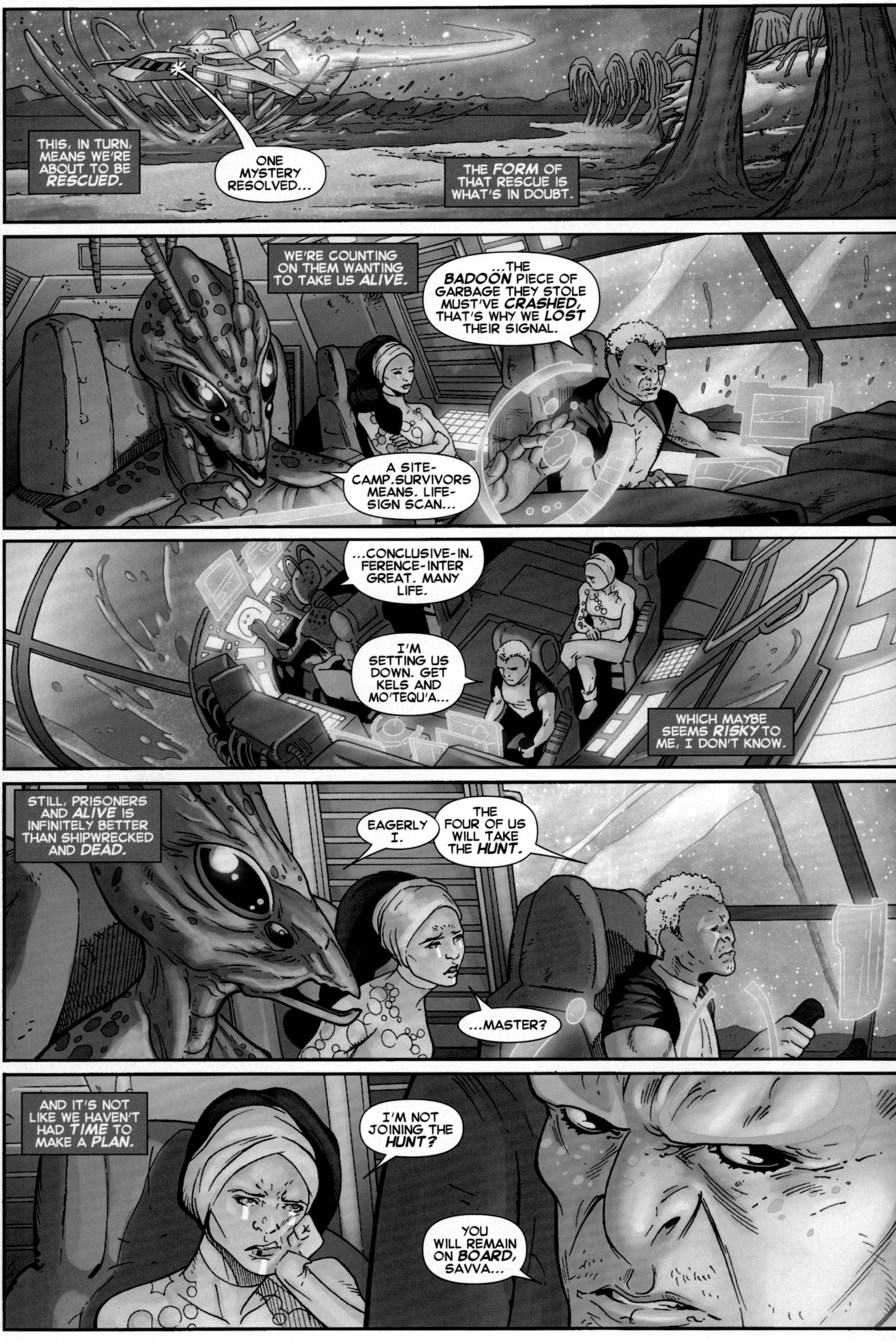
THIS, IN TURN, MEANS WE'RE ABOUT TO BE RESCUED.
ONE MYSTERY RESOLVED...
THE FORM OF THAT RESCUE IS WHAT'S IN DOUBT.
WE'RE COUNTING ON THEM WANTING TO TAKE US ALIVE.
...THE BADOON PIECE OF GARBAGE THEY STOLE MUST'VE CRASHED, THAT'S WHY WE LOST THEIR SIGNAL.
A SITE-CAMP.SURVIVORS MEANS. LIFE-SIGN SCAN...
...CONCLUSIVE-IN. FERENCE-INTER GREAT. MANY LIFE.
I'M SETTING US DOWN. GET KELS AND MO'TEQU'A...
WHICH MAYBE SEEMS RISKY TO ME, I DON'T KNOW.
STILL, PRISONERS AND ALIVE IS INFINITELY BETTER THAN SHIPWRECKED AND DEAD.
EAGERLY I.
THE FOUR OF US WILL TAKE THE HUNT.
...MASTER?
AND IT'S NOT LIKE WE HAVEN'T HAD TIME TO MAKE A PLAN.
I'M NOT JOINING THE HUNT?
YOU WILL REMAIN ON BOARD, SAVVA...

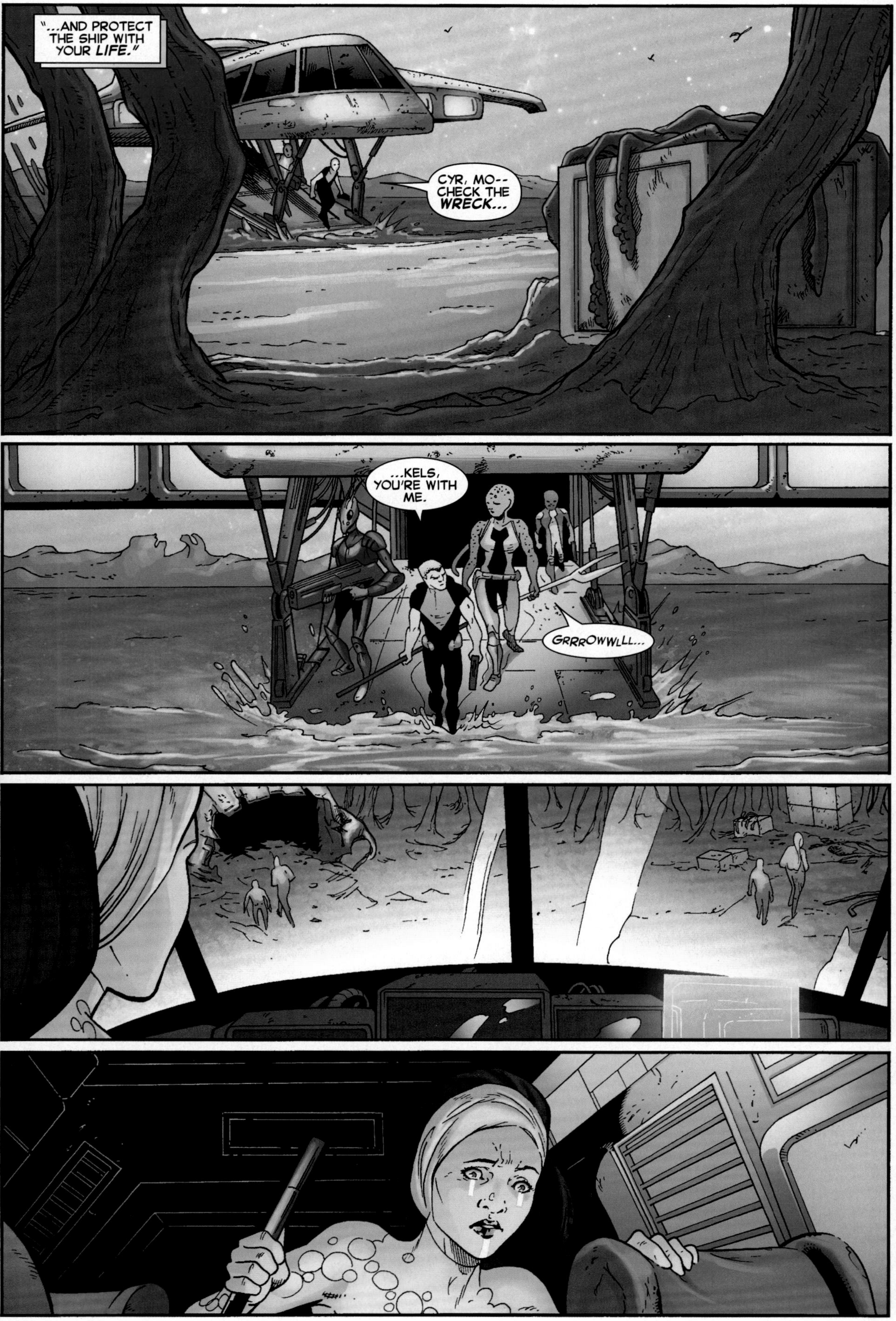
"...AND PROTECT THE SHIP WITH YOUR LIFE."
CYR, MO-- CHECK THE WRECK...
...KELS, YOU'RE WITH ME.
GRRROWWLLL...

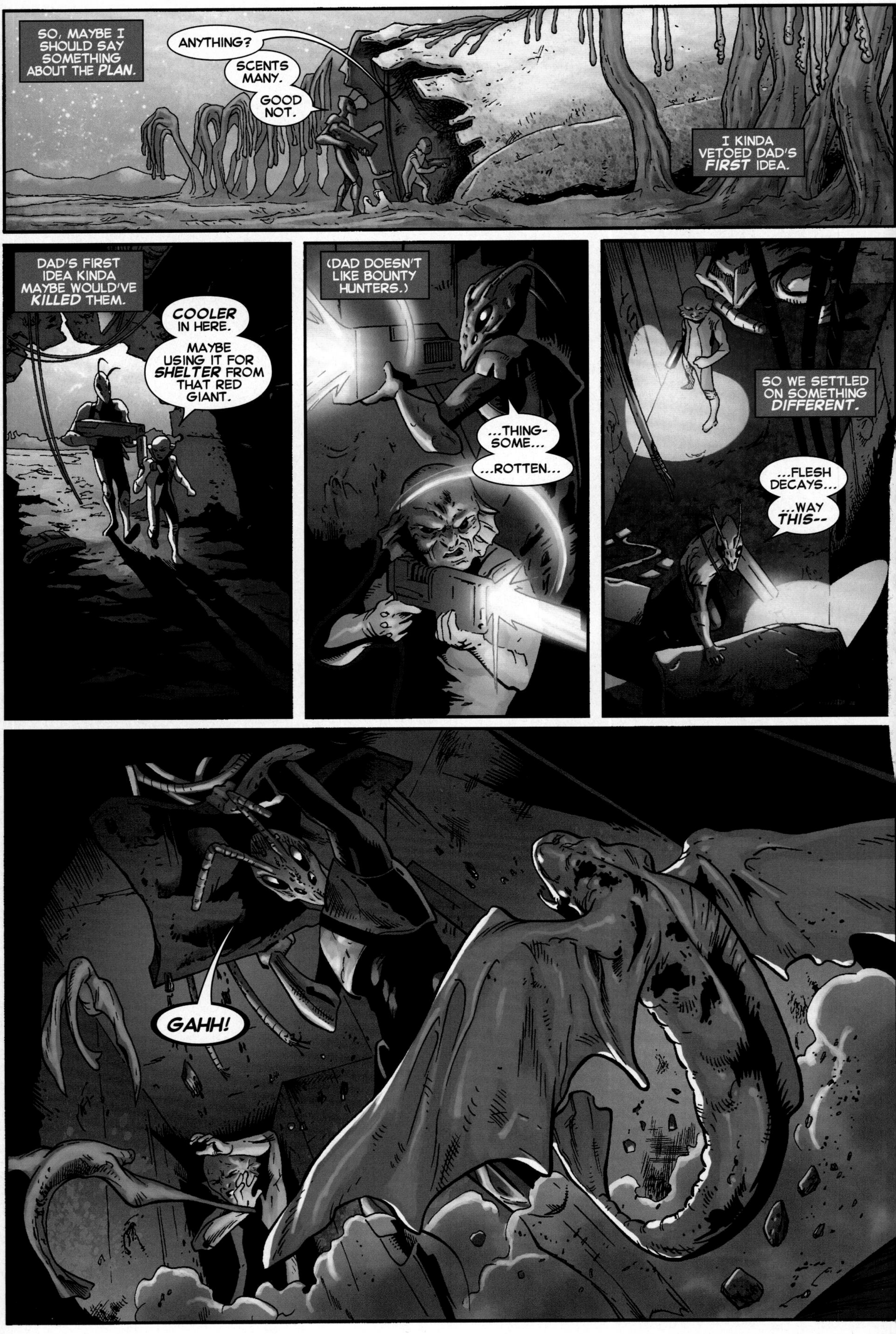
SO, MAYBE I SHOULD SAY SOMETHING ABOUT THE PLAN.
ANYTHING?
SCENTS MANY.
GOOD NOT.
I KINDA VETOED DAD'S FIRST IDEA.
DAD'S FIRST IDEA KINDA MAYBE WOULD'VE KILLED THEM.
COOLER IN HERE.
MAYBE USING IT FOR SHELTER FROM THAT RED GIANT.
(DAD DOESN'T LIKE BOUNTY HUNTERS.)
...THING-SOME...
...ROTTEN...
SO WE SETTLED ON SOMETHING DIFFERENT.
...FLESH DECAYS...
...WAY THIS--
GAHH!

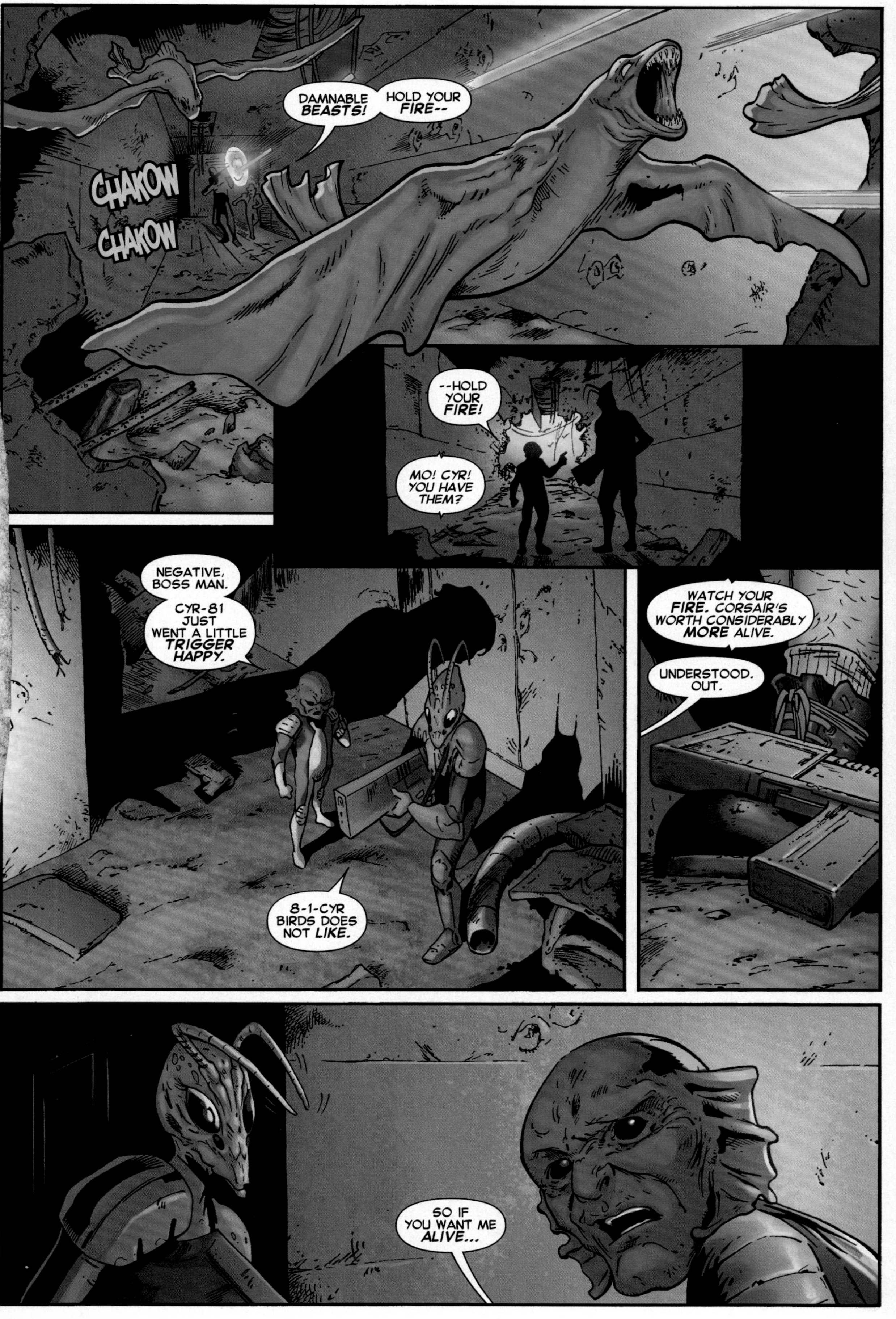
DAMNABLE BEASTS!
HOLD YOUR FIRE--
CHAKOW
CHAKOW
--HOLD YOUR FIRE!
MO! CYR! YOU HAVE THEM?
NEGATIVE, BOSS MAN.
CYR-81 JUST WENT A LITTLE TRIGGER HAPPY.
8-1-CYR BIRDS DOES NOT LIKE.
WATCH YOUR FIRE. CORSAIR'S WORTH CONSIDERABLY MORE ALIVE.
UNDERSTOOD. OUT.
SO IF YOU WANT ME ALIVE...

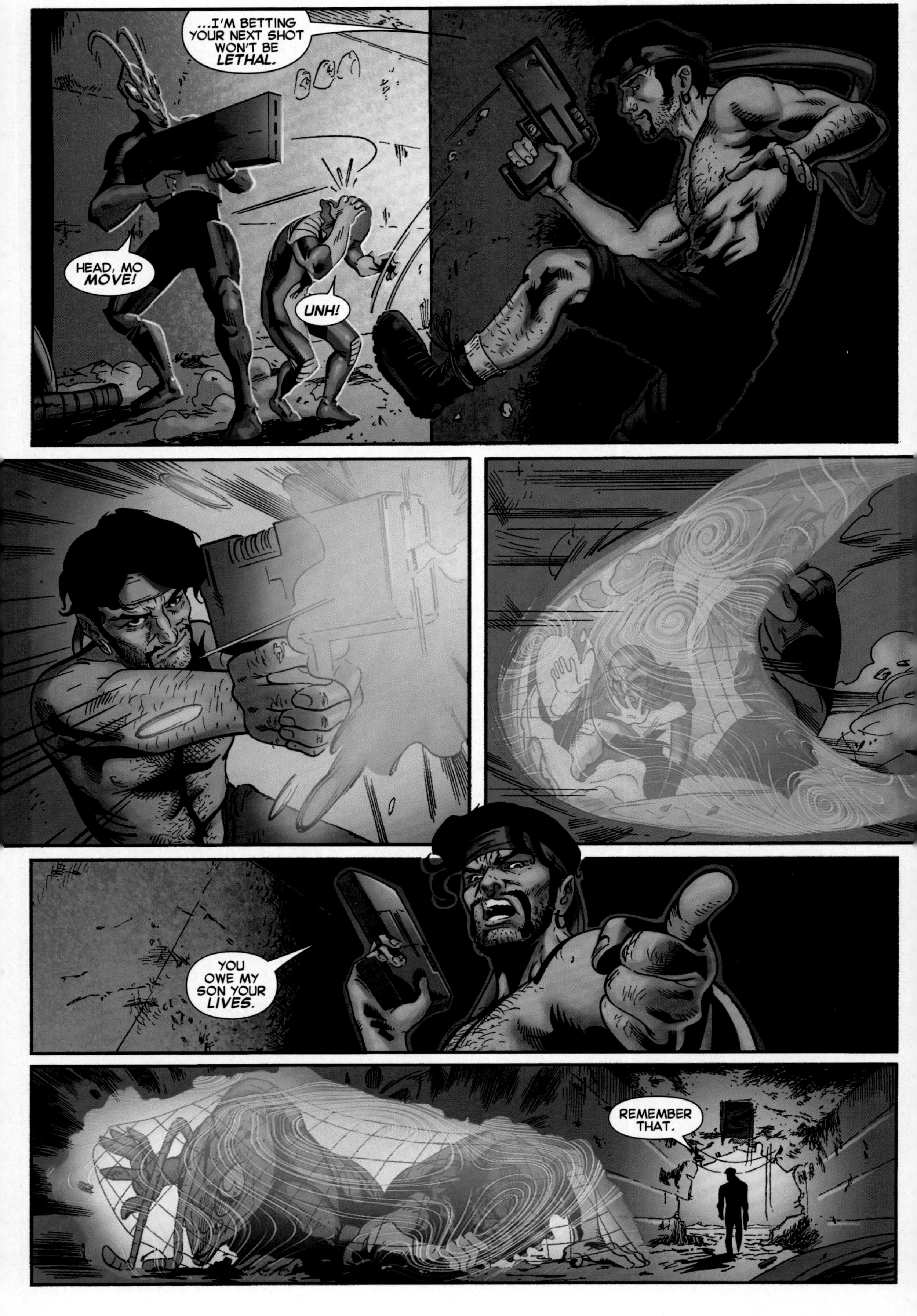
...I'M BETTING YOUR NEXT SHOT WON'T BE LETHAL.
HEAD, MO MOVE!
UNH!
YOU OWE MY SON YOUR LIVES.
REMEMBER THAT.

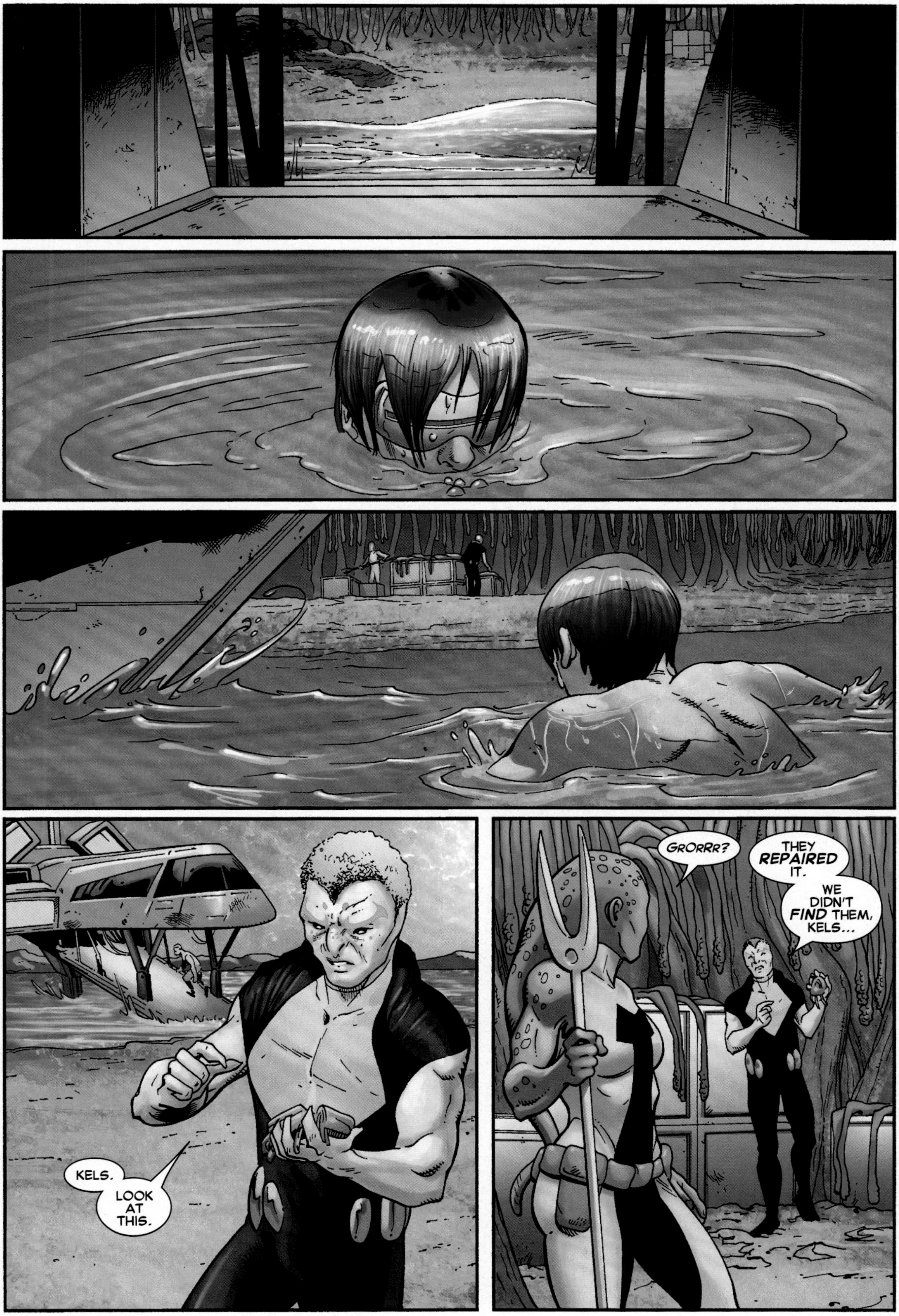
KELS. LOOK AT THIS.
GRORRR?
THEY REPAIRED IT.
WE DIDN'T FIND THEM, KELS...

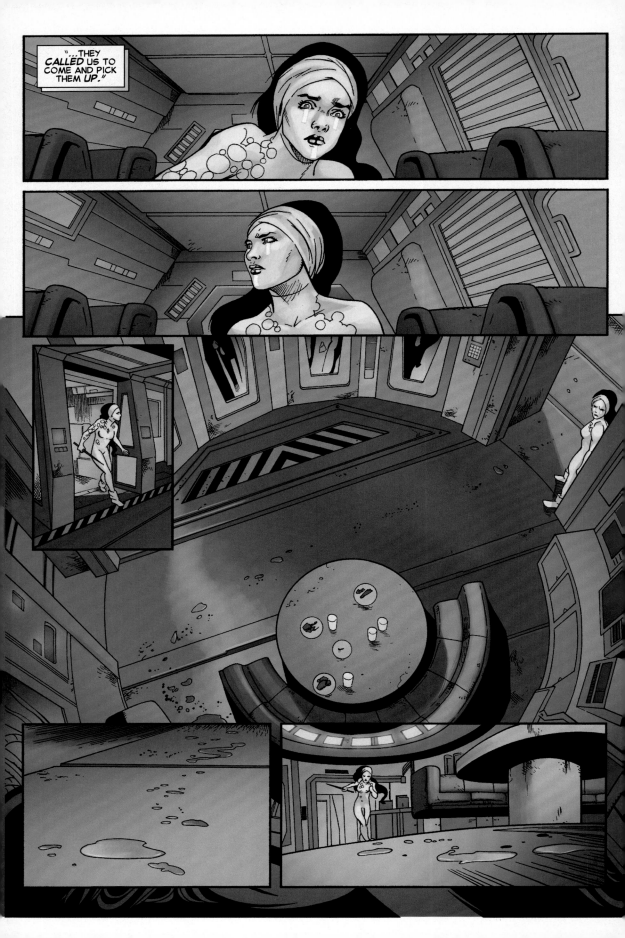

"...THEY **CALLED** US TO COME AND PICK THEM **UP**."

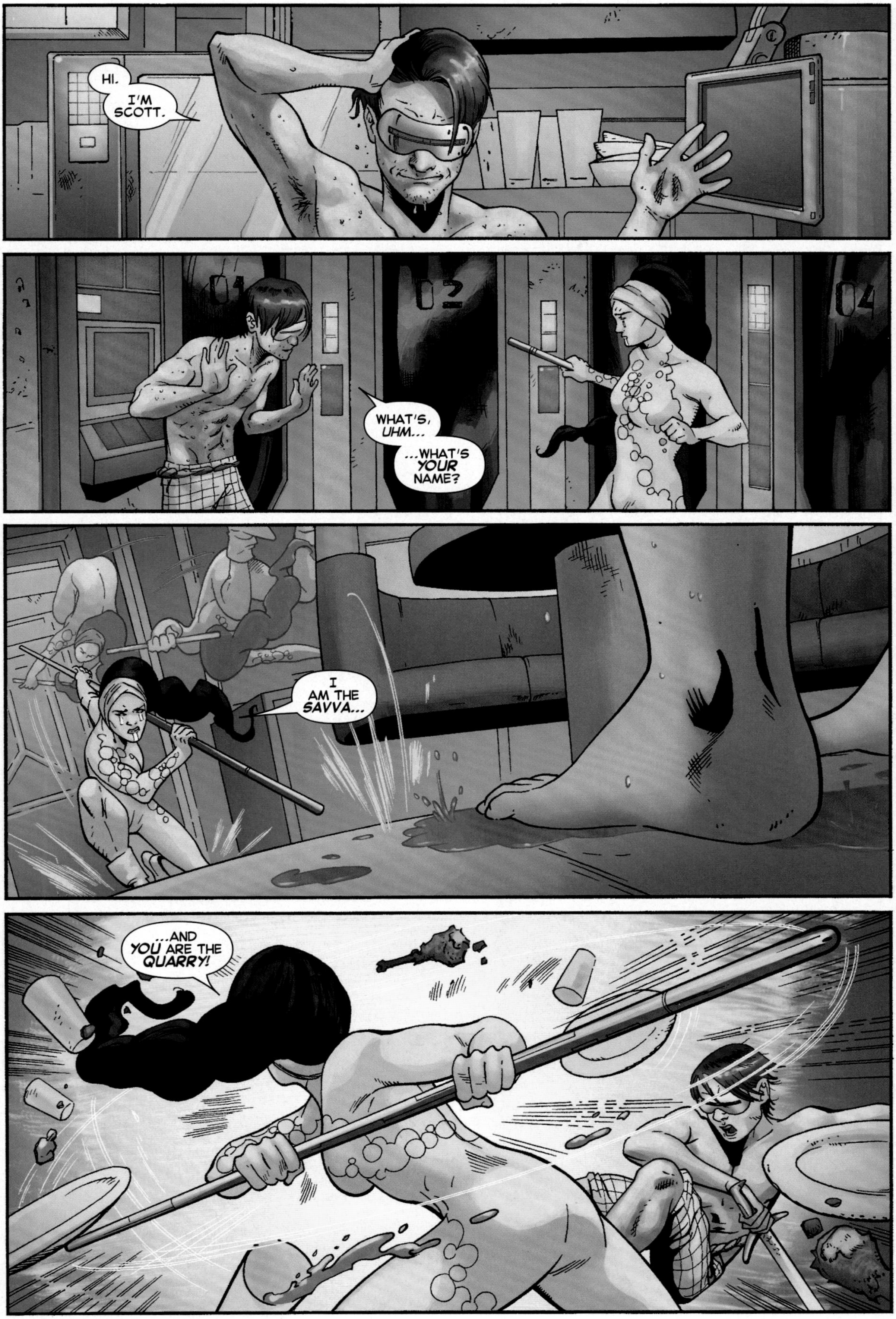
HI. I'M SCOTT.
WHAT'S, UHM...
...WHAT'S YOUR NAME?
I AM THE SAVVA...
...AND YOU ARE THE QUARRY!

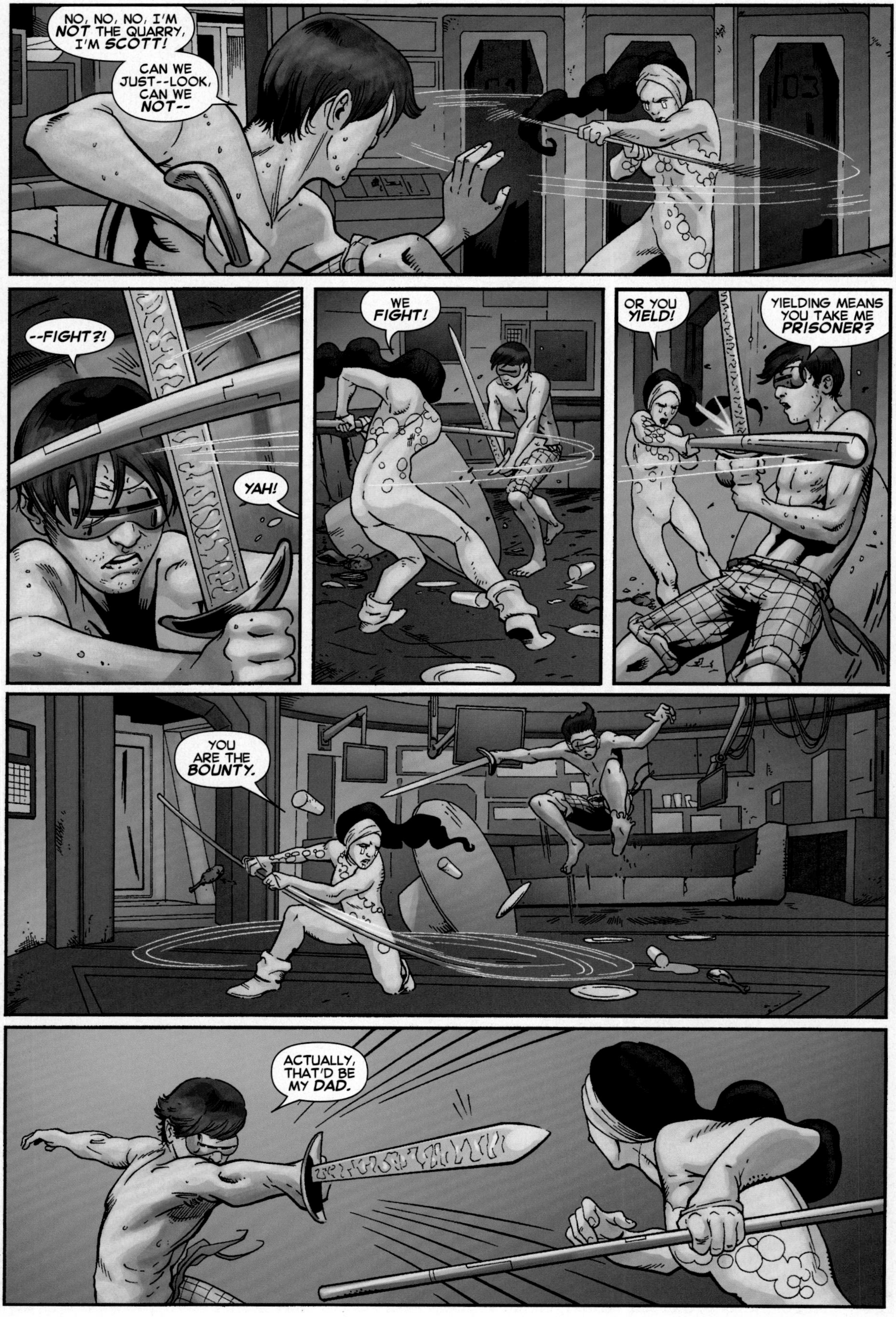
NO, NO, NO, I'M NOT THE QUARRY, I'M SCOTT!
CAN WE JUST--LOOK, CAN WE NOT--
--FIGHT?!
YAH!
WE FIGHT!
OR YOU YIELD!
YIELDING MEANS YOU TAKE ME PRISONER?
YOU ARE THE BOUNTY.
ACTUALLY, THAT'D BE MY DAD.

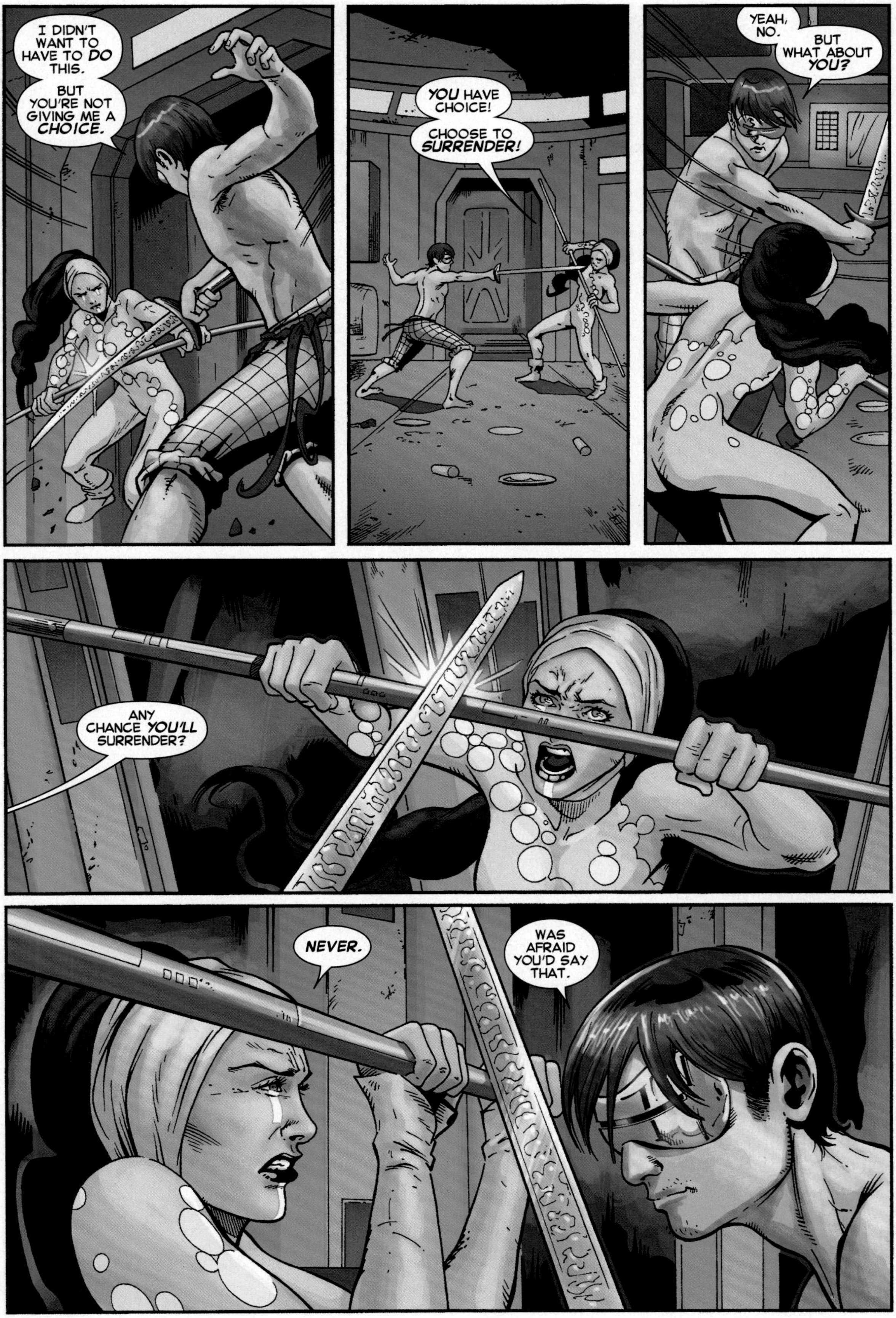
I DIDN'T WANT TO HAVE TO DO THIS.
BUT YOU'RE NOT GIVING ME A CHOICE.
YOU HAVE CHOICE!
CHOOSE TO SURRENDER!
YEAH, NO.
BUT WHAT ABOUT YOU?
ANY CHANCE YOU'LL SURRENDER?
NEVER.
WAS AFRAID YOU'D SAY THAT.

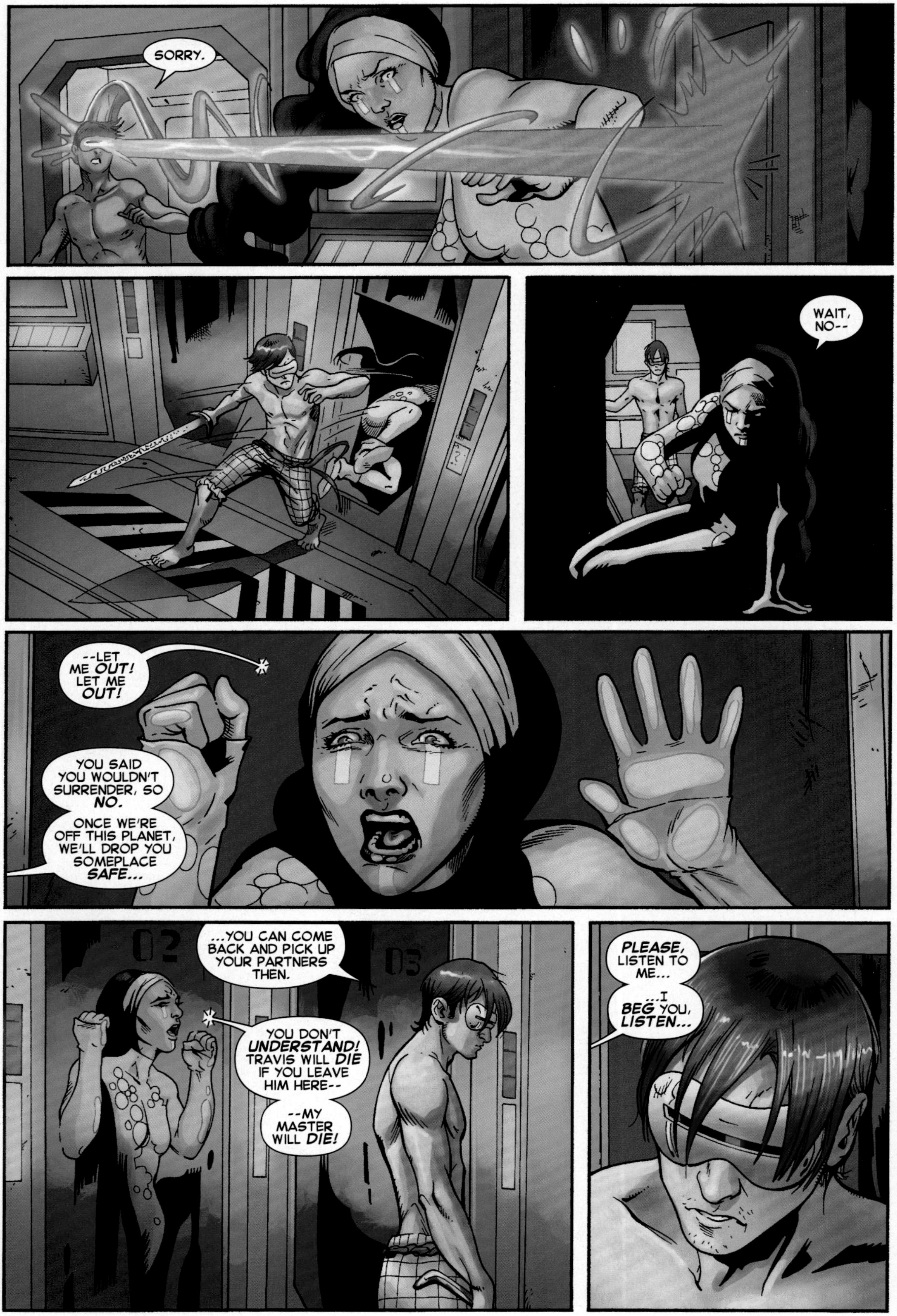
SORRY.
WAIT, NO--
--LET ME OUT! LET ME OUT!
YOU SAID YOU WOULDN'T SURRENDER, SO NO.
ONCE WE'RE OFF THIS PLANET, WE'LL DROP YOU SOMEPLACE SAFE...
...YOU CAN COME BACK AND PICK UP YOUR PARTNERS THEN.
YOU DON'T UNDERSTAND! TRAVIS WILL DIE IF YOU LEAVE HIM HERE--
--MY MASTER WILL DIE!
PLEASE, LISTEN TO ME...
...I BEG YOU, LISTEN...

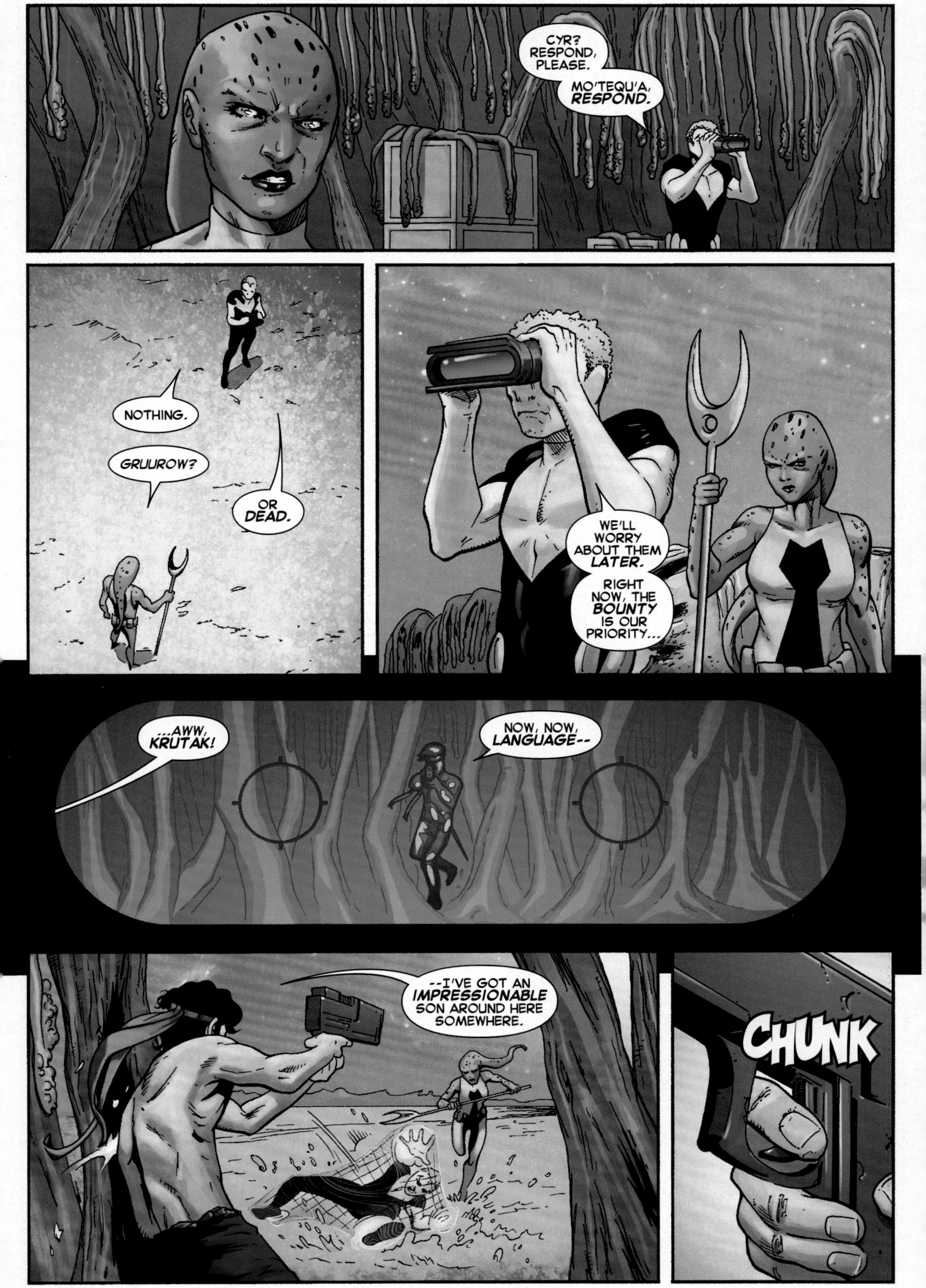
CYR? RESPOND, PLEASE.
MO'TEQU'A, RESPOND.
NOTHING.
GRUUROW?
OR DEAD.
WE'LL WORRY ABOUT THEM LATER.
RIGHT NOW, THE BOUNTY IS OUR PRIORITY...
...AWW, KRUTAK!
NOW, NOW, LANGUAGE--
--I'VE GOT AN IMPRESSIONABLE SON AROUND HERE SOMEWHERE.
CHUNK

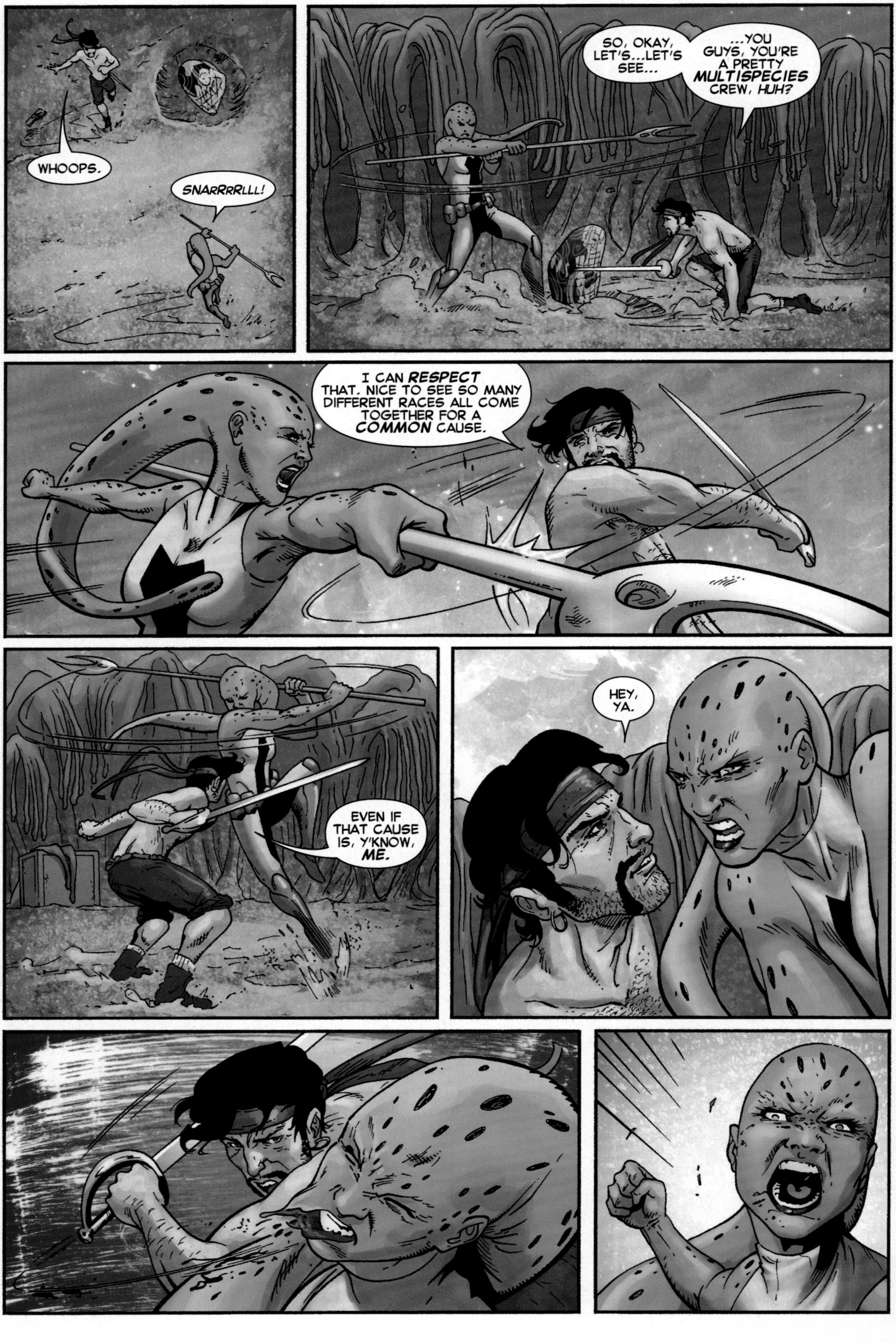
WHOOPS.
SNARRRRLLL!
SO, OKAY, LET'S...LET'S SEE...
...YOU GUYS, YOU'RE A PRETTY MULTISPECIES CREW, HUH?
I CAN RESPECT THAT. NICE TO SEE SO MANY DIFFERENT RACES ALL COME TOGETHER FOR A COMMON CAUSE.
EVEN IF THAT CAUSE IS, Y'KNOW, ME.
HEY, YA.

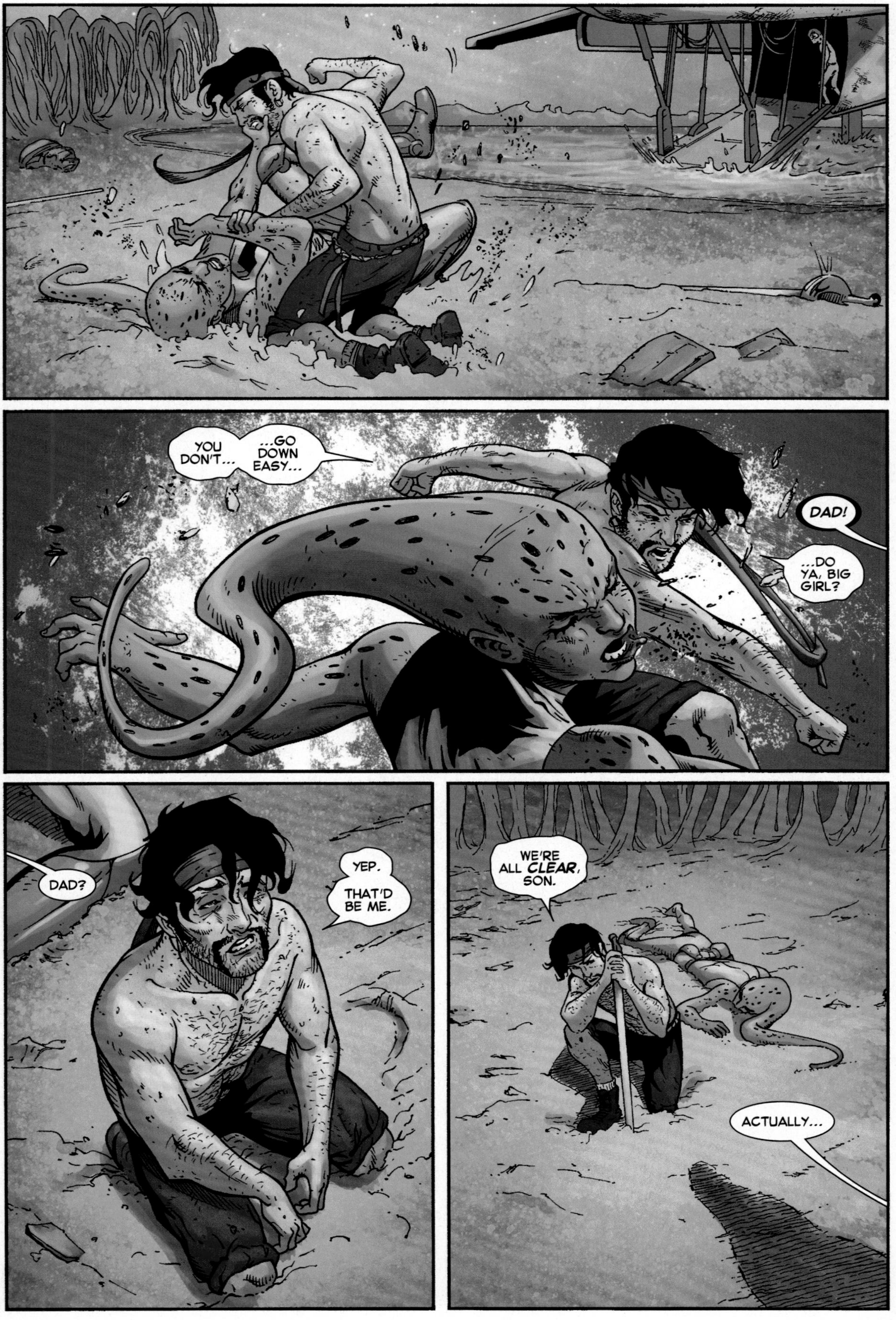
YOU DON'T...
...GO DOWN EASY...
DAD!
...DO YA, BIG GIRL?
DAD?
YEP.
THAT'D BE ME.
WE'RE ALL CLEAR, SON.
ACTUALLY...

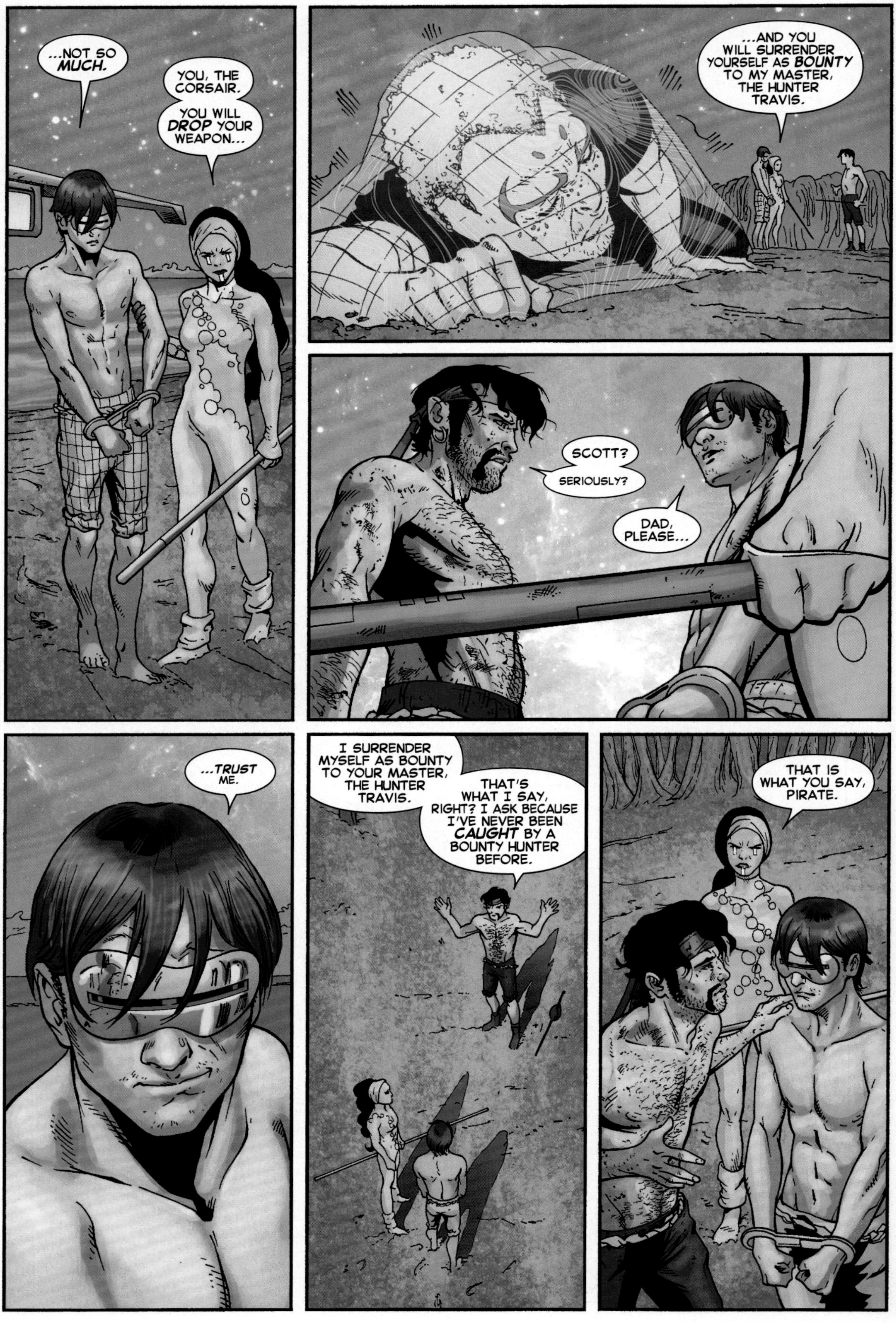

...NOT SO MUCH.
YOU, THE CORSAIR.
YOU WILL DROP YOUR WEAPON...
...AND YOU WILL SURRENDER YOURSELF AS BOUNTY TO MY MASTER, THE HUNTER TRAVIS.
SCOTT?
SERIOUSLY?
DAD, PLEASE...
...TRUST ME.
I SURRENDER MYSELF AS BOUNTY TO YOUR MASTER, THE HUNTER TRAVIS.
THAT'S WHAT I SAY, RIGHT? I ASK BECAUSE I'VE NEVER BEEN CAUGHT BY A BOUNTY HUNTER BEFORE.
THAT IS WHAT YOU SAY, PIRATE.

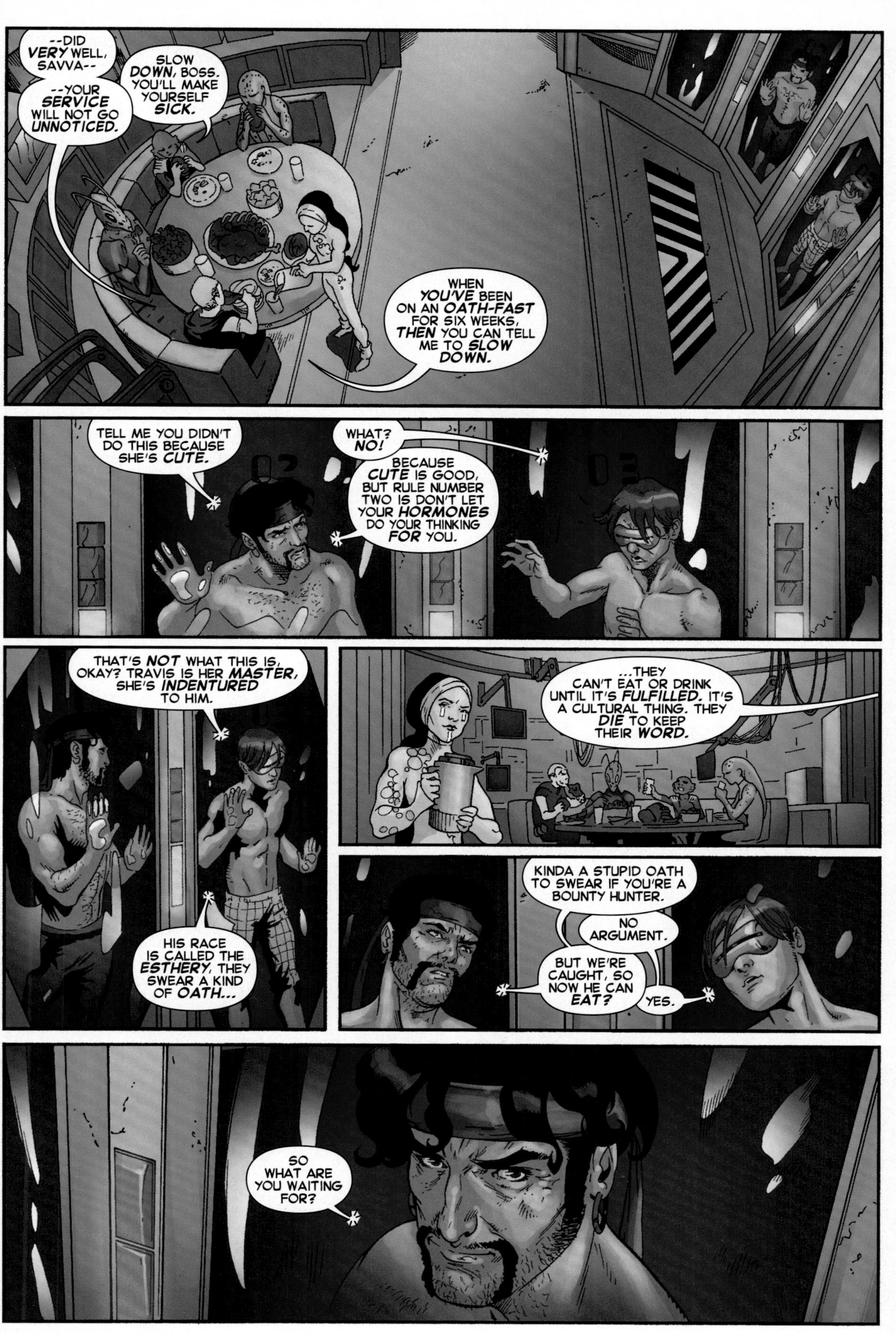
--DID VERY WELL, SAVVA--
--YOUR SERVICE WILL NOT GO UNNOTICED.
SLOW DOWN, BOSS. YOU'LL MAKE YOURSELF SICK.
WHEN YOU'VE BEEN ON AN OATH-FAST FOR SIX WEEKS, THEN YOU CAN TELL ME TO SLOW DOWN.
TELL ME YOU DIDN'T DO THIS BECAUSE SHE'S CUTE.
WHAT? NO!
BECAUSE CUTE IS GOOD, BUT RULE NUMBER TWO IS DON'T LET YOUR HORMONES DO YOUR THINKING FOR YOU.
THAT'S NOT WHAT THIS IS, OKAY? TRAVIS IS HER MASTER, SHE'S INDENTURED TO HIM.
HIS RACE IS CALLED THE ESTHERY, THEY SWEAR A KIND OF OATH...
...THEY CAN'T EAT OR DRINK UNTIL IT'S FULFILLED. IT'S A CULTURAL THING. THEY DIE TO KEEP THEIR WORD.
KINDA A STUPID OATH TO SWEAR IF YOU'RE A BOUNTY HUNTER.
NO ARGUMENT.
BUT WE'RE CAUGHT, SO NOW HE CAN EAT?
YES.
SO WHAT ARE YOU WAITING FOR?

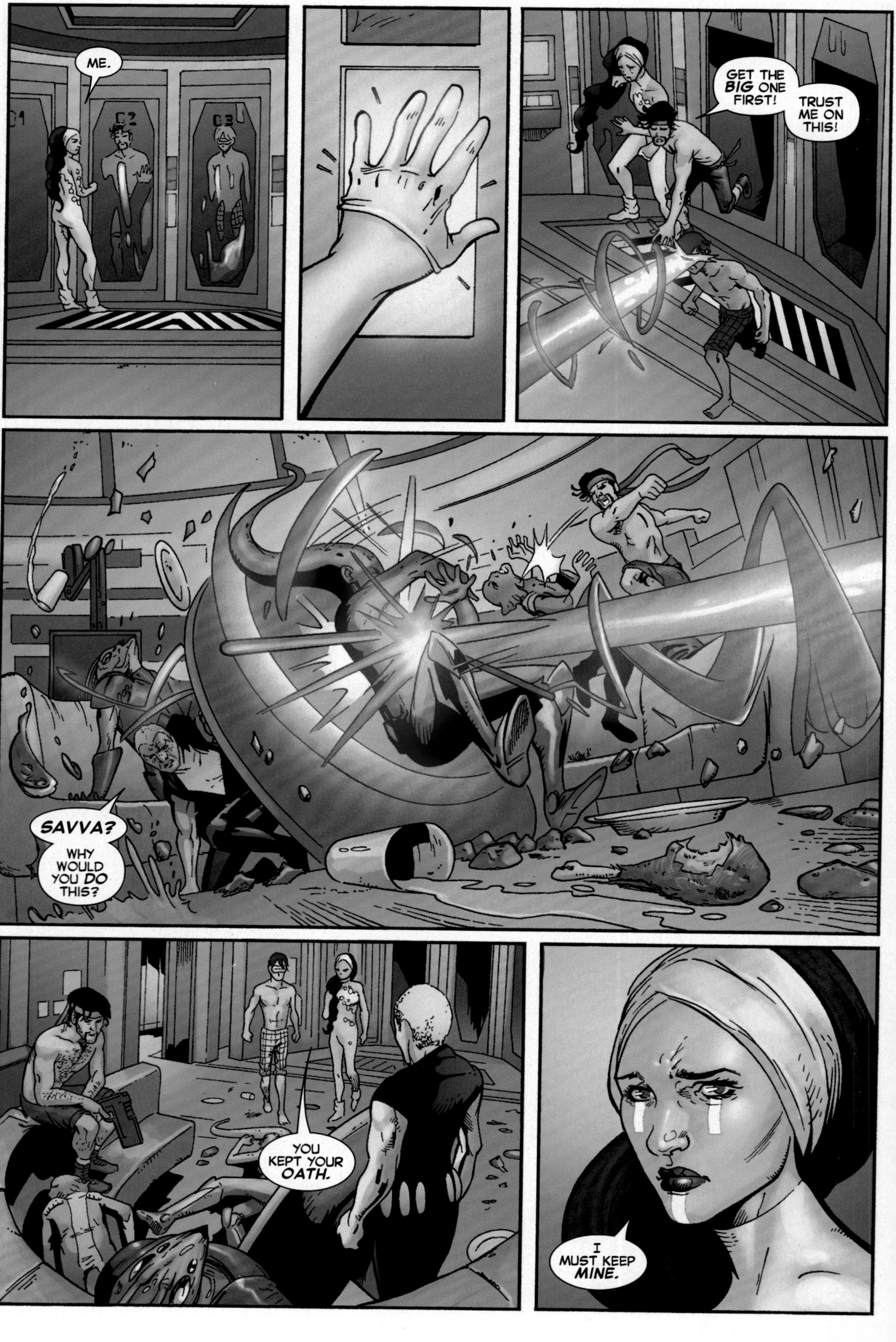
ME.
GET THE BIG ONE FIRST!
TRUST ME ON THIS!
SAVVA?
WHY WOULD YOU DO THIS?
YOU KEPT YOUR OATH.
I MUST KEEP MINE.

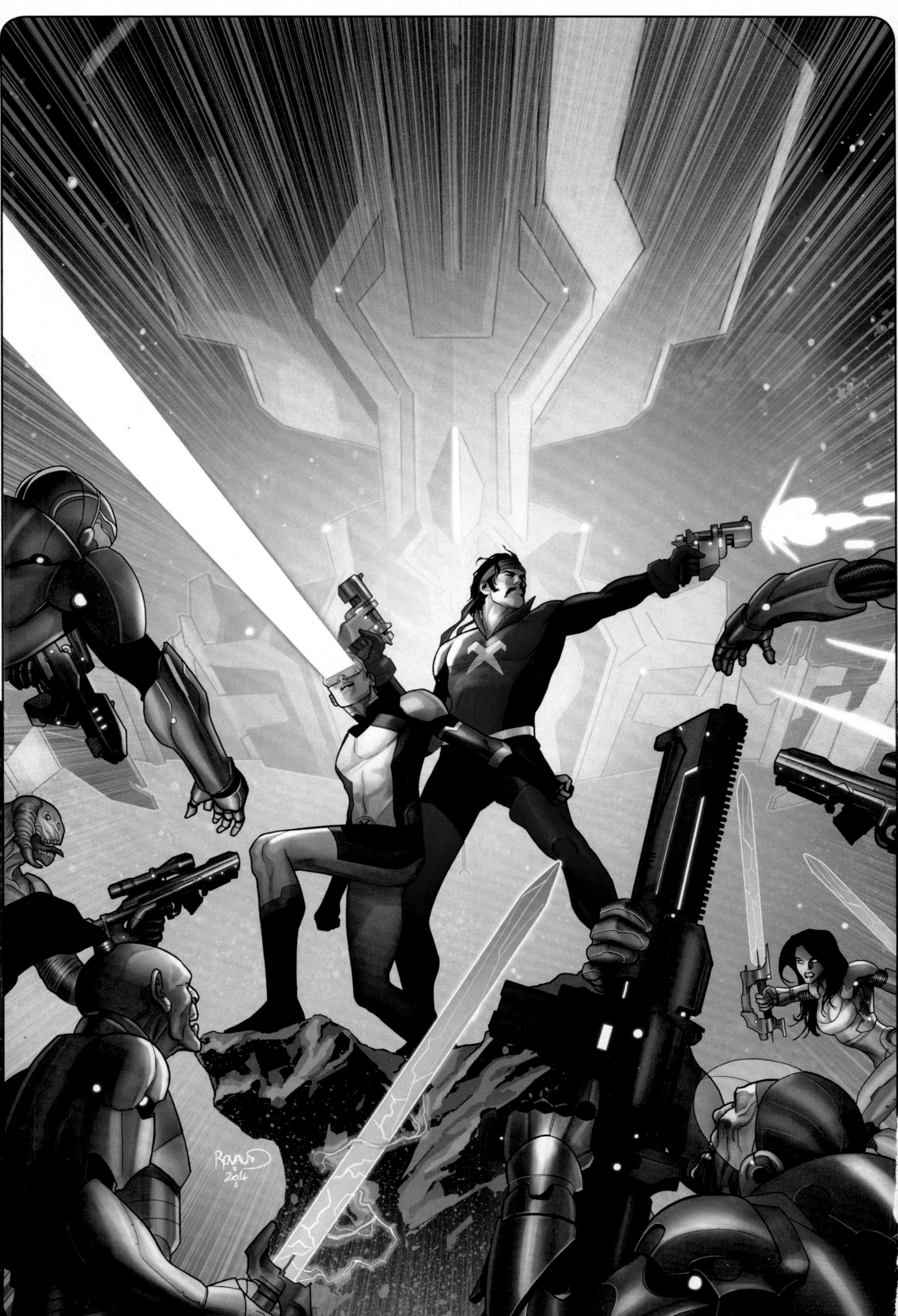

CYCLOPS #3 VARIANT
BY PAUL RENAUD

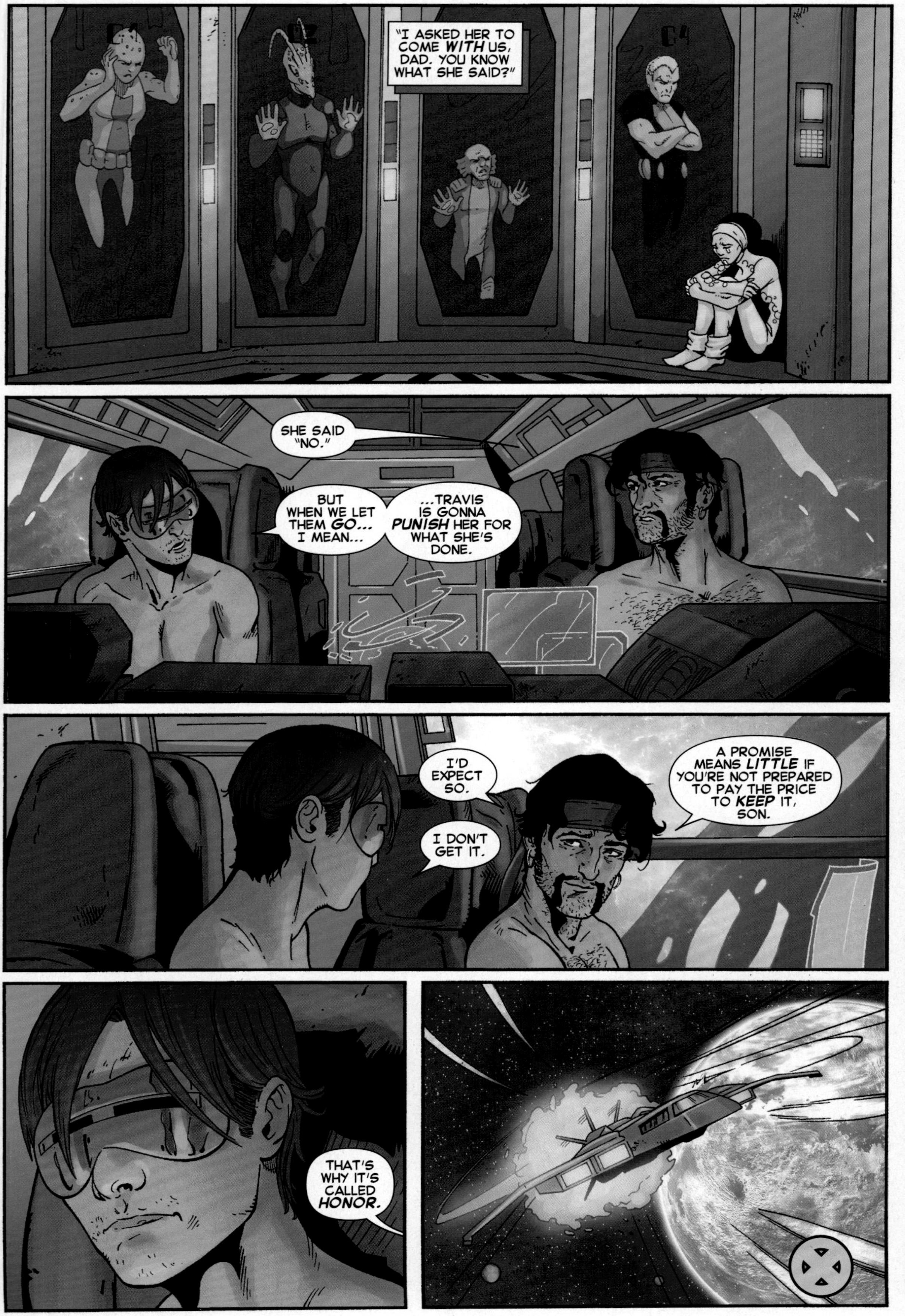
"I ASKED HER TO COME WITH US, DAD. YOU KNOW WHAT SHE SAID?"
SHE SAID "NO."
BUT WHEN WE LET THEM GO... I MEAN...
...TRAVIS IS GONNA PUNISH HER FOR WHAT SHE'S DONE.
I'D EXPECT SO.
I DON'T GET IT.
A PROMISE MEANS LITTLE IF YOU'RE NOT PREPARED TO PAY THE PRICE TO KEEP IT, SON.
THAT'S WHY IT'S CALLED HONOR.